D1133772

HIDDEN WYNDHAM

Life, Love, Letters

AMY BINNS

GRACE JUDSON PRESS

This book is dedicated, with much love, to Richard, Rosie and Tommy.

First published by Grace Judson Press, 2019.

Copyright Amy Binns, 2019.

All rights reserved.

The moral right of the author has been asserted.

Cover design by Gary Buckland.

Cover photograph self-taken by John Wyndham, 1938.

Printed and bound in Great Britain by Clays Ltd, Elcograf S. p. A.

Typeset in 10.5pt/13pt Garamond.

ISBN 978-0-9927567-1-0

When the minds have learnt to mingle, when no thought is wholly one's own, and each has taken too much of the other ever to be entirely himself alone; when one has reached the beginning of seeing with a single eye, loving with a single heart, enjoying with a single joy; when there can be moments of identity and nothing is separate save bodies that long for one another ... When there is that, where is the word? There is only the inadequacy of the word that exists.

"We love one another," I said.

The Chrysalids, John Wyndham

"Darling, whose book is this to be?"

"Ostensibly yours, my sweet."

"I see - rather like my life since I met you?"

"Yes darling."

The Kraken Wakes, John Wyndham

CONTENTS

Part One

1903 - 1939

Prologue:
Edgbaston, Birmingham
March 1911

Childhood is for everyone, I suspect, happier in recollection than in reality – and youth, too, for the matter of that. Actually it is continual lesson-time, and many of them are painfully learnt – and yet, unless one sets out deliberately to recall the miseries, humiliations, and frustrations, it is the pleasant recollections that usually dominate. But to a newcomer to a strange world everything matters too much.

I should hate to have to go through it again. Yet, as I recall it, I was as happy as most, and a lot more so than some.

- *John Wyndham, in interview with Sam Moskowitz.*

A bolt scrapes back within one of the new detached villas facing the road. A pretty housemaid, neat in black and white uniform, opens both halves of the gothic split door. It is a Sunday, the day above all for the muted display of wealth that confers respectability. And the show is needed: the family is teetering on the edge of bankruptcy and disgrace.

Inside the hall stand the boys: John Wyndham Parkes Lucas Beynon Harris, aged almost eight, and his little brother, Vivian Parkes Lucas Beynon Harris, four. Jack and Viv are dressed in the bane of the Edwardian boy's life: white sailor suits with HMS Colossus picked out in gold on the hat brims. Nominally based on naval workwear, they are in fact a complex construction of tapes and stiffening that explodes from a hat box every Sunday.

Nurse Hatton has spent more than half an hour cramming them

into these outfits and she is still straightening their collars when Father appears. She shifts slightly to stand behind Jack, her hands on his shoulders. He looks up. She is the youngest of a young staff, aged only 20. She is usually the most fun, but now her mouth is compressed into a firm line. Jack knows she doesn't like Father. He doesn't know why. Jack isn't sure how he feels about him, Father has so little to do with him. Jack doesn't realise, but Grandpa Parkes made sure of that years ago.

Now they are just waiting for Mother. Father fidgets, sighs, pulls out his watch. He gazes at Nurse. Impervious, she folds her arms and stares out of the door. Father turns his attention to Lily, the maid.

Viv is bored. He discovers the brass whistle on the scarlet cord which completes the outfit, takes a tentative toot. Father's head jerks around. Swiftly, gently, Jack removes the whistle, whispers in Viv's ear. Viv chuckles. Father restricts himself to a growl. Now is the worst possible moment for a domestic row. They are on their way to see Mother's parents for afternoon tea.

And at last, here is Mother, sweeping down the stairs without apology. At 42, Mother is well into middle-age by Edwardian standards and has never been a beauty. She would be prettier without the pince nez, but her clothes are the latest cut. Father stands back to allow her to step out first. He has learnt hard lessons in the treatment of ladies. As a barrister and former politician, he understands about image. Whatever tensions lie within the house, they will not be visible beyond the front door.

Father walks out and the boys trail behind him. The walk is a short one. The Parkes grandparents live close by. They bought the villa for their daughter and her family, as they have bought houses in the neighbourhood for their other children. Sunday tea is a regular fixture and all the family must attend their suburban mansion.

It is no hardship for Jack, Viv and the cousins: just as Grandpa supplies cartloads of coal to his children's homes every week from his foundry, so Grandma supplies every delicacy from her kitchen. When the children are bored, they can disappear to the glasshouses to filch more fruit behind the gardener's back.

Meanwhile, beneath the ornate plaster ceilings of the drawing room, maids circulate with trays amongst the Parkes clan: Mother's three sisters, brother and their spouses discuss trade, politics and the doings of the many Methodist chapels they support. Father has little to add on these occasions. His legal career is only middling, he does not own any factories, he is no longer a politician. He is not even a Methodist.

Stuffed with cake and fruit, the boys trudge back behind their parents to their own, more modest villa, and are put to bed by Nurse.

But the day is not yet over. Jack is half asleep when he realises Lily is in the night nursery, telling him to wake up, Father wants him downstairs. Viv is already snoring. He stands up, unsure what time it is. Lily is holding his dressing gown, and he puts it on as she wakes Viv. He walks through to the day nursery. Nurse is standing in rigid silence by the fire, holding her mending.

She watches the boys hustled out of the room towards the stairs and at the last moment seems to change her mind and follows after them. Lily pushes them towards the dining room.

Father is sitting at the table and beckons Jack forward to stand between his legs. Jack considers him. He has rarely seen him this close. At 47, he is still a neatly built, smart man, close-shaven, almost dapper. He smells of cigars and something bitter. He is smiling.

Mother says: "Don't, George!"

Jack looks at her for the first time since he entered the room. She is standing by the sideboard, flushed. She seems both furious and frightened.

"He is seven years old! You mustn't!" she cries. Jack catches her fear. He doesn't know what is going to happen, but he wants her to make it stop. She does not move.

George chuckles slightly and smiles again at Jack.

"Please, George!"

"Now, now, Gertrude," says Father, without turning. His eyes are still merrily fixed on Jack, but his knees are squeezing tighter round his body. "Your mother doesn't understand. I've just got something for you. Something you'll like. A treat! Here you are."

He hands Jack a glass. It's a beautiful, fragile one, the kind he is usually forbidden to touch. Lights catch and flash in the pattern of the crystal. Inside, a gleaming brown liquid clings to the sides as he tips it.

He knows what it is. It is liquor.

Jack has heard sermons on the demon drink by his great uncle, the Rev Stephen Parkes. He has seen lantern lectures on its evils. Methodist children are encouraged to sign the pledge, promising to abstain for life. His other great uncle, Sir Ebenezer Parkes MP, is campaigning with local women's Temperance organisations for children under 14 to be prevented from entering licensed premises.

But Father is not an abstainer. And tonight, he wants to make a point.

"Drink it," he says. He is still smiling, but there is an edge to his voice now as he pushes the glass closer to Jack's mouth. It's not a bad smell, but it is strong with a strange undertone, like the sweetness of almost rotten fruit.

"George!" says Mother. Her voice is high and pleading.

"It's only sherry," says Father.

Jack says: "No."

Father swears and suddenly grabs the back of Jack's head, tipping it up, pushing the glass into his mouth. It's drink or drown. Jack splutters, swallows. Father's hand drops from his head to his shoulder, pats, squeezes.

"There," says Father with a smile. "Not so bad, is it? Go on. Let's see you drink the rest."

Jack is still trapped between Father's knees. Nervously, he takes a small sip. It's not so bad. Father is still watching, his face close. Jack thinks of medicine, screws himself up and swallows the rest at a gulp. Father laughs. Someone gasps. Jack looks up.

Mother is staring at him. All her fear and anger has vanished. In its place is horror and grief. For one terrible moment, Jack thinks something has happened to his face to cause her to stare so. Is the demon drink already inside him? Is it looking out at Mother through his eyes? He twists between Father's knees. Lily has her hand over her mouth. Nurse's lips are pressed together so tightly they have disappeared. She is holding Viv's hand. Now she bends to pick him up and hold him close.

Jack turns back to Father. He leans back. He is not smiling any more, but laughter and triumph glint in his eyes. "Go to bed," he says.

Nurse takes them upstairs and tucks them in without a word. After a few minutes, Jack hears Viv's breathing slow into sleep.

Jack thinks. He decides there is not a demon inside him, despite the terrible warnings of his great-uncles. Apart from a lingering bad taste in his mouth, he feels little different. A tendril of doubt about the teachings of the Church begins to unfurl.

There are other puzzles here. Mother didn't want him to drink the sherry. Neither did Nurse, or Lily. But it didn't make any difference. None of them stopped Father. The servants can't of course, or they will be sacked, as Father sacked a maid before when she spoke to him disrespectfully. But what about Mother? Can Father sack Mother? What would happen to him and Viv then?

Didn't Mother know how frightened he was? Is she not allowed to stop Father? Jack has heard sermons on the impurity of women as often as on the evils of drink. Is it God then, who forbids Mother from interfering?

That night, something within Jack changes. He knows now how he feels about Father. But suddenly, he is no longer sure how he feels about Mother.

1

Edwardian Scandals

John Wyndham's life began in secrecy and subterfuge. What began as a reaction to events would become a habit engrained within him, until it coloured his entire life.

He was unfortunate in his parents. George Beynon Harris and Gertrude Parkes had little in common but their self-centredness. Theirs was never a match made in heaven. There was a whiff of second best about their relationship from the very start.

But they did give him some gifts. George Harris gave him a talent for writing and invention. Gertrude gave her love, however inadequate the rest of her mothering. Perhaps most importantly, the remnants of her family's fortune would be just enough to keep him afloat during the many tough years ahead.

Maybe the Parkes family also gave him something else: though quiet and diffident, he had an inner core of stubbornness through failure and success that may have come from his relatives' iron backbones. For the Parkes of Edgbaston, Birmingham, were a force to be reckoned with.

They were literally non-conformist, belonging to the Methodist church that had rejected state authority along with the Baptists, Quakers and other, usually working-class, dissenters. The Victorian establishment held these 'chapel-goers' in a contempt that masked an uneasiness with their growing strength. Establishment disdain meant nothing to families such as the Parkes. As the nineteenth century marched on, some of these foundrymen became factory owners, with brass in their pockets and a rock-solid sense of self-worth.

Jack's grandfather and great-grandfather were amongst these newly wealthy industrialists. Whilst earlier social climbers had tried to distance themselves from 'trade', men such as Jack's great-grandfather, Israel Parkes, were proud of their achievements and the source of their wealth.

Israel Parkes was an ironmaster, whose factories made tips and heels for boots, tin tacks and corrugated iron. His staunch Methodist faith didn't stop some occasional sharp practice. When facing bankruptcy, he transferred raw material worth thousands of pounds to his son and settled property on his wife to keep it from creditors. He was heavily criticised in court for destroying his own records and claiming to be unable to remember details which would have made him liable to pay.[1]

But he built himself up again, and by the time of his death in 1901, two years before Jack was born, Israel Parkes had founded a dynasty. His daughter was married to an Alderman, and his three sons were: Sir Ebenezer Parkes, factory owner and Liberal Unionist MP for Birmingham Central; the Rev Stephen Parkes; and Wyndham's grandfather John Israel Parkes, Justice of the Peace, with his own cut nail factory.

John Israel followed in his father's footsteps, running a business with enough profit to endow several Methodist chapels and generally maintain his position as a pillar of the community. His religion wasn't just show – morning prayers were heard in the dining room. His grandson Vivian would remember him as "a tower of strength on all occasions with only one weakness, which was Grandma, whom he worshipped as if she wasn't the beautiful, selfish, loveable woman she was."[2]

John Israel and his wife Eliza Parkes lived in one of the finest houses in the area: Mayfield, on Harborne Road, Edgbaston, Birmingham. This is a street that has not lost value in the intervening century. Ten bedroomed mansions cluttered with bay windows, gothic gables and fancy brickwork still sell for millions.

Here, Jack's mother, Gertrude, born in 1868, lived as a provincial princess with her three sisters and brother in the lap of luxury.

This was the life that George Harris aspired to. He was born in 1863, the eldest of several children of Ruth and Evan Harris, a schoolteacher turned postmaster. They lived in the house attached to the post office in a tiny village on the Gower Peninsula.[3]

George was ambitious. He trained as a solicitor in Cardiff. He was only 29 when asked at short notice to stand as a Conservative councillor for Cardiff Town Council. He lost, but impressed enough to be asked to stand again a year later. He was unashamedly populist and a good speaker. His energy and style did not recommend him to everyone, as the South Wales Daily News editorialised:[4]

> When on the war path, fully armed in his political paint, we found him to be a red-hot Tory, bouncing and aggressive . . . and habitually mistaking strong words for strong argument. We have for the present Cardiff Town Council sufficient good will to fervently hope that Mr G Beynon Harris will never officially become a member of their body, and all the harm we wish to Mr G Beynon Harris himself is that he may become wiser in thought and more restrained in speech as he grows older.

Nevertheless, he won, a victory that the Western Mail reported as being "most popular".[5] He was greeted with a rousing reception and the burning of coloured lights at the Central Working Men's club, and he showed no sign of becoming more restrained. For several years he regularly appeared in the columns of the local newspapers as the leader of the "young bloods", witty, cocksure and irreverent. Their favourite activity was baiting the Aldermen, and "unseemly squabbles" and protests in the council chamber were reported.[6]

His style didn't stop him being competent and likeable enough to be made assistant to the Town Clerk, a prestigious appointment. He was also corporation prosecuting solicitor for the police courts, a reliable source of income. He added 'Lucas' to his name in order to link himself to a well-known local family.

But after a minor scandal he was obliged to leave Cardiff, losing his carefully nurtured connections. He was forced to start again, practising law in Birmingham. It was a major setback for a man approaching middle-age. He had few prospects beyond the daily grind. When Gertrude met him, he was living in a double-fronted terrace in Greenfield Crescent – respectable, genteel, but several rungs down from Mayfield.

He was an unlikely match for an heiress, but there seemed few choices, despite her wealth and her family's prominence. She had been 24, almost an old maid by Victorian standards, when she had been first married and swiftly widowed. Her husband, Thomas William Hunt, was an eligible 32-year-old from the family of a local chemical manufacturer. He caught a cold while out driving on their honeymoon in Lynmouth, North Devon, and died of complications. She was rescued for the first of many times by her father, and installed back in her old home in Birmingham. [7]

Deaths from chest infections were not uncommon but this was more unusual – the doctor recorded underlying tuberculosis on the death certificate, which Gertrude surely must have been aware of before the wedding. Active TB typically develops over at least a year, and was well understood in Victorian times as consumption. Did Gertrude know he was doomed, but want to marry him anyway, no matter what the risk to her own health?

That risk was worse than she had known. Her son Viv later wrote that Hunt had infected her with venereal disease on the honeymoon, a fate suffered by many Victorian brides. She did not rush to remarry and was said to have had a lengthy course of treatment.[8]

So by age 32 she was still living at her father's house. She had some private income, and passed the time with a series of holidays, which allowed her to escape her parents and the inevitable comparisons with her more successfully married siblings. She seemed on the shelf, but into this new era, the 20th century, had come George, introduced to the family by Gertrude's sister, who had met him at a chapel.[9]

George became friendly with John Israel and for a year visited the house. A year later George asked him for permission to marry Gertrude. John Israel was reluctant. Despite their acquaintance, he knew nothing of George's background. Perhaps he sensed George was not everything he seemed. He requested the name of some gentleman in Cardiff who could vouch for him.[10]

George hesitated. He didn't tell John Israel why he had left Cardiff, but eventually gave him the name of a reference. John Israel visited Cardiff, made inquiries, and was shocked by the result. George's life-changing scandal was a short tale which would have been laughably trivial for most of the 20th century, but is oddly relevant in the #MeToo era, when a report of a hand on a knee or a drunken lunge can again spell career-ending disgrace.

Back in the 1890s, George's career in Cardiff had been shaping up well. He had become a well-known lawyer and politician with a bright future – perhaps a little too well known. His bumptious style had brought him attention but also made him enemies.

One lively civic ball was all it took to bring him crashing down. He and a young lady slipped away from the crush into the privacy of an adjacent room. We cannot know exactly what happened – an innocent flirtation, a drunken fumble or worse – but when other guests entered, she was sitting upon his knee. She screamed.

George insisted that nothing improper was taking place, that the young lady had perched there "in perfect innocence" due to a lack of chairs. He claimed she screamed not out of fear of him, but to save her reputation.

Nothing further happened that night, but after the ball, the young woman told her family enough to throw a more serious light on the affair. A summons was issued, charging George with indecent assault. Though the matter was kept out of the press, his political rivals made capital out of it. George later claimed he "took the honourable course". He resigned his position as an official of the Corporation by letter, and left town aged 35 to set up all over again in Birmingham.

John Israel challenged George with his new knowledge. George said: "There is another side to that matter."

John Israel replied: "I have heard quite enough to satisfy me."

He extracted a promise from George never to ask Gertrude for her hand again. George asked to see her once more to say goodbye. It's not clear if John Israel told his daughter what he had learnt. If he kept it from her, he had cause to regret it.

A week later, John Israel received a telegram. George and Gertrude had eloped. They had married by special licence at a Church of England church in the Lake District, on 27 August 1902.

The Parkes family were shocked, but the marriage was now a fait accompli. They announced the marriage in the local newspaper in the usual way and made the best of it.

It's not known exactly what the newlyweds did next. They returned to Birmingham, but whether to George's terrace or another rented home is unclear.

John Wyndham Parkes Lucas Beynon Harris, known to his family as Jack, arrived ten months later, on 10 July 1903. His birth certificate gives the address simply as Dorridge, a village ten miles south-west of Edgbaston, Birmingham. This may have been a friend's home or a nursing home. Gertrude would have been given the best medical attention. As well as her wealth, she would have been considered at higher risk because of her medical history and her age. She was then 34 and had never given birth before. Soon after, the family moved to a newly-built semi-detached house in Fountains Road, Edgbaston.[11]

Within a year, George was showing Gertrude his true colours. If she displeased him, he would refuse to speak to her for days. On holiday with her family, he was so rough in his handling of baby Jack that Gertrude was distressed and her sister left the room in anger, telling him he had no idea how to treat a wife.[12]

John Israel made up his mind to do what he could to save the situation. He gave the family a cheque for £100 on Jack's birth, and another on the birth of Jack's younger brother Vivian three years later in November 1906.

He also made George a regular allowance. George had a mortgage on property in Cardiff, which he was struggling to finance; John Israel offered to take over the deeds. Through this, and George's involvement in John Israel's business schemes, their finances became deeply entangled. George became dependant on his in-laws.

By 1908, when Jack was five, John Israel had built them a substantial detached villa on the main Hagley Road. This protected his grandsons from his son-in-law's lower standard of living, while shoring up his own social position. It also established him as the paterfamilias and put his son-in-law even more firmly in his debt. Every week, two carts of coal were delivered from his Smethwick factory and tipped into their enormous coal house.

Now demolished, the site of that Hagley Road house is a waste ground of overgrown trees, surrounded by low-budget restaurant chains. The remaining house next door gives an idea of how it would have been before this road became an artery to newer suburbs.

It was three storeys, brick above and rendered below with an assortment of gables and chimneys. It faced the main road across a front garden, with a curving path to a gate flanked by stone pillars. The top storey gave spacious accommodation for Edith Winter, the 23-year-old cook; Louise Hatton, nurse, aged 20; and Lily Beresford, parlour maid, aged 25.

The garden had a pond: one of Viv's earliest memories was of falling in and Jack holding him up by his hair until Nurse Hatton rushed up to rescue him.

The house had been built in hopes of a large brood, but this was not to be.[13]

The family lost two babies, who died before they were even named. It is likely one was born between the two boys and one after Vivian. This pattern of live and stillbirths is common in women infected with syphilis. Many years after infection, the disease is transmitted to the foetus about 40% of the time, resulting in malformations which can be fatal. It may have been these half-remembered losses that bonded Jack to his younger brother despite Vivian's later difficult behaviour.

Meanwhile, promoted to the cream of Birmingham society, George made some attempt to live up to expectations. He finally qualified as a barrister, though didn't have much success. He appeared occasionally in the local paper. In a public debate, he spoke against Welsh nationalism, astutely siding with his Birmingham audience over his native land. He also spoke against the Government's treatment of imprisoned suffragettes. He built up a property portfolio of rented houses, albeit with Gertrude's money. He even wrote a book, a legal tome on tender which he shrewdly dedicated to the Lord High Chancellor.

In a more blatant display of brown-nosing, he appears to have dedicated the boys themselves to his erstwhile career. Windham, spelt with an i, was the name of one of George's many brothers, but both Wyndham and Vivian were the names of prominent politicians in Cardiff, George's former mentors. By giving his son the name Wyndham, George was trying to claim an aristocratic connection as he did in a later book.

Windham Wyndham-Quin, Fourth Earl of Dunraven and Mount-

Earl, was an inaugural member of Glamorgan County Council, the district surrounding Cardiff. He represented Bridgend as a Conservative between 1889 and 1892. He was also a successful journalist, army officer and huntsman. An elegant glass-roofed arcade in Cardiff is still named after him.

The Vivian family, linked by marriage to the Wyndham-Quins, were wealthy industrialists who held every possible civic title between them. Members included Henry Hussey Vivian, first Baron of Swansea, also a founder member of the Glamorgan County Council and its first chair, as well as being an MP for 40 years. Sir Arthur Vivian was an MP, JP, lieutenant-colonel, county councillor for Glamorgan and Fellow of the Royal Geographical Society, amongst many other titles.

This was the society George dreamed of. Perhaps he hoped to keep these illustrious connections alive. Maybe he even thought he could return in glory to preside in Cardiff's magnificent new city hall. But he had not done so, and despite his intelligence and energy had failed to generate real income. He continued out of harmony with the Parkes dynasty.

Thanks to them, he was outwardly financially secure, but without substance. George was bored: frustrated by middling success when he had glimpsed the peaks, and tired of playing second fiddle in someone else's family.

George had always been a 'ladies' man'. Now, his sexual advances to the servants became routine, though it is not clear with how much success. Nurse Hatton complained that he put his arm around her waist, and later tried to get into the nursery while she was asleep there. Another servant, trapped by him on the stairs, threatened to break his neck if he didn't let her go.[14]

In one instance, whilst Gertrude was ill, he dismissed a girl for "the way she addressed him" – probably a curt rejection. Sacking servants was an unusual thing for a husband to do – management of servants was a wife's domain.

When John Israel Parkes heard of it, presumably after complaints from Gertrude, he objected. He said that he was funding the household and had a right to have his say. One of John Israel's friends tried to act as peacemaker between them. To humour his father-in-law,

George ended up signing a letter drafted by John Israel's friend, promising not to interfere with the servants, the training of "Jackie" (then aged four) or domestic affairs generally.

The man who had once been written of as "one of Cardiff's most promising sons"[15] was not even master in his own home, nor permitted to manage his own son. Relations were turning sour.

Unlike his Methodist in-laws, George had never been an abstainer. Now he drank more heavily. Gertrude may also have found her new role as a mother tedious after many years of holidays. It may be at this time that she too began a lady-like tipple.

Still, some things were sacrosanct, and George was pushing against the boundaries. The terrible evening when George forced Jack to drink sherry in front of his mother was still remembered by Viv 70 years later.

It was, like everything George did even under the influence, an instinctively canny choice. It would be sweet enough not to disgust the child, but strong enough to show his mother who was in charge.

It was also, like everything George did, a short-sighted attempt to score points without a strategy for the long-term game. Nothing could have been more likely to turn the Parkes family against him, especially given the family's Temperance campaigning.[16]

For Jack, caught in the middle, this could only be confusing. The dynamics of his parents' relationship must have been opaque to him, but its imbalance was clear. All Gertrude's beliefs, her morals and motherhood, her emotions and desires – in short, all that made her who she was – counted for nothing compared to his father's drunken, manipulative whim. Even her money and connections weighed little in the balance.

One result of living in this toxic household was to turn both boys against the institution of marriage. They would both enter long-term, committed partnerships, but without legal ties. For Jack, marriage was slavery, explicitly so in his short story "Dumb Martian" (published in *Galaxy*, 1952).

As adults, Jack and Viv would dismiss their father from their lives, referring to him only as George and gradually losing touch with him. The hole this created would be visible in several of Jack's stories with missing fathers. In *The Midwich Cuckoos*, a never-seen alien impregnates the women and leaves. In *Chocky*, the adopted boy doesn't know either of his biological parents. The thousands of cloned siblings in *Plan for Chaos* never discover their father's identity, while fathers are entirely erased from the reproductive process in *Consider Her Ways*.

Their relationships with their mother would always be more complicated and were at the root of Jack's fervent but frustrated feminism.

Gertrude was rich, educated and supported by her family. Yet she was weak, ineffectual and incapable of protecting her children. She produced nothing – even her motherhood was only of reproduction. The tough, creative work of raising the boys was handed to servants and schools: a style of motherhood which Jack would criticise in *The Day of the Triffids*.[17]

> In spite of generations of talk about the equality of the sexes there has been much too great a vested interest in dependence for women to dream of dropping it . . . It will no longer be considered that a woman has fulfilled all her social obligations when she has prevailed upon some man to support her and provide her with a niche where she can irresponsibly produce babies for somebody else to educate.

Gertrude didn't seem to want to drop her dependence. Her only solution to her problems with her manipulative husband was to throw herself back on her controlling father.

Jack's romantic heroines would be the polar opposite: strong, independent women happy to break with social conventions and abandon religion. His most famous heroine would be Josella Playton in *The Day of the Triffids*, the notorious author of a racy novel. She sees no value in traditional marriage. She is willing to countenance polygamy as long as she is in charge, then settles for a permanent, loving union without a wedding. She is supremely resilient. When the leaders of a new group outline their unorthodox plans for repopulating the world, the narrator is taken aback:[18]

> I looked to Josella. To my astonishment she was grinning impishly.
> 'What do you find funny about this?' I asked, a trifle shortly.
> 'People's expressions mostly,' she replied.

His mothers, on the other hand, would be shown as incapable of caring even for themselves, let alone their children. Mother are loving but obtuse in *Chocky* and *The Midwich Cuckoos*; distant and oppressed in *The Chrysalids*; and helpless parasites in *Consider Her Ways*.

Strange, alienated children appear throughout his works. These children are 'other' – biologically unrelated to their families in *The Midwich Cuckoos* and *Chocky*; evolved beyond them in *The Chrysalids* and his pre-war short story "Child of Power" (published in *Fantasy*, 1939).

By the time Jack was eight, the situation was so bad that the Parkes family had closed ranks against George. When he suggested moving his family to London, John Israel vetoed the plan, again probably at Gertrude's request. Instead, he suggested that if George liked to further his career in London chambers, he would be happy to fund him an extra £3 a week to stay in a hotel alone during the week.

Grandma Eliza Parkes also stepped in. She was anxious to have Gertrude and the boys' company on a series of holidays in the country. Alas, she claimed to be uncertain of the addresses. They would be sure to send George a note when they arrived. Perhaps he could join them later, when work allowed? Unless they had moved on.

George may have been an outsider, but he would not be brushed off easily. Where his own interests were concerned, he had grit. He insisted there were no problems. He claimed he and Gertrude were in perfect harmony.

But his financial position was precarious, and he could not maintain his home without money. John Israel withdrew support. The situation was made worse when a friend of the Parkes family – the same who had drawn up the letter reconciling John Israel and George – pressed George for immediate payment of four years' owed interest on a mortgaged property. George did not have the money and now faced bankruptcy.[19]

Gertrude left, returning to Mayfield with the boys. George watched as the Parkes' gravy train pulled out of the station without him.

In yet another attempt to re-start his career, he wrote a second book, ostensibly a memoir of his life in South Wales called *When I was a Boy*. It was an expensive hardback production by Routledge with many illustrations. It's a romanticised version of a country childhood in a remote, unnamed village on a peninsula facing the sea.

The narrator is the only son of an ancient family whose name is commemorated on many tablets in the church. His mother is descended from this grand family and has inherited the ancestral home, a turreted mansion with a coat of arms over the door. This is significant, as it allowed George Harris to lay claim to a genteel descent without having to account for a humble name.

His father is less stately and more fun, taking young George shooting and fishing on their extensive lands. Life is full of donkey rides, circuses, ponies and dogs. George enjoys the country round of hunting in winter, birdnesting in spring and swimming in summer. He goes away to school, and makes friends with a boy called Vivian, who is an ace with a catapult.

Of course, George was not the only male offspring of an ancient family, nor did his father manage an extensive estate. His family were respectable, but not blue-blooded or even well-off. The details of country life and the taste of salty snowflakes blown inland from the sea may have been factual; the turreted ancestral home and upper class boarding school were pure fantasy.

When I Was a Boy is a charming read, a perfect Edwardian Sunday School prize. It's also a sad, narcissistic fantasy of a different past in which George was on a level with the wealthy families he briefly knew, and socially superior to his wife's family. It may have been partly intended as a present to his sons – the heritage he wanted them to have.

The dedication is opaque: "To Wyndham and Vivian this volume is fondly inscribed. 'The sun of memory glowing through my dreams' – Byron". It is not clear if this means his sons or the grandees of Cardiff. The rest of the family never called Jack by the name Wyndham.

If George hoped his former colleagues could be flattered into offering him a second chance at political success, he was disappointed. The Birmingham Methodists might admire a self-made man, but to the blue-blooded Wyndhams and their ilk, he was the worst kind of social climber.

No further books followed. George was virtually ruined. But he was still a lawyer. He knew his rights, or thought he did. He had little to lose.

In March 1913, in a stroke of shameless, self-destructive brilliance, he sued John Israel and his respectable friends for a conspiracy to "deprive him of the custody, control and society of his wife and children". It was not illegal for a wife to leave her husband, but it was illegal for others to coerce her to do so. He thought he had a case and he was determined to prove it.

Why did he do it? Was it anger, or desperation? Or did he count on his wife's family paying up rather than face an embarrassing court appearance? In this, he was wrong. Victorian industrialists did not make their fortunes without a degree of bloody-mindedness. However furious John Israel may have been at finding himself as a defendant in the Victoria Assize Courts, Birmingham, he was not going to be the first to blink. The Parkes fought back.

As if it was no more substantial than a doll's house, the whole front of the Edgbaston villa swung open, revealing everything of the lives inside to the voyeuristic eyes of the agency journalists. The case was a gift to the press, with all its intimate details of misery and Machiavellianism amongst the high and mighty. Dozens of column inches were wired to newspapers all over the country, from Scotland to London, every day of the four-day hearing. Jack was almost ten and attending a day school, where the pupils would certainly have known about the case.

To win, the Parkes family had to prove that Gertrude had plenty of reasons to leave her husband irrespective of any influence from her family. No case could be brought against her, only against the 'conspirators': her family and their friends.

First, the Parkes' lawyers told the whole tale of George's sudden departure from Cardiff, the summons for indecent assault, John Israel's discovery of his past and the elopement. The Parkes' lawyers claimed that George concealed the assault case before Gertrude married him, and she was horrified when she discovered the facts after their wedding. This proof of immorality was reason in itself for her to leave him. George said that prior to the wedding he fully disclosed all the circumstances to Gertrude, which were, in any case, totally innocent.

Libel laws meant this 15-year-old gossip could never have been publicly said except in court. There, the Parkes' lawyers were freed by absolute privilege to claim what they liked without fear of being sued. By providing the Parkes with a risk-free public platform, George had allowed them to irreparably blacken his name.

Nor did the Parkes' lawyers hesitate to weaponise Gertrude's distress. Her rather melodramatic letters to her mother were read out as evidence of her misery:

> I don't look forward to any happiness; all I want is peace. I feel completely worn out. Life has been too much for me. If it were not for you and the children I would be very glad to be at the end of it. Please tell father how grieved I am. Don't doubt how much I love you and how much I would do if I were able to spare you all this trouble.

George fought back. He claimed Gertrude had described John Israel as a petty tyrant. He claimed his wife's letter to her mother was forged, and produced other letters from his wife affectionately calling him 'Toodlems'. He brought up his mother-in-law's machinations for separating the family on those country holidays, and the suspicious timing of the sudden demand for payment from John Israel's friend. His lawyers claimed John Israel had prompted his friend to ruin his son-in-law and force the separation. John Israel's own business and financial dealings with George were dissected: [20]

> Mr Parkes again entered the box.
>
> Mr Vachell (cross-examining) – Had the question of your daughter's separation from her husband been discussed by you with either your wife, your son, or Mrs Holt [his daughter]?
>
> – No, not a word about it. She meant to leave.
>
> – Did it seem to you that if your son-in-law were made a bankrupt he was practically bound to consent to a separation?
>
> – I did not know he was going to be made a bankrupt...
>
> – Was it your object in making plaintiff a bankrupt to utterly ruin him?
>
> – It was to get my rights. I thought he had some private resources somewhere. I have no desire to ruin any man.. I did not intend the matter to be made public...
>
> Mr Vachell next asked the witness why he wrote to his

daughter, pointing out his financial position.

– Why did you not leave husband and wife alone?

– You must remember that if she was Mr Harris's wife, she was also still my daughter. I felt that Mr Harris, although her natural protector, was not a protector.

George scored a few points, but he was hopelessly outgunned. If he had counted on the Parkes being unwilling to air the family's dirty laundry in court, then he had underestimated John Israel's anger and determination to be rid of him.

The reporters in court eagerly anticipated Gertrude's turn in the witness box, detailing her plum coloured dress, sealskin coat and pince nez. But by the time Gertrude stepped up to give evidence, the jury had already heard enough. They refused to watch her further humiliation. They asked to retire, finding against George Harris.

So the Parkes had won, but there was little to celebrate given the embarrassment the hearing had caused and the money it had cost. George was now out of their lives, though he showed up occasionally to try and cadge more money out of Gertrude. She never attempted to divorce him, but he faded from view to the point where his sons never knew where their own names had come from.[21]

Gertrude was free; but freedom didn't really suit her. She had never supported herself financially, emotionally or practically, nor did she want to now.

Her father found her yet another, more modest, house nearby, and agreed to fund her with £300 a year. This was not poverty: a rural vicar might earn a similar amount and raise a family with careful management. It was enough for a cook and a nursemaid, but it was a long way from the glories of Mayfield.[22]

Jack had been attending a local day school, Miss Woodward's Private School. He had then moved to the nearby Edgbaston High School for Boys. This was a disaster. Whether the publicity surrounding the case was the reason or not, he was badly bullied.

Vivian wrote in his memoir:[23]

I was too young to realize what was happening, but I am sure it worried Jack a great deal. But schools worried him a great deal more for he had already acquired the outlook on life that stayed with him always. He weighed everything against the standards of logic and fair play that were his plimsoll-mark of behaviour, and if it was found wanting he would say so in no uncertain terms . . .

[This] didn't suit the conventional day school to which he was sent . . . like most day schools of the period it was riddled with bullies and gangs so that he had a rough time to a point where he received a blow which affected his health for years.

His nose often bled copiously and he walked in his sleep giving my nurse a nasty turn when she came down in the morning to find him fast asleep in the kitchen chair.

His behaviour became more risky. Desperate to prove himself brave enough to stand up to the bullies, and also to force his mother's attention, he began jumping from his first-floor bedroom window into the flowerbed below. These personal 'dares' became a lifelong habit, leading to a series of risky climbs as an adult over roofs, up Little Orme and even Beachy Head, often followed by his frightened but determined brother.

The bullying taught him a lesson in self-concealment. An interviewer once asked him about his relationships with other children when he was young. He replied:[24]

It is a wise defence to pretend an interest in the interests of the majority. Having learnt this fact painfully by the age of 11, I managed to get by all right with only occasional lapses into statements of honest opinion. (This process is now known, I believe, as social integration. I don't think it had a name then.)

This was a fib of a kind. He was not 'socially integrated' in the least. Nor did he want to be integrated into a system he disliked. He had learnt enough to appear to conform outwardly. Inwardly, he was laying down the foundations of a lifelong habit of secrecy, rigidly separating out the strands of his life. No-one would know the whole, real Jack. He would constantly re-invent himself, hiding behind a series of names that changed even when he was internationally famous.

The public humiliation of the court case and the bullying that followed it had left him with a desire for privacy that would one day result in his being known as "the invisible man of science fiction". All his sensitivity was walled away from view, protected from prying, jeering eyes.

Gertrude was also unhappy. Living in Birmingham, she continued to be surrounded by the family who had suffered through her disgrace, and the close-knit society who now knew every detail of the failure of her marriage. Her days as a provincial princess were over.

She found domesticity in reduced circumstances even more tedious than in luxury. She decided that after all, she preferred hotels. So she removed the boys from the day school and sent them away to board, and embarked on an endless tour of spa town hotels and seaside boarding houses.

Jack found himself in an institutionalised, genteel state of homelessness that would last almost his entire life.

References

1   *Birmingham Daily Post* (1872) "The Affairs of Israel Parkes", May 3, p.8.

2   Vivian Beynon Harris, *Jack and Me: Growing up with John Wyndham.* Only the first chapter exists of Vivian's planned, long biography. It was published with detailed annotations by Prof David Ketterer in *Foundation, the International Review of Science Fiction,* 28:75, Spring 1999, alongside another short and rather chaotic biography by Vivian, *My Brother John Wyndham 1903-1969.* This covered more of Jack's life. Both originals are in the University of Liverpool's Special Collections Archive, alongside Jack's letters, manuscripts, audio tapes and much more. This book is largely based on these archival materials.

3   These details come from their marriage certificate and their 1881 census returns. The house still exists.

4   *South Wales Daily News* (1893) "Cardiff Municipal Election", October 23, p.4.

5   *Western Mail* (1893) "Local Muncipal Elections: Riverside, Brilliant Conservative Victory", November 2, p.5.

6   *Cardiff Times and South Wales Weekly News* (1896) "Baiting the Aldermen: Young Bloods of Cardiff Council", March 14, p.6.; and *South Wales Daily News* (1895) "Cardiff Town Council: Another Personal Dispute", November 4, p.4

7   *Hull Daily Mail* (1893) "Death on the Honeymoon", October 25, p. 3.

8   Vivian Beynon Harris, ibid.

9   Many of the details about the marriage in this chapter, including George's history, are drawn from reports of the later court case, in particular the articles: *Leamington Spa Courier* (1913) "Remarkable Family Dispute", March 7, p. 4.; *The Londonderry Sentinel* (1913) "Case Stopped by Jury", March 11, p. 8.; and *Supplement to the Manchester Courier* (1913) "Claim for Wife: Jury Intervene in Strange Action", March 10, p. 3. Similar articles were published in many other local newspapers around the country. They are available on the British Newspaper Archive website.

10   *Birmingham Gazette* (1913) "Barrister's Suit", March 8, p.10. John Israel described in court his conversations with George before and after his visit to Cardiff, and his shock at receiving the telegram.

11　As another researcher has queried this birth certificate as vague, and suggested he was born earlier out of wedlock, I submitted it to a professional genealogist, Anne Mealia of the Association of Genealogists and Researchers in Archives. In her judgement, the certificate is correct. She said the lack of a street address was not that unusual at the time. Although street names were normally given, it wasn't uncommon for just a village to be recorded. She pointed out that the registration process was well established by 1903, and to fail to register a birth in order to register it later would have been difficult to do at that time (and illegal).

12　"Remarkable Family Dispute" ibid.

13　The servants' names and ages were recorded on the 1911 census. Parents were asked to record the numbers of both living and dead children. Only living children resident in the house were listed by name. As there are no birth certificates for the dead children, it is likely they were stillborn. Birth certificates were not required for stillbirths.

14　During cross examination in the later court case, the Parkes' lawyer went into details of various servants' allegations, which George denied. *Birmingham Daily Gazette* (1913) "Conspiracy Suit", March 7, p.5.

15　*Western Mail* (1892) "The Municipal Elections", October 28, p.7.

16　*Birmingham Daily Gazette* (1908) "Local Petitions", February 8, p. 6.

17　John Wyndham (1951) *The Day of the Triffids,* p.177 to 178. First published by Michael Joseph. All quotes come from the Penguin 1981 edition.

18　*The Day of the Triffids*, p.120.

19　*Pall Mall Gazette* (1913) "Deprived of his Wife's Society", March 5, p.10.

20　*The Northern Whig* (1913) "Barrister's Claim to a Wife; Jury Stop the Case", March 10, p.12; and *Manchester Courier and Lancashire General Advertiser* (1913) "Claim for Wife", March 10, p.12.

21　Vivian Harris, ibid. The brothers didn't know much about their father's younger life before he appeared in Birmingham. Years later, Jack thought Wyndham had some South Wales connection, while Vivian speculated that it came from Wyndham's theatre. This was named for the Liverpool-born theatrical impresario Sir Charles Wyndham (who had himself changed his name by deed poll from the less aristocratic Culverwell) This seems much less likely than that it reflected George's attempts to memorialise his days of glory.

22　Ibid, p18.

23   Ibid, p18.

24   Magazine editor Sam Moskowitz wrote short biographies of several science fiction writers. He sent Jack a list of 30 questions, which he answered in writing. The profile was published in *Seekers of Tomorrow* in 1966. The full text of the Q&A is in the Liverpool archive, Wyndham 11/2. The quote at the head of this chapter also comes from this Q&A.

2

Discovering Utopia

Sensitive, imaginative boys rarely enjoy their schooldays. Jack would probably have had a rough time in any case, but he was particularly unlucky in being saddled with a mother who, though loving, was undomesticated and lost in her own problems.

George was also a problem. He and Gertrude never reunited but neither did they divorce, and he continued intermittently to pursue Gertrude for money. Gertrude moved from hotel to hotel, while the boys were sent to so many schools, they later couldn't agree on the number.

Jack thought it was seven altogether. After leaving Edgbaston, he had two or three brief experiences of boarding before arriving at the age of 12 at Shardlow Hall, Derbyshire.

His arrival there may be the inspiration for his bleakest short story. Almost all his stories have some element of fantasy – Jack enjoyed playing with ideas. "Lesson" is unusual in being a straightforward tale of a bullied boy arriving at a new school. It's a sympathetic treatment of an unhappy, lonely child desperately trying to fit in, with a shockingly violent ending. There's no evidence Jack ever tried to sell it, though he had it typed.[1]

The protagonist, eleven-year-old Michael, arrives at the latest of several schools with his mother, who habitually deposits him and snatches him up again during her travels. Michael is frustrated and angry with her. The previous school had been a disaster, partly because she had sent him with the wrong kind of kit.

This time Michael has prepared carefully. He has succeeded in a desperate fight for pants and vests instead of childish combinations. Toys which he dearly longs to bring have been left behind, others he cares nothing for have been diplomatically brought. Michael is grimly aware that being a comfortable nonentity is not always possible. The first days at his new school will allocate him a role of some kind – he wants it to be the right kind.

Despite Michael's warnings, they are too early – Mother doesn't want to travel back in the dark. They are politely entertained to lunch by the headmaster and his wife:

'What delightful panelling!'

'It is charming, isn't it?' the headmaster's wife agreed. 'But how they'd treated it! We had to strip off fourteen coats of paint before we reached it.'

The ensuing talk continued to rove over the characteristics of the house, interspersed with minor historical allusion of no interest to Michael, save that he could see his mother was impressed with it and gaining confidence in the rightness of her decision to send him there. He did not understand what the age of the house could have to do with this, nor did he greatly try. He was only, and keenly, aware that this was another school, and, as such, still an unknown quantity. Somehow or other that appeared to be the one aspect upon which the conversation did not touch.

As he sat there, his replies to questions were seldom more voluble than 'yes' or 'no', but he took thoughtful care that they should be the kind of answers that school-masters expected, irrespective of truth...

A car called for his mother. He kissed her goodbye and it carried her away down the drive, stationwards and homewards. The pricking in his eyes became almost too insistent, but he managed to master it. His voice he could not control, but that did not matter much: shaky words were not cardinal. Tears or no tears was one of the strictest of adult ready-reckoners.

Over the next few hours, Michael waits in a classroom that slowly fills up with boys. He watches them, without drawing attention. If he speaks to a boy who is not new, he will be classed as cocky: "Why so natural an action should be wrong, he did not understand, but he knew it for one of those outstandingly significant details where first judgements were concerned." But he knows he cannot stay quiet either, that would class him as odd. He finally chooses a boy and starts up a conversation. The boy responds civilly.

> Michael was quite inclined to like him, but he had business on hand. The boy got up, revealing himself as an inch or two the taller. That was satisfactory: adult standards would approve.
>
> It was easy to take offence at a remark – though he could never afterwards remember what the remark had been. Then, with a cold hatred of what he was doing, he went for the boy. He pummelled him hard in the middle, hit out at his face with its silly look of surprise, pitched into him, and drove him backwards across the room.

The others pull Michael off him. When he turns, the crowd parts to let him through. He locks himself in the toilet to weep:

> He knew what he had done: before any role could be thrust upon him, he had chosen one . . . He despised what he had done. He knew it for the mean thing it was, a deliberate fake, made to satisfy the standard that admired the right fakes.

But though he weeps, the deception is a success: "In his three years at the school only two more fights were necessary – and both of them were half won by prestige before they started."

Of all his stories, this is the harshest. There is nothing to redeem the misery. Peace is gained only by violence brutally meted out on the innocence. And it is a peace that precludes friendship. He has succeeded in being left alone only by donning a mask of cruelty.

It is clearly largely biographical – how far it is true cannot be known. But it is a fact that Jack had two years of comparative peace at Shardlow Hall. He loved the surrounding farmland and tolerated the rest. It was there he discovered the works of H G Wells. For the rest of his life, to re-read them would be to return to the Derbyshire countryside.

Then Gertrude's father, John Israel Parkes, who had been a rock throughout her life, died. This separated the little family permanently from their base in Birmingham. Protecting – or perhaps controlling – his daughter to the end, he left her and her children a quarter share of his fortune of £53,538. It was the equivalent of about £3.5million today but was tied up in a trust fund managed by Gertrude's brother and brother-in-law. This meant the capital was protected from George, but he could still badger Gertrude directly for a share in the income.

A few months later, in January 1918, Jack started at the most disastrous of his schools, Blundell's. He was 14. More than 20 years later, trapped in the institutions of war, Jack was to recall the lessons in camouflage and ostracism he learnt there.

It was a very traditional boys' school which had just celebrated its 300th anniversary. The fagging system meant older boys could tyrannise the younger ones, and severe corporal punishment was routine.

It was probably at Blundell's that he was confirmed into the Church of England under pressure from his schoolmasters. He later wrote: "Went to communion the following Sunday. Was so shocked and nauseated that I have never been since. Don't, on the whole, like religions. Power tends to corrupt them. Have a suspicion that they may be the Achilles' heel of humanity."[2]

This loathing of religion would appear in some form in nearly every story he wrote. One of his early pulp stories, "The Venus Adventure", directly sets the marvels of science against religious dogma.

Jack was also haunted by the consciousness of the Great War. More than 200 old Blundell's boys are now commemorated in the school's war memorial, and their regular appearances in the casualty lists were a stark reminder of where Jack could be heading. Two of Jack's older friends shot themselves when called up. By 1918, civilians were also feeling the effects of food shortages. Vivian recalled:[3]

> [Blundell's] was the last place for my brother . . . He had to join the Officers Training Corps, there wasn't enough food, there was fighting, and, of course, my brother's way of thought didn't fit in. He lost weight, he lost spirit, and was not at all himself. . . the ever present fear that he would be of call-up age before the war ended made him ill.

Fortunately, the family doctor stepped in. He insisted that Jack be removed from Blundell's after only a few months. What to do next was unexpectedly solved by Gertrude, who chose a new type of school opened by a visionary headmaster in Hampshire. Perhaps her father's death had left her freer to make her own choices regarding her sons.

41

As a fellow non-conformist, the school's non-denominational stance also appealed to Gertrude.

Although both boys were close to Gertrude all their lives, her shortcomings as a mother are revealed in Vivian's remark: "Now, completely uncharacteristically, she did the one thing that was absolutely right for him. She sent him to Bedales co-educational school, where the whole pattern of his life was altered and laid down."[4]

Bedales was, by the standards of the time, a bold educational experiment, most noted for its warm relations between pupils and staff. It was led by J H Badley, now acknowledged as an educational genius and a typically confident and energetic late Victorian. A former Rugby pupil, he studied at Cambridge then entered teaching, but after only a term at a public school he decided he wanted to create a very different establishment.

He was influenced by the socialist and early gay activist Edward Carpenter and by the politics of William Morris, now best known for his Arts and Crafts design work but also the author of the utopian *News From Nowhere*. When only 28, in 1893, Badley became headmaster of his new school, with three boys and three teachers plus domestic staff.[5]

The second master, and Badley's lifelong friend and colleague, was Oswald Powell, known as Osbos. He was also heavily influenced by the Arts and Crafts movement, with a love for bookbinding, handweaving, gardening and bee keeping.

By the time Jack arrived in 1918, the school had grown to more than 200 pupils, of whom about a third were girls. It was internationally recognised as a beacon of modern methods; and was now housed in a purpose-built building near the village of Steep, in Hampshire, with the girls' dormitories in a separate house in the grounds. Much of the outdoor work, such as levelling the football field and even some bricklaying of the outbuildings, had been done by the children themselves.

There were fewer formal lessons than in most public schools, with a reduced emphasis on Greek and Latin. In their place was a core curriculum of maths (including book-keeping), grammar, geography and "elementary knowledge of... the machinery and laws of the State,

"Bedales", Petersfield.

and of natural laws". Greater emphasis was placed on outdoor life and practical skills such as market gardening and carpentry. Pupils of Jack's age were expected to do about 15 hours 'Head Work' a week, plus six hours of 'Hand Work' – either music or handicrafts – and six hours of physical exercise. Every day included half an hour reading.

The school was non-denominational, with a Sunday evening service of readings and varying music ranging from the Psalms, plainsong and popular hymns. Readings were from Walt Whitman, Thomas Carlyle and John Stuart Mill. The services also included what another Bedalian of Jack's time, Jocelyn Brooke, recalled as rather tentative, apologetic prayers: "God, one inferred, was addressed rather hypothetically; at mention of His name, the speaker would usually pause, ever so slightly, as though adding, silently, the cautious qualification: 'If You exist'." [6]

A central feature were Badley's 'Jaws', in which he discussed the ongoing war, other contemporary issues or discussions of human values. These were usually in Christian terminology, but Badley didn't hesitate to mention other religions, with an emphasis on spiritual values rather than dogma.

In a pamphlet written for new members of staff, he wrote: "The school life is to be a practical lesson in religious toleration . . . Whatever be the idea that God calls up in the mind of the speaker or hearer, whether it be an idea of personality or power, of creative intelligence, of a stream or tendency, one thing is certain, it represents to us our ideal."[7]

Badley and his 'Jaws' about the world as it is and as it should be are recreated in the portrait of Michael Beadley in *The Day of Triffids*, the organiser of a band of survivors which plans to set up in a "country house or boarding school". Beadley, a conflation of Bedales and Badley, ultimately becomes the leader of the new society, freed of the conventions of the old world. The narrator, Bill Masen, describes him:[8]

> He was lean, tall, broad-shouldered, and slightly stooping with something of the air of an athlete run to books. In repose his face took on an expression of mild gloom from the darkness of his large eyes, but it was seldom that one had a glimpse of it in repose. The occasional streak of grey in his hair helped very little in judging his age. He might have been anything from thirty-five to fifty.

Wyndham's Beadley is perceptive, practical and likeable, a charismatic speaker without oratorical tricks: "When he spoke, it was in a pleasant, practised voice, with a fireside manner." This kind manner conceals an absolute determination on his own course.

His vision is of a completely new world: "We aren't out to reconstruct – we want to build something new and better."[9] Ultimately, he succeeds where all others fail, and his vision of the new world becomes a reality.

For J H Badley, success was on a smaller scale than a new world order, but no less absolute. He became known simply as 'The Chief', a spare, ascetic figure, always dressed in grey flannel bags and tennis shoes, which later had a hole cut in one to accommodate his bunion. One old boy described him as a cross between Jesus Christ and a Roman senator. He had so much control that he had only to point silently at a piece of paper on the floor for the nearest boy to immediately pick it up. Yet he was understanding of children's failures and misdemeanours. He was warm and good fun, roaring with laughter at crude Latin jokes and drenching pupils with water while doing the washing up on camping trips.

His central belief was in the importance of self-fulfilment, as he once wrote to his father: "The best and most useful work one can do is that which springs from one's own personality as outcome of an inner need. The man . . . who is seeking to liberate himself from what he feels to be intolerable constraints and soul-destroying conditions thereby does most to liberate others."[10]

His ideals were mocked by many. In modern terms, it was a school for snowflakes – every child precious and unique – and it was derided as such. Comments included: "Enthusiastic amateurs dealing with the children of cranks" and "Bedales? Oh, yes! That's where they drink cocoa and eat brown bread as if it were the Eucharist."

But after seven unhappy, disrupted years, the school and village were to be a lodestone to Jack for the rest of his life. Many years later, he recalled his first sight of it in a collection written by former pupils and staff to celebrate Badley and his school. It's a piece that speaks as much about his experience of school life to date as it does about his new home. It is also notable that Jack arrives at Petersfield station and walks the last mile and a half to his new school alone – Gertrude does not accompany him.[11]

> 'Bedales?' said the porter. 'Just you follow those three there.'
>
> So I grasped my overnight bag and, at an unobtrusive distance, tagged along. Surprisingly they stopped and waited for me. 'Bedales?' said one in a friendly way. 'Yes, come along with us.' After a while we came in sight of a building dominated by a tall window. 'That's Bedales,' said the boy beside me; even then something in his tone struck me. Far from creeping like a snail, he seemed glad to see the place.
>
> They took me up to Flat [the boys' dorms], found my name on the list, showed me G dormitory, recommended the choice of a particular bed and told me there would be tea at six.
>
> I found my way to the dining hall. It was full of noise, a huge, rather formidably bare room, ornamented by a couple of portraits, and four butter pats stuck to the ceiling. I slid tentatively into an empty seat, expecting a possibly rowdy ejection. Instead, someone passed me a jug of tea...

I remember that there was plenty to eat, but not what it was. I was too interested in my surroundings. In all my previous experience the return to School had been accompanied by a subdued mood, but there was nothing subdued about the crowd in the dining hall. They seemed pleased, to *enjoy* being together again... the whole thing was very unreal... I had discovered a school that expected civilised behaviour and had miraculously succeeded in making the wretched business of growing up a largely enjoyable process.

From a distance of a hundred years, it is hard to understand the chasm that marked out Bedales from the methods of most boarding schools of the time, but Jack and Vivian were not the only pupils to feel the difference.

The naturalist author Jocelyn Brooke, whose own school career and late-blossoming success as a writer mirrored Jack's life, wrote of the change he experienced in himself after arriving there shortly after Jack. He also had suffered at a prep school, then a public school, King's. He was removed after running away twice in two weeks and sent to Bedales.

Like Jack, he was amazed to find a world where people were habitually pleasant to each other, and where newcomers were made to feel at home. More than 30 years later, like Jack, he wrote of King's:[12]

The ferocious initiation ceremonies, the petty cruelties and indecencies, the perpetual sense of injustice and irrational guilt... immunised me successfully against any possible horrors which the future might hold in store . . . The worst I had to fear from the war was that it would be as bad as going back to King's School again: but it never was.

Reading the innumerable accounts of the experiences by refugees who have escaped, either before or during the war, from a totalitarian to a democratic country, I have felt, over and over again, a sense of familiarity with the emotions they describe. For this was precisely my own experience when I left King's School and went to Bedales... The perpetual cloud of fear and suspicion – which I had known at St Ethelbert's as well as at Canterbury – was suddenly, miraculously lifted. I had not thought it possible to be 'happy' at school: but at

Bedales I learnt, to my astonishment, that it was not only possible but easy.

Life at Bedales may have been a paradise compared to other schools, but it was not a soft option. Badley had a strong Puritan streak. Life there was vigorous with few indulgences. An account by an Old Boy who was also there in the 1920s, recalls a world that was "strange but thoroughly friendly".[13]

The day began with the nurse and her assistants taking everyone's temperature – raised temperatures meant a trip to the Sick Room. Boys then stripped off their clothes in the dormitory and ran to the bathroom to plunge into cold baths and out again. Boys dressed in jackets and knitted ties. Girls wore gymslips, they were forbidden to wear stays, and hair had to be parted in the middle. Pupils made their own beds (wooden slats made in the school's workshops), had breakfast and then had to use the toilets in sets. These were the most basic of earth closets which required the pupils to squat over a cast iron frame. It was considered vital for health that they moved their bowels at the same time every day.

The morning continued with academic lessons, but over a much wider curriculum than most public schools. The midday dinner was preceded by an inspection of hands – they must be free from ink and hair well brushed. Badley himself ate in the same room as the boys, always drinking a glass of milk. After lunch was a 30 minute siesta in the dorms, followed by outdoor work on the estate farm and orchard, and PE classes, with cross country runs when it was too wet for games.

In the evenings were more relaxed activities, such as chess, Badley's own courses in classical history, well remembered as brilliant storytelling sessions, plus homegrown entertainment. There were senior and junior orchestras, choirs and stage performances, particularly Shakespeare. The school was so small that most people were pressed into service to fill gaps.

Many activities took pace in the Quad, a glassed-in central courtyard surrounded by the school buildings. Those not involved would often stand in the upper corridors surrounding the Quad, looking down and chatting.

Concerts and informal 'Merry Evenings' of songs and sketches often took place in the Lupton Hall, built a few years before Jack arrived in the style of a barn. This is now Grade 1 listed as a superb example of Arts and Crafts. On most evenings, the day was brought to a close here with a ritual of hand-shaking, when each child filed past and said "Goodnight" to each member of staff, including the Chief.

The days ended with washing in cold water in handbasins in the dormitories, which had at least five beds occupied by a mixture of ages intended to mimic family life. Lights went out at 9pm, though chattering and storytelling often went on later. All dormitory windows had to be wide open at all times.

There was virtually no privacy at all. Communal life was the rule.

But within this Spartan and energetic framework, there was little cruelty. Prefects had far less power than in other schools, and though the Chief occasionally beat a boy, punishments were not severe. Even the PE teacher – often the most dreaded figure of school life – was Mr R E Roper, later remembered by pupils as the kindest man in the school.[14]

Badley had discovered the secret of contentment used by most boarding schools today: a programme so packed with activity that there was little room left for misbehaviour or homesickness.

Weekends were filled to the brim with horseback riding, games, classical and folk music concerts. There were occasional trips out, such as to see the Naval Review on the Solent, or to Cambridge to see professional plays.

There were the usual sports teams, though success in these was not fetishised. Jack's experience fending off bullies came in handy on one occasion when he competed as a boxer, recorded in the school magazine as a wild slogging bout:[15]

> Gardiner rushed to the offensive at once, repeatedly running his nose against Harris' ever-ready left, indeed the latter never seemed to use his right much. Despite a bleeding nose, Harris won as the result of a steady defensive, an exceptional tactic in the Gym.

Jack loved the whole day "senior expeds" on bicycles or on foot into the Hampshire countryside on Sundays. It was almost certainly here that he encountered the puffballs that would be a motif of his early work, finally morphing into the triffids.

Puffballs are one of the strangest phenomena in the English countryside. They can grow to be well over a metre in diameter, lying alone and as unaccountably as if they have fallen from the sky. When young they are solid white flesh all through, and are safe to eat, but as they grow the inside turns yellow, then purple and brown. At this point, they are just millions of spores, held together by a paper-thin skin. If disturbed, they explode, severely irritating the lungs and eyes. A single raindrop can cause spores to shoot out in a cloud above the puffball.

Jack was fascinated by them. They recur in his work, starting with one of his earliest short stories "Sphere of Hell", later retitled "The Puffball Menace". It was one of the first depictions of biological warfare, published in 1933.

A fictional Eastern state seeks revenge on the British Empire. They send seeds of a modified fungus to keen British gardeners throughout the South West, encouraging them to compete at nurturing their own doom. The puffballs have been crossbred to combine both types of fungus – the parasites such as ringworms that live on living flesh and the mushroom-type saprophyte that grows on rotting vegetation. Their poison kills their victims, and more puffballs grow from the rotting flesh.

Jack used puffballs as weapons again in his lost tribe novel *The Secret People* in 1935. The men make slits in the skins of ripe puffballs and throw them at their enemies, sending them coughing and spluttering away. Jack probably learnt the trick messing about with his friends in the fields.

The puffballs' exploding spores would be mimicked by the triffids' seed pods:[16]

> When it burst, it did it with a pop . . . The white seeds shot
> into the air like steam, and began drifting away on the lightest
> breeze . . . Looking down on a field of triffids in late August
> you could well get the idea that some kind of desultory bom-
> bardment was in progress.

It was this disturbing contrast between the alien menace and the beauty of the English countryside that would always be a feature of his work.

Bedales was nurturing of creativity. Visits from guests were common, usually musicians or artists, who might stay for a few days to help with concerts or productions. While Jack was there the great Bengali poet Rabindranath Tagore visited and gave a reading.

There was a well-equipped darkroom for photography, which also became one of Jack's passions. Various newsletters and journals were run by the pupils, along with other clubs. Bedales Wireless Society had been set up by Peter Eckersley in a hut soon nicknamed Wavy Lodge. He went on to become the first BBC Chief Engineer.

Even the formal curriculum included a fair amount of freedom. Except for timetabled 'Head Work' lessons, teachers were stationed in each room and would instruct any pupils who chose to attend. This was meant to allow individualism, but inevitably some activities – carpentry, book-binding, art – were more popular than others.

It suited Jack, who was naturally good with his hands and who enjoyed the craftsmanship of the studios and the opportunities to 'tinker'. He learnt a great deal that stood him in good stead all his life. His brother Vivian later recalled how practically useful he was in the Army, travelling through Europe after the Normandy landings. He made beds that kept him off the ground and used abandoned German materials and kit to make life tolerable. Vivian wrote:[17]

> The young men who came from working homes and had been to day schools didn't know how to live in a community and had no idea how to clean boots, sew on buttons or make beds; Mother had always done it for them, so my brother's cleverness with his hands was a matter of awe to them. He could bind books, do leather work of all sorts . . . He kept a drawer full of bits and pieces and he never bought a gadget if he could make it himself, and if he did buy a gadget he invariably improved it.

Jack was already writing, and at the age of 16, he had his first publication printed in one of the school magazines, *The Bee*. Titled "Vivisection", it is the first part of a horror fantasy, and draws heavily on the H G Wells story, *The Island of Doctor Moreau*.[18]

It is told, like most of his future novels, in the first person. The narrator is invited to stay in the country house of Professor Langley, a man with ideas about vivisection which the narrator thinks impossible. His first night is disturbed by the cries of animals:

> ...not plain, ordinary animals such as one hears at the Zoo, but mixed; there was one which sounded like a combination of a lion's roar and the bellowing of a bull and other curious noises. Suddenly arose a most frightful scream of pain, the sound of a tortured soul.

He rushes to the landing where he hears a pony trotting inside the house, then mounting the stairs. He is horrified to be confronted by two faun-like creatures and flees back to his room. The half-human creations keep coming – the housemaids are a kind of black dwarf, while the formal gardens are inhabited by an eight-feet tall creature dressed in an overall and straw hat, which ambles off into the trees: "I stared after it and then at the ground before me. . . . The prints upon the ground were those of horse's hooves; no others were visible."

Here, the story breaks off, and part two is not forthcoming in later issues. The story has a Victorian feel of *Dr Jekyll and Mr Hyde*: the rational narrator visiting a man he believes to be as educated and civilised as himself, only to be confronted by a spectacle of horror. Like H G Wells, and like the future works of John Wyndham, it contrasts the apparent peace of an English scene – velvety lawns and walled gardens – with a nightmare.

It also prefigures what was to be one of his later obsessions: the creation by humans of hybrids and mutations. Like the triffids, the title makes clear these creatures are not formed by Nature or God – they are the result of scientific meddling. And like the mutant children of the *Chrysalids*, it is not clear that they are monsters. Jack's sympathy is not totally with the narrator.

Jack found encouragement for his writing at Bedales. He later said that he often wrote stories when set to write essays "and frequently got away with it".[19] The year he arrived, he won a writing competition, but apart from this small success, he was not a star in the school. He left little trace, and rarely appears in the school's official or unofficial magazines.

Though a strong swimmer and athlete, he disliked team games and wasn't in any of the teams. He very rarely appeared in plays, and didn't join any committees. In a 15-strong jazz orchestra, Jack was on the triangles. On the staff of the school magazine, he was a back issue salesman.[20]

Viv, on the other hand, was in everything and loved it. He was on the cricket team and was awarded the silver medal by the Life Saving Society. When he appeared in *The Merry Wives of Windsor*, the reviewer noted: "V Harris as Sir Hugh Evans had scope for his inimitable buffoonery."[21] Viv would always be an entertainer.

He joined the Boys' Fire Brigade as soon as he arrived and rose through the ranks to be a popular and efficient Captain. This was no sinecure. The year Jack arrived there was a small but significant fire caused by overheated pipes in a bedroom. It was gleefully put out by the Brigade, who flooded the room and dining hall below it. The boys held practice alarms at least once a week, often at night, and Viv's experience would shape his future in the Second World War.[22]

But all this fun and creative freedom in a beautiful setting came at a cost: a fair number of academic failures, as recorded by many who were there at the period. One of Bedales' more successful alumni, the childcare campaigner Lady Allen of Hurtwood, loved her time at Bedales, worshipped the Chief, and stayed on for an extra year as Head Girl. Nevertheless, she titled her autobiography *Memoirs of an Uneducated Lady*.

Jocelyn Brooke recalled: [23]

> It was possible to slack almost to one's heart's content. Once I had passed the School Certificate and Responsions[24], nobody cared a hoot what I did – with the result that, when I got to Oxford, I was totally unable to construe a simple bit of Latin prose, and consequently distinguished myself by failing in the Law Prelim, at the end of my first year.

Even the staff of the time were conscious of the lax academic standards. Geoffrey Crump, who joined the staff from the Army a year after Jack arrived, had been disturbed by the orgy of waste and misery of the Great War. As an English teacher at Bedales, he was at first overjoyed to find a school that was fundamentally different in terms of all its conventions, then concerned by its failures. He said:[25]

> Its most immediately striking characteristic was the atmo-
> sphere of freedom and contented activity... There was a holi-
> day feeling about the whole place; everybody was healthy and
> happy and full of interest. It was like a big family: all on the
> best of terms, and all devoted to their home; it was difficult
> to believe that one was a member of a school staff, and a
> newcomer at that...
>
> The boys and girls, as a whole, were contented with inferior
> achievement in all their activities and there was a strong and
> fairly universal determination to do only what they wished to
> do . . . A certain dissatisfaction could often be detected espe-
> cially among the older ones. They were beginning to feel that
> they were not getting anywhere.

Academic work was not the only area where the school struggled to
combine freedom and responsibility. As one of the very first co-educational boarding schools, Bedales had to find a way to create healthy
relations between the sexes that did not include any actual sex. This
was a very difficult balancing act. Any suggestion of impropriety, let
alone any unwanted pregnancies, would have been a catastrophe for
the individuals themselves and for Bedales' growing reputation. It
could easily have led to the failure of the school.

Even Badley himself was remembered by pupils of Jack's generation as remote, his more extrovert side only really coming to the fore
as he got older and Bedales' success was assured. As the head of a
ground-breaking co-educational school, he knew he had to be beyond
reproach, and any hint of intimacy with pupils would have sounded
warning bells, justified or not.

Girls and boys had to live as siblings and 'good chums', getting
to know and value each other, without any sexual aspect. Adolescent
passions had to be kept in check, both by practical rules such as the
separation of boys and girls into different buildings at night, and by a
subtler, more insidious method of social control.

The main method was to minimise the importance of sex, which
Brooke described as creating an emotional vacuum in pupils' minds.[26]

> To be attracted to a girl or boy and to show it was considered
> *silly*. In cases where 'affairs' seemed likely to have serious

developments (and there were surprisingly few of these), the two parties concerned were treated to serious and sympathetic lectures in which it was pointed out that 'all that' was mere silliness; that the aim of co-education was to promote a 'healthy, natural comradeship' between the sexes, and that any deviation from this 'healthy' attitude was a kind of disloyalty to the headmaster. How such 'comradeship' between a young man and a normal adolescent girl could be 'healthy' yet entirely sexless, was not explained. Nor did one gather why 'all that' presumably ceased to be 'silly' when (at the age of eighteen or nineteen) one left school.

Other old Bedalians also remembered that there was little revolt against these ideals. Girls and boys might pass notes in class, or even 'corridor' together when 'saying goodnight' in the passages above the Quad, but this minimisation of sex was largely accepted. Badley himself had so much prestige, and the relationships between staff and pupils were so close, that there was no natural rejection of their values by a rising generation. One old boy said:[27]

> There was a myth of freedom, but so far from being free we were in truth being indoctrinated extremely efficiently by an insidious culture . . . How damaging it in fact was is too difficult to say; it is revealing though that Bedalians of that generation, contrary I am sure to theoretical expectation, do not seem since to have been conspicuously successful in sexual or emotional relationships.

Some girls were surprised and discomfited when they later met young men who did not want to be 'good chums'. Boys also struggled to make the leap from a world where "all that was mere silliness" to romantic relationships with young women. Though well-versed in the politics of gender equality, they could be even more shy and clodhopping with women than their peers educated at traditional schools.

So a co-educational school, though doubtless creating much closer and more comfortable relationships between the sexes than the single sex public schools, in some ways had to be even more repressive.

Bedales boys were among the first to experience a very modern problem, now visible as a lack of passion in a post- #MeToo world.

Relationships can be smothered at birth by anxiety about respect and permission. The greater the desire for equality, the harder it can be to make the jump from friends and equals to romance and sex. Jack's circumspect five-year-courtship of his future lover, surely agonising for them both, is a case in point.

And sex was not the only snake in Badley's Eden. A public school headmaster who critiqued the school summed this up:[28]

> At Bedales you have begun to solve our greatest problem – that of intellectual apathy; you seem to have got everybody interested in everything, though you have done so at the expense of such things as fatigue, dissipation of energy, and a lowering of academic achievement. You have also made school life a thing which is thoroughly happy, and thoroughly healthy, another thing that we have not achieved. But it seems to me that in your principle of liberty you are catering for an ideal state which is not in existence, and in that sense you cannot be said to be giving children the best training for life as it now is.

This last remark was the core of Bedales' problem. Was this really a suitable preparation for adult life in the challenging years of the 20th century, with economic depression, fascism and war ahead? How would Bedales snowflakes manage in a world that wanted cogs for the machinery of Empire, or even just cannon fodder? In the coming decades, Jack, Viv and their friends would have to find out.

By creating an almost utopian community of liberty and equality between boys and girls, children and staff, its pupils were unprepared for the realities of life outside – or for the people outside their self-regarding bubble.

Several old Bedalians have written that these principles of equality never extended to the pantry staff, grammar school boys or the local villagers. Snobbery always remained – with an elitism even more rigid than that of the average public school boy due to the Bedalian belief in their school's uniqueness and superiority. It's a condescending type of prejudice that's even more common today – the 'we know best' attitude of the well-educated liberal elite.

The fact that this egalitarian society could only be accessed by the very wealthy was a paradox that the school could never resolve. The pupils were given little political education to understand this, or to truly help in the establishment of a wider and more equal society as William Morris and his peers of the Arts and Crafts movement had envisaged. Neither did their 'spiritual' teaching and tolerance leave them equipped to understand evil or totalitarianism, as a grittier religious training would have.

And though the venture was the result of high fees paid by parents, the children were ill-prepared to replicate their parents' success. One old boy of the 1940s wrote: "Tap enough money boxes and you can make a social island... Bedales teaches you to appreciate the good things of life without giving you any of the means to acquire them." [29]

One result of creating a school better than the society surrounding it was a large number of pupils who, in one way or another, never really left. Badley's social engineering experiment was all too successful. He had created a bubble that no-one wanted to pop.

One said: "It's surely revealing (and depressing) that people seem to remain Bedalians even more than people remain Etonians or Wellingtonians, but it's not surprising: it was a school that was bound to induce just this kind of immaturity."[30]

Another Bedalian wrote: "After school the cold air of capitalism blew many of us into depression, nostalgia, or back to individual versions of Cockshott Lane [a pleasant spot near the school]. The microcosm could not be re-created, and many of us were totally unfitted for the more general project."[31]

Jack Harris certainly fitted into this category. Well hardened to Puritan standards, he spent much of his life in a Quaker-founded London club that was an adult version of the Spartan but comradely life of Bedales. He was continually popping back to the village of Steep to stay with friends (some of whom actually lived on Cockshott Lane), until he finally returned to live just outside the school grounds for the last few years of his life.

But the lasting pull of the Bedales vision was far from being purely negative. Badley's belief that a better world was possible through intelligent organisation would run like a golden thread throughout Jack's work. Even after living through the horrors of war, he would still believe it. He writes of destruction over and over again – his worlds are obliterated by plagues, drowning and nuclear bombs – but his heroes seek to replace them with something better.

He never abandoned Badley's central tenet that "the best and most useful work one can do is that which springs from one's own personality as outcome of an inner need". He never settled to a life of nine-to-five grind.

There would be decades of scrabbling a living as a magazine and pulp fiction writer, and hundreds of rejection letters for unpublished novels and stories, before he would be rewarded with the outstanding success of *The Day of the Triffids* and all that followed. In those early years, he could easily have given up or sidelined his writing and taken up a more profitable career. But he did not. A modest room, like-minded company and creative freedom were enough.

References

1   The manuscript is held in the University of Liverpool archive.

2   It may seem strange that Jack should have been so horrified by Holy Communion, but it is less common in Methodist churches. It may be an occasional rather than weekly occurrence. It is sometimes a simple sharing of bread and a non-alcoholic drink, rather than being expressed as "blood and body of Christ".

3   Vivian Beynon Harris, *My Brother John Wyndham,* p.19, see note to Chapter 1.

4   Harris, ibid, p.19.

5   For more about Bedales and Badley, see James L Henderson's *Irregularly Bold, A Study of Bedales School,* published by Andre Deutsch in 1978. Unless otherwise indicated, most of the first person accounts and details of Bedales life in this chapter come from Henderson.

6   Jocelyn Brooke's *The Military Orchid,* his account of his obsession with botany and one particular flower, was first published by The Bodley Head in 1948. It was reprinted by Little Toller Books.

7   Henderson, ibid, p.45.

8   *The Day of the Triffids,* p105. Thanks to David Ketterer for this insight of Badley as Beadley.

9   Ibid, p.258.

10   Henderson, ibid, p.18.

11   John Haden Badley 1865 – 1967, *Bedales School and its Founder.* Edited by Gyles Brandreth and Sally Henry. Published by the Bedales Society, 1967.

12   Brooke, ibid, p.82.

13   Henderson, ibid.

14   As visionary as Badley, Reginald Roper became a major influence in physical education, publishing many books and papers about the importance of organised play, and the individual within the community. In contrast to most PE teachers, he was particularly concerned for weaklings, and that every individual should reach their optimum development.

15   *Bedales Chronicle,* p.18, May 1919, vol 12.

16   *The Day of the Triffids,* p.50.

17   Vivian Harris, ibid, p.24.

18   Held in Bedales archive as hard copy, not digitised at time of writing. Thanks to archivist Jane Kirby for showing me this.

19   Interview with Sam Moskowitz, see note to chapter 1.

20   *Bedales Chronicle,* p.1, July 1921 mentions Harris on the staff; and *Bedales Chronicle,* p.57, June 1921, mentions his role in the orchestra. *Bedales Record* 1919, issue 31, lists him as a writing competition winner.

21   David Ketterer, "Introduction", p.8, *Foundation*, vol 28, no 75, Spring 1999.

22   *Bedales Record*, no 36, 1923-24, p.64.

23   Brooke, ibid, p.86.

24   The Responsions was the first of three examinations once required for the University of Oxford. It included relatively simple questions in Latin, Ancient Greek and mathematics.

25   Geoffrey Crump, *Bedales since the War,* London, Chapman and Hall, 1936. Quoted in Henderson, p.54-56.

26   Brooke, ibid, p.84.

27   Henderson, ibid, p.136.

28   Crump, ibid.

29   Henderson, ibid, p.130.

30   Henderson, ibid, p.135.

31   Henderson, ibid, p.130.

3

Love Without Chains

Jack left school to an uncertain future typical of Bedales graduates. Thanks to his mother's wandering habits, he was rootless as well as directionless.

He first became apprenticed to a famous sheep breeder near Banbury. But as he said later, the sheep had little conversation. He disappeared nightly into Oxford on an ex-government surplus motorbike for company. Within a couple of years, he needed a change.

His parents again demonstrated their total obtuseness regarding their son. His mother wanted him to try accountancy; his father suggested the Church on the grounds that he would be able to hunt two or three times a week. George seemed not to realise that his son despised religion and was uninterested in either horses or the social status conferred by the hunt. They compromised on law, and Jack went to Oxford to cram for the exams he had failed to take at Bedales.[1]

He enjoyed his time there because he could rush through the work then go to the next-door science museum, but he failed the first exams. His next step was a desultory attempt at a career in advertising. He later summarised this period of his life: "After school tried farming and learned something about sheep. Started to read law, and learned a little more about sheep. Gave that up for advertising, and learned a great deal about sheep."[2]

Meanwhile, he rented a pair of old railway carriages on farmland near his old school and used them to go back every weekend to see Viv and his other friends. This was the start of a lifelong habit of retreating to the countryside he loved and the people he understood.

Viv graduated from Bedales with more of a plan. He enrolled at the Royal Academy of Dramatic Arts to train as an actor. Both brothers headed for London. Gertrude anxiously consulted her hotel acquaintances, and a Quaker recommended the newly opened Penn Club, then at 8, 9 and 10 Tavistock Square, Bloomsbury, London. The brothers moved in to share a room together. It would be Jack's home for 30 years.

The terraced building had been leased and renovated by the Quaker community in 1920, who wanted to do something for the damaged generation of young people recovering from the war. It grew partly from the club of men who had been ambulance drivers in France, often after refusing to fight. It was open to any young person "in sympathy with the Friends' ideals" seeking convivial accommodation in the capital.[3]

Many residents were former pupils from Quaker or progressive schools. It was used for Bedales' Annual Meeting, and for old boys' dinners. Jack joined in 1925 as a permanent resident, paying 50/- (£2.50) a week for a single room, bed and board. This was slightly more than the average weekly wage. The Penn Club was not aimed at the working class, but it was cheap enough to allow Jack to live on his allowance and write.

There was no luxury. A typical room had a bed, washstand, dressing chest, table and chair, with linoleum on the floor. Gas fires had meter boxes for payment. Washbasins with running water were available in only a few rooms.[4]

But it must have seemed comfortable enough after the compulsory cold baths and wide-open windows of Bedales, and the communal rooms formed a lively heart to the club.

These were modified as the club became more financially secure: a wireless and loudspeakers were bought in 1926, a year later the old-fashioned billiard table was replaced with table tennis. Regular dances with bands or hired gramophones were held; tennis parties used the grassed square outside. There were fireside talks and lectures and games of bagatelle. Residents, including Jack, joined in play readings of radical dramas such as J M Barrie's *Admirable Crichton*.

Committee meeting minutes show attempts to keep some kind of lid on the 40-odd young people determined to have a good time: table tennis bats were locked away at 11pm, and the playing of gramophones and musical instruments in rooms banned after 11.30pm.

It was cosmopolitan: as well as students and long-term residents, it became a favoured destination for liberal visitors from all over the world seeking like-minded souls in London. It has been described as a miniature university common room. Viv wrote:[5]

> The club was ideal for him…. he met distinguished and ed-
> ucated minds and there were always members to talk with.
> Talking and people were two of my brother's great interests.
> Also he was a very curious person and whenever he came
> to stay with us he would always wander round peering into
> cupboards and hidey holes to see what was inside. I think he
> perhaps gained some sort of estimate of people's character
> by their hidden life behind cupboard doors.

While Jack dug in at the Penn, for a few years Viv's life seemed to be taking off. He spent two years at RADA, moving out of the Penn Club to digs where he could work with his friends. He then appeared in a number of London productions at the new Children's Theatre, and at the Apollo and the Royal Court theatres. He toured Scotland with Shaw's *Major Barbara*[6].

For his 21st birthday, Gertrude gave him £50 to furnish a flat in Chelsea and paid the first year of a seven-year lease. Viv continued to perform, but a year later over-reached himself as stage manager and actor in a production of *The Brass Paperweight,* loosely adapted from Dostoevsky's *The Brothers Karamazov.*

It got mixed reviews, but when it closed, Viv considered it a failure. Physically and mentally exhausted, he went down with flu and started to run a very high temperature. Alone in his flat, he began hallucinating that someone was walking around outside reciting religious texts "of a singularly depressing theme".[7]

He called Gertrude, who took charge. She moved with him to Smedley's, a vast Derbyshire spa hotel that specialised in 'hydrotherapy': a system of baths and saunas at varying temperatures. Viv later wrote: "I never returned to my flat. Something had happened to me. What had been a vague feeling of insecurity became a fully blown anxiety neurosis – the driving ambition and confidence built into me by my time in the theatre was dissipated."

The next 20 years of Viv's life would be dominated by Smedley's, a forbidding Victorian pile looming over the little town of Matlock. It covered several acres, with 260 bedrooms, catering for more than 400 guests, plus any servants they brought. Fewer than half were invalids, it also offered rest and relaxation for those who could afford at least £4 per week. It advertised "Healthy comfort without boredom or stuffiness; amusement without fatigue; the hearty geniality of communal life yet with privacy for those who prefer it."[8]

There were winter gardens and billiard rooms for poor weather; tennis courts, bowling and croquet in the summer. Boating, fishing, riding and golf were offered. More than 60 staff worked in the Russian and Turkish baths alone, plus 12 trained rubbers (masseurs).

There were also regular concerts, theatricals and tableaux. Gertrude decided that Viv should "keep his hand in" by working in the small theatre, and he set to work painting new flats and props. Amongst the entertainment staff was 36-year-old actress Lila Gann, stage name Grettan. Lila's family disapproved of her work, thus her change of surname. She had taken a job at Smedley's after a modest career with a touring company.[9]

Soon, Viv and Lila were appearing on stage together, raising the standard to the point where non-residents were coming to see the plays at weekends.[10]

Lila was to be Viv's partner for the next 45 years, a loyal love that didn't include marriage. Gertrude must have cursed the day she brought Viv to Smedley's – she never liked or trusted Lila. For the rest of their lives, Jack would have to act as a buffer between them, relaying information without revealing the source.

Viv arranged to write up Smedley's social events for the local paper. For this valuable publicity, the hotel allowed him to stay for a minimum charge.

Both Gertrude and Viv forgot about the Chelsea flat. Viv couldn't sub-let it, and Gertrude had refused to pay any longer. The result was that Viv was made bankrupt at the age of 24.[11]

A middle-aged, third flight actress and an embarrassing bankruptcy in the press: where Viv was concerned, Jack's iron sense of standards, logic and fair play did not apply. Cemented together by trauma, Jack would never turn his back on his younger brother. There was no allowance he would not make, nothing he would not forgive. In return, Viv worshipped Jack, following behind on his hair-raising climbs up Little Orme and Beachey Head despite his own terror. When they were older, Viv would save every press cutting mentioning his brother, proudly preserving them in leather albums without a trace of envy.

Viv's fragility may have had a bracing effect on Jack. As a writer, Jack would suffer doubt and self-disgust all his life. He also had periodic depressions, which were particularly acute during the war. But in a small family, at least one person has to be responsible. Gertrude and Viv had seized the roles of delicate invalids. Jack was therefore forced to be the grown-up of the little group, a part which probably strengthened him in his determination to be some kind of success.

Decades later, Viv would recall their holidays together in what could have been a metaphor for their relationship. Viv would sit on the carrier of Jack's motorbike, which didn't have quite enough power to take them both up steep hills. As it started to fail, Viv would repeatedly hop off and, as the bike gathered speed again, leap back on, until he inevitably missed: "I sat down in the road and he went to the top without me. And we laughed at this. We always laughed together. We both had the same nervous inhibitions but he could control his and I couldn't control mine. But always he was a special indestructible part of my life."[12]

Viv's choice of lifestyle – an unofficial yet faithful relationship with an actress 13 years older – may have been unconventional, but for him it worked. She was the support he needed, as much mother as mistress. He had found the love of his life and they were free to form their own kind of bond. They would never have children, so Viv would always be the baby. It's not clear why they didn't marry but Viv probably found Gertrude and George's example uninspiring. Gertrude may also have forbidden it, and she controlled the purse strings.

Lila accepted the situation. Having already disappointed her family, she had little to lose, and she was old enough to make her own decisions. Viv was something of a catch for her. Apart from his private income, he was slim, affectionate and funny. He was a skilled raconteur and fellow professional. Amongst Viv and Lila's theatrical friends, their relationship was not so shocking. It was a rather different story at the Penn.

Unusually for its time, it had accommodation for men and women, with the proprieties observed by separating them into opposite ends of the terraced building. The Quakers believed in equality but were shy of outright permissiveness. In the early days, one young couple stayed up to the early hours to chat and snuggle on the sofa. They were firmly told to go to their rooms by the warden. They refused to budge. The next day an emergency committee meeting was held and they were asked to leave.[13]

Taken altogether, it was an only slightly more adult version of Bedales school, but change was in the air.

All around the Penn Club lived the Bloomsbury set, experimenting with new kinds of marriages and ménages; and with a fixed belief that "to thine own self be true" was the only maxim worth living by. The literary surroundings may have made the Penn Club attractive to Jack, as an aspiring author. Virginia Woolf, already famous in the mid-1920s, lived at 52 Tavistock Square. She was inspired to write *The Lighthouse* while walking in the gardens the same year Jack arrived. Psychoanalyst and editor James Strachey lived and practised around the corner.

Though far from religious, they swam in the same waters as the liberal Quakers. Jack never became part of the Bloomsbury set, but many of their offspring went to progressive schools. Writer and Bohemian Julia Strachey, niece of the historian Lytton Strachey, was at Bedales at the same time as Jack. She once horrified a prefect by playing Boston one step jazz on her gramophone before breakfast.[14]

The nearby Slade School of Art produced many complex relationships: painter Dora Carrington married Ralph Partridge but fell in love with Lytton Strachey. He was gay and more interested in Ralph, but the three managed to make a triangular relationship work. This was enlivened by other lovers such as artist Mark Gertler, who was obsessed with Carrington.

The king of the Bohemians, painter Augustus John, was notorious for attempting the seduction of almost anyone with a pulse. He adored the many children that resulted. His wife, their five children, his mistress and their two children all lived together, with other lovers and their children slowly added over the years.

These were extreme examples, but through the 1920s and 30s there was a more widespread movement towards banishing Victorian ignorance and acknowledging and embracing sexuality: sexologist Havelock Ellis claimed "congenital inverts" – homosexuals – should not be blamed for the way they were born; Marie Stopes astonished the English-speaking world with her discovery of the clitoris; Freud's ideas, at first shocking, became mainstream.

A more practical reason for the sea change was the vulcanisation of rubber, allowing the production of contraceptive caps and condoms. Marie Stopes promoted these through her clinics in the 1920s. For the first time, the spectre of unmarried motherhood receded. In theory, contraception was only available to married women, but some friendly private doctors did not demand wedding certificates. Even more radical was the intrauterine Grafenberg ring, which has been described as "being to the Twenties what the Pill is to the Seventies".[15]

Contemporary writer Douglas Goldring wrote of this period: "An army of girl-graduates descended on London, each with her contraceptives in her handbag and a grim determination to rid herself as soon as possible of her repressions."[16]

University students had invested in their education and were determined to make use of their new freedom. They did not want to end up "having to get married" any more than their male counterparts did. The sisterhood of graduates shared practical information and contacts, as well as philosophies about the rights of the New Woman.

One girl graduate to arrive at the Penn Club was Grace Wilson, who had studied English at Oxford. She had a true vocation as a teacher and would be devoted to her work all her life.

Grace was from a modest but respectable background. She was just a few weeks younger than Jack, born on 26 August 1903 in Antsey, Hertfordshire. She grew up with two brothers attending local schools. Her father Josiah had been a baker, grocer and lay preacher in a non-conformist church. He became a full-time minister when she was eight at the village Congregational chapel of Braughing, Hertfordshire, then in Newport Pagnell, Buckinghamshire.[17]

He was an energetic and responsible man and was elected as a member of the local Board of Guardians, which administered workhouses and rural sanitation. When Grace was 18, he was a delegate to the World Brotherhood Congress in Prague. His grandchildren remember him as a genial man, but Grace's diaries suggest he was a strict father and could preach sermons ex tempore if his children displeased him.

When she was 20, Grace left home to become one of the first female full members of the University of Oxford, with a right to take a degree. She graduated third class, but in her reference, her tutor said her work was usually of high second class standard. Perhaps the exam room brought out her nerves. Her tutor, Margaret L Lee, wrote:[18]

> She was always a pleasant pupil on account of her keenness and power of enjoying the best, both in life and literature . . . I consider that Miss Wilson should make an ideal teacher, for she has the outlook and spirit of youth combined with much thoughtfulness and sympathy and a strong desire for service. She will always keep in touch with her pupils, and her enthusiasm is of the infectious kind, and is moreover strongly practical.

While Jack was shuttling between Bedales and the Penn, Grace spent several months living in France and Scandinavia – she would love Danish design all her life and often wore Danish costume jewellery. A year after graduating she took a job teaching English at an independent girls' school in Inverclyde, Scotland. While there she wrote children's stories. One, "Salmon and Shrimp", was accepted by the BBC for reading on *Children's Hour*.

After three years, she sought a new position, and her headmistress wrote: "Her own enthusiasm for her subject communicates itself to her pupils and she gains and keeps their interest and willing co-operation so difficulties of discipline never arise."[19]

Grace came to London to teach English at Blackheath Girls Public Day School in 1930, the same year Viv met Lila. Grace was then aged 27, tall and slim, intelligent and good fun. She moved in to the Penn because her cousin was Basil Burton, a permanent resident and the honorary treasurer. He worked at the Midland Bank in the city. Basil was a Quaker and had been imprisoned for more than a year as a conscientious objector during the Great War.[20]

Grace may also have been drawn by Bloomsbury's literary reputation. She was a great admirer of Virginia Woolf, and once wrote to
her: "May I thank you for the beauty and truth of 'The Waves'. To read
it gives me the keenest joy, and I am filled with exultation that such a
lovely thing should be."[21]

Grace later moved to teach at Roan Girls' School, where she would
remain for the rest of her working life. Both her brothers married and
had children, who remembered her as a very glamorous and attentive
aunt, generous with trips to the theatre and even occasional cheques.

She loved elegant, tailored clothes and modern jewellery but she
was no slave to fashion. While most women were chopping their hair
into bobs, she kept her mane piled up. It would be even more striking
when she went prematurely grey.

Gerald Hodgett, a resident of the time, remembered: "She was
a very elegant person, always impeccably dressed, a very clubbable
sort of person. I think everybody liked Grace. I am not inferring that
people didn't like Harris, but he wasn't the easiest of men to get on
with."[22]

Grace was more radical than Jack. While he was Liberal, she was a
socialist. Where he was still shy and reserved, especially around wom-
en, she was a welcome addition to any party.

They shared many of the same views on literature and enjoyed arguing about politics. A friendship slowly grew. Jack was a 'good chum'
in the Bedales fashion. Grace had little time for romance – all her
horizon was filled with her career and her forthcoming trip to see the
fruits of the revolution.

In the summer after she arrived, she was to visit Russia with the
Fabian Society to view socialism in action as part of a teachers' delega-
tion. It was not to be in the luxury that George Bernard Shaw enjoyed
that same summer of 1931 with the Fabians in Moscow, but for her
it was the trip of a lifetime. She travelled to St Petersburg and on into
Siberia. They went 'hard class', packed like sardines into carriages with
bare benches. She wrote to her family: "We are having a marvellous
time and finding it interesting beyond rashest expectations."[23]

The evening before she set off, she walked with Jack around Soho
Square. Like most fellow travellers, she didn't believe the stories in

the capitalist press about food shortages and starvation. But Jack was worried. He talked about his fears for her safety, and for the first time Grace had some inkling of his interest in her. [24]

Nevertheless, they knew each other for years more before they became lovers in May 1935, when both were aged 31. They did not flout convention, just discreetly took a walking holiday together in Switzerland.

Why did it take them four years to finally get round to it, when they were seeing each other daily? Jack's diffidence must have played a role here – he was so timid that fans remarked on it even when he was an international success. It is also much higher risk to try and move out of the friendzone when sharing accommodation. If Grace had rejected him, he would have had the awkwardness of seeing her every day. His refuge at the Penn Club would have become a torture.

However, when they ultimately found each other, it was a momentous occasion for Jack. For years he wrote her anniversary poems in May, along with birthday and Valentine's poems. It may have been his first sexual relationship. He had other female friends, notably the author Molly Cathcart Borer, but there's no records of previous affairs and he was usually shy around women.

What drew them to each other? Jack was physically attracted to Grace, who was a very good-looking young woman. He always noticed the details of women's clothes, and Grace liked taking care over her appearance. She was his intellectual equal, politically interested in building a better world, and a great reader like him. She always read and criticised his work. Beyond this, he needed her to steady him. And behind Grace's cool assurance, she was also a little more vulnerable than she appeared.

Grace's later diaries reveal her anxieties about her health, and her occasional depression. When she could not sleep, she wrote of going next door to eat biscuits with Jack and be soothed by him: "Last night I had a ridiculous hysterical fit and J was quite marvellous. We said how lucky we were that when one had been inclined to histrionics the other had always been calm and affectionate."[25]

Grace admired Jack's commitment to his writing. As an English graduate, she did not think it strange to give up a 'proper' career for a financially precarious life as a struggling author. She didn't want children and wasn't domestic enough to want her own home. Grace always had admirers and even a proposal of marriage but turned them all down. She told her sister-in-law Nora: "I've never met any man I like as much as I like Jack."[26]

Given their devotion, it may seem strange that they did not marry, but there was logic behind it. Jack was just as unimpressed as Viv with Gertrude and George's example. Grace also had a good reason for being willing to break with convention. The marriage bar on women teachers stated that they had to give up their jobs if they wed. Many chose to live quietly with the men they loved in order to go on working.[27]

In an interview after Jack's death, Grace claimed their motives for not marrying were financial.[28] Jack had a small private income from his inheritance but much of this was swallowed by his mother and brother – Viv's nervous breakdown was the start of a long life of intermittent, unproductive dependence.

If they had married, Grace would have lost her job. Jack's own earnings were irregular and meagre, certainly not enough to set up a household and pay for a wife and possible children. Nor was he willing to settle for the kind of steady job that would pay more money. Despite only limited success, he was determined to live by writing.

But Jack and Grace's motives were not only about work. If they had been, they could have married in 1938 when the marriage bar was lifted. Many women teachers did just that. Together, Jack and Grace could have earned enough for a private home. But they continued to live in separate, sparsely furnished rooms with a bathroom two floors down. Their true reasons went far deeper.

A hidden relationship suited Jack. He would remain secretive all his life, compartmentalising his work, friends and family. Grace was placed in a further compartment which was strictly separated from the others. This enabled him to keep his most private feelings hidden from view. A public avowal of their relationship seemed impossible and he convinced himself it was unnecessary; and that marriage was one of society's strictures which didn't apply to them.

His views are voiced by Gordon Zellaby in *The Midwich Cuckoos*, in a lukewarm toast on Zellaby's daughter's engagement:[29]

> "Let us now drink," announced Zellaby, "to the adjunction
> of fond spirits. It is true that the institution of marriage as
> it is proclaimed by Church and state displays a depressingly
> mechanistic attitude of mind towards partnership – one not
> unlike, in fact, that of Noah. The human spirit, however, is
> tough, and it quite often happens that love is able to survive
> this coarse, institutional thumbing. Let us hope, therefore . . ."

Jack didn't want his private feelings coarsely thumbed by the state.
He would stubbornly refuse to play the game.

In her own way, Grace was as private as Jack, even in her writing.
She destroyed her earlier diaries believing them immature. Even in
later life, she kept her daily journal safe at home when visiting friends,
although she recorded little more than external events. She probably also destroyed all her letters to Jack after his death: none survive,
though he frequently mentions them in his letters to her, which she
kept.

Yet this meant they missed out on the advantages of marriage,
which does at least put matters into black and white and provide security. For years Jack suffered from a fear that he had failed to tell Grace
what she really meant to him, and that she might leave him. While they
were separated by war, he wrote to her a week after they had managed
to meet:[30]

> Darling,
>
> I started this yesterday, and then broke off because I was so
> clumsy – I don't suppose I'll do much better this time though.
>
> A week ago . . . yes, I suppose it really was, but it's difficult
> to relate the compartments to one another – and there ought
> not, one really feels, to be compartments; yet there very much
> are.
>
> And when I'd seen you, Sweet, it didn't seem that I'd seen
> you at all – I'd said none of the things I'd meant to say, and
> felt I'd been stupid and loglike.
>
> Once more it seemed as though I had expected you to di-
> vine the things I didn't say: and I kicked myself for it, as often
> before. Why, Darling, why the hell am I such a dumb one?

71

You know, don't you, Sweet, that you are flying along on a parallel course. And I keep on looking across to make sure you're still there. Sometimes it gets sort of thick and murky, and I look across in a panic, because if you weren't there, well, there just wouldn't be any course any more. I think I'd just wallow, and come to a kind of lurching stop.

Then I open my mouth to tell you something – and hear myself talking about the weather – or food – or –

Sweetle, it's nearly as hopeless to try to write about it, too. But you do feel it a little, don't you? I know it's unsatisfactory to have a bloke whose tongue goes all clay when he opens his lips, but I'll try, Sweetle, I will try.

Grace also paid a price for her privacy – she missed out on support from family and friends who were shut out of large chunks of her life. Over time, Viv and Gertrude were introduced to Grace and accepted her. Grace told her sister-in-law Nora, and presumably her brothers, about Jack, but she could not tell her parents. They would not have understood.

Her father was a non-conformist preacher, whose regular sermons predicted hellfire for sinners. Nor could her colleagues know. Living in sin would render her instantly unsuitable for the moral care of the young. Unlike the flamboyant Bloomsbury artists, their relationship had to be kept secret.

Apart from Jack's secrecy, he had other reasons for rejecting marriage. He saw it as a bondage that diminished women into little more than brainwashed slaves. His own mother, Gertrude, acted as a terrible warning. Her whole life had been a passive dependency on a series of men. Even after her father's death, her inheritance had been placed in the hands of her brother and brother-in-law as managing trustees. She had never worked or created anything. She played almost no part even in the raising of her own children. Viv's bankruptcy had been partly down to her failure to control his finances. For decades she lived a bored, boring, lonely life in a succession of hotels, sustained by sherry and games of bridge.

Jack was not the only person to believe marriage had a crippling effect on women's personalities. A short story by Saki, "Tea", depicts a woman's descent from cheerful, creative independence into yet another wife "tinkling behind a teapot".

But neither was the Bloomsbury set's much vaunted liberation much of an improvement for women. By 1930 it was becoming clear that many promising women artists had ended up in identical servitude to their married sisters.

Bloomsbury men universally believed in free love: none of them believed in shared housework.

Dora Carrington may have achieved sexual and personal fulfilment, but with all the various men, straight and gay, sharing her house, she was the one who emptied the chamber pots.

Augustus John's wife Ida had welcomed his lover Dorelia partly out of sheer relief that someone would share the childcare, exhausted as she was by constant pregnancies. When Ida died after her dreaded fifth confinement, Dorelia took over the raising of all seven children. Two more girls of her own followed. John permitted none of them to go to school, as he felt Dorelia was a rare genius who would raise them to be brave, beautiful and free. Dorelia's own artistic talents were sacrificed to this.

Bloomsbury diaries and letters are full of women artists whose careers faded away. The painter Stella Bowen claimed to be proud to give up her art to be housemaid to novelist Ford Madox Ford. Artist Nancy Nicholson was less grateful when her husband Robert Graves complained her housework intruded on the space he needed to write. Author Katherine Mansfield was desperate with frustration at her role as a skivvy to John Middleton Murry. The list goes on and on.

As a writer, Wyndham is often compared with H G Wells. Wells' books about free love are less read now than his science fiction. *Ana Veronica* (1909), based on his then lover Amber Reeves, depicts a young woman who throws away her respectability to live with a married man. A series of other racy fiction and non-fiction books expanded on Wells' belief in a utopian socialist future, where women would be as free as men to love where and when they chose. He was denounced in pulpits and editorials as corrupting young minds.

Jack first read H G Wells' novels in his Derbyshire prep school. They inspired him throughout his life. Wells was his hero: many times, Jack proudly acknowledged his influence. He may have believed Wells' manifesto and never realised the extent of his hypocrisy. Their private lives couldn't have been further apart.

Wells married briefly as a young man but divorced on falling in love with his student, Amy Catherine. He rechristened her Jane when they married. He saw her as the perfect, fragile helpmeet, too delicate for his energetic sexuality. Whilst she competently managed their family and income, he had a series of affairs, including two children by prominent feminists: scientist Amber Reeves and writer Rebecca West.

Jane was obliged to be pleasant to these mistresses and congratulate them on the births of their children. She had to do her best to help Wells avoid scandal. In return, her position as wife was inviolable. His mistresses' role was to keep him sexually entertained regardless of the demands of their reluctant motherhood. When discarded, they had to prop up their damaged careers as best they could.

As Katie Roiphe wrote, despite his revolutionary ideas, he had "fallen into a life of fairly traditional hypocrisy . . . based on the usual lies."[31]

By comparison, Jack and Grace's relationship was truly radical. Jack appears to have been totally faithful to Grace his entire life, not because he had signed a marriage contract, or feared public disgrace if he strayed, but because he loved her. This was not self-indulgence masquerading as freedom, but a true equality.

Jack appears to have felt this very deeply. During the war, he was very conscious of the length of time the post took – it defined how far they were apart in time as well as space. They were the same age, but his birthday came earlier. He always experienced this as the opening of a gap between them, which didn't close until she "caught him up". On one birthday he wrote:[32]

> Once more we're on a level plane
> Today you've caught me up again,
> T'is sweeter far to have you near
> Than all a year away.
>
> And, though these anniversaries
> Lack thrills they had in nurseries,
> I hope that you will have, my Dear,
> A very happy day.

One cannot imagine Wells, addicted to lovers less than half his age, feeling the same sensitivity of connection.

Of course, Jack and Grace's arrangement did not liberate everybody. Domestic drudgery was transferred to the Penn Club servants, who lived in damp rooms in the basement. One housemaid, depressed at losing her father and wanting to remain a few days with her mother, was told to return to work at once as she was needed. She was granted one day off for the funeral.

But the couple's decision to forego the comforts of a private home did mean they could preserve an equal partnership. Grace could continue her hard-won career and enjoy her own income. So could Jack. Neither of them had to clean the floors or organise the laundry or cook endless meals. They didn't even have to make their own beds until the war caused a servant shortage.

Their letters show they were generous in treating each other, arranging little surprises of hoarded sugar and eggs throughout the war. But neither was dependant on the other for paying the bills.

For Grace, it was an arrangement that echoed the ideals of communist Russia, where blocks of flats were being built without private kitchens. Canteens took the strain from working women. For Jack, raised between boarding schools and hotels, the communal life must have seemed both normal and a reassuring continuation of the happy days at Bedales.

He was a practical man, and this was a practical solution. Over the years, he quietly became a lynchpin of the club. He often withdrew from socialising to write, but he is regularly mentioned in the club records as being asked to fix lino and doorbells, while Grace joined the committee.

Mollie Raymer, a resident from 1939, remembered: "Harris was ever the mainstay of the Club, being a great handyman. He helped us to fit curtains round the wash basins. I think he was the only person who knew where the fuse boxes for the various landings were located, as these were in a variety of weird places. A story goes that he once fused all the lights and so went out for the day!"[33]

These were happy years. Viv had made a brief return to the London stage in 1934 but had then returned to Lila and Matlock. Viv visited Jack and Grace regularly in London, and they would all go out to a restaurant and a show. Their mother Gertrude also moved to the hydro in Matlock for a time with Viv, and Jack often visited them there, sharing Viv's room.

The brothers had lost touch with their father George by the time he died in 1934 in a Brighton nursing home, but he left them a small legacy. Viv paid off his debts, then spent his share on a car, which the brothers used to tour England every summer, finding places to stay by chance. They swam off the beach at Eastbourne, explored Cornwall and climbed Hadrian's Wall.

In 1938 Viv joined the nearby Alderwasley Fire Service. Small villages like this were commonly served by 'retained' firefighters. They didn't remain at the fire station for regular shifts, but were paid a small amount to train and be on call during certain hours. They received extra payments if they attended a fire. It suited Viv who had loved his time as Captain of the Bedales Boys' Fire Brigade.

Jack had formed a friendship with another old Bedalian, Harry Barker, known as Biff. He had been living abroad, but he returned with his wife Eileen in 1930 to run the Bedales workshop. Jack had always popped back for weekends; now he started a pattern of lengthier visits.

Biff was a talented silversmith and taught woodwork, metalwork and technical drawing. He and Eileen moved into Row Cottage, a roomy Arts and Crafts house at the school gate. Grace spent Christmas and Easter with her family, so Jack would stay in Steep with the Barkers. In the summer he always appeared in time for the Old Bedalians social weekend and sometimes stayed for weeks. The Barkers kept his typewriter in the sitting room, which became Jack's room. He would type through the day and reappear in the late afternoon.

He was soon "Uncle Jack" to the Barker girls, Tess and Jean. They fondly remembered how he always arrived with gifts, occasionally danced the Charleston with Eileen to a gramophone after dinner, and frequently disappeared to the pub with Biff.

He was also welcome at the weekend retreat of his old school friend Arthur Sykes, known as Bill, and his wife Leslie. Like Jack, Bill was into science fiction, with a practical, mechanical mind. He worked for the family shoe firm of Lilley and Skinner, in London. Leslie, a graduate, was a geography teacher, a keen vegetable gardener and member of the Soil Association.

They were both passionate about rural life and left London for weekends to stay at an old workers' cottage until they managed to buy the grand Red House in 1935. It had been designed and built in the Arts and Crafts style for poet Edward Thomas, who was killed in the Great War.

Leslie was a striking and intelligent woman with a slightly formal, didactic way of speaking. She would later be the model for the Zealand woman in *The Chrysalids*: "She was sure of herself, with a serenity of confidence that made Rosalind's self-reliance seem like bravado... Against the thrown back white hood, her beautiful face looked as if it was framed by a halo."[34]

Bill and Leslie adopted a son, David, after trying for a child for some time. A few years later, they had a biological daughter, Mathilda. Jack would use this set-up as a model for *Chocky*, the tale of an outsider within a loving but obtuse family.

David also remembers Jack's generous presents. They were always strictly functional: a Roberts radio, a specially designed Aga kettle, or a massively heavy hedgetrimmer.

Grace did not join these sociable weekends. As unmarrieds, their relationship was still unacknowledged.

By the end of the 1930s, the Penn Club's official attitude to such relationships shifted from the shadow of Victorian prudery. The new policy on arrangements such as Jack and Grace's was more "don't ask, don't tell". When the lease ran out on the Penn Club's Tavistock Place quarters in 1938, the club moved down the road to the current premises. This is another Georgian terrace of houses from 21 to 23 Bedford Place, off Russell Square. Here, men and women were no longer separated into opposite ends of the building.

Grace and Jack were quietly allocated adjacent rooms, numbers 44 and 45. They were tucked away on the top floor, separated by staircases and service rooms from any others. These rooms were to be theirs for another 25 years.

References

1   Q&A with Sam Moskowitz , see note chapter 1.

2   Letter sent to T Stanhope Sprigg, editor of *Fantasy*, to be used as author's bio in the magazine.

3   David C Maxwell (1996) *The Penn Club Story*. Published by The Penn Club.

4   Details about the club come from committee notes and correspondence in the Penn Club archive, which manager Fergal Crossan kindly allowed me to view.

5   Vivian Beynon Harris, *My Brother John Wyndham 1903-1969*. See note chapter 1. Transcribed and annotated by David Ketterer.

6   *The Illustrated London News* (1928) "On Stage Noises, The Young Generation", 22 September, p.516; David Ketterer (1999), Introduction, p.8, *Foundation*, vol 28, no 75; *The Scotsman* (1927) 'Glasgow and West", 18 August, p.5.

7   Viv's memorandum book, which includes memories of his and Jack's lives, is in the University of Liverpool archive.

8   Smedley's brochure from 1925 is available online at http://www.andrewsgen.com/matlock/pix/matlock_smedley_1925_brochure.htm. Accessed 12 May 2019.

9   Notes by Ketterer on Vivian Harris's biography, ibid. Lila's age is taken from my own researches through the General Records Office.

10   *Derby Daily Telegraph* (1930) "Matlock Rotary Concert", 28 November, p.11.

11   *The Derbyshire Times* (1932), "Lease of a Flat", 19 March, p.7; *Nottingham Journal* (1935), "Actor Pays in Full", 27 June, p.15.

12   Vivian Beynon Harris, ibid.

13   Penn Club archive, ibid.

14   Virginia Nicolson (2003) *Among the Bohemians: Experiments in Living 1900-1939*, Penguin.

15   Nicolson, ibid, p.58.

16   Douglas Goldring (1945) *The Nineteen Twenties*. Nicholson & Watson. Cited in Nicolson, ibid.

17   Details about Grace's life come from conversations with her neph-

ew's widow, Ann Wilson, and her niece Hilary Wilson, who generously gave their time and shared their family records and letters. I am also grateful to Neil Pollard, a Wyndham researcher who has written about Grace in his forthcoming book of guided walks, *In John Wyndham's Footsteps*. He was kind enough to share a draft copy with me.

18   Letter dated March 1927. Held by Ann Wilson.

19   Letter dated 11 March 1930, by Beatrice S B McMurtie of St Columba's School, Kilmacolm. Held by Ann Wilson.

20   Neil Pollard, *John Wyndham's London*. Unpublished.

21   Letter by Grace Wilson sent from the Penn Club in December 1931, quoted in Beth Rigel Daugherty (2006) Letters from Readers to Virginia Woolf, *Woolf Studies Annual*, vol 12, p.110.

22   *John Wyndham: The Invisible Man of Science Fiction* (2005), BBC4. Directed by Mick Conefrey.

23   Postcard to her sister-in-law Nora Wilson, 25 August 1931. Held by Hilary Wilson.

24   Diary entry August 25, 1969. Grace's diaries are held by Professor David Ketterer, who kindly allowed me to read the first volume, and the later volumes from 1963 to 1966.

25   Diary entry Sunday March 6, 1949.

26   Private communication from Hilary Wilson, daughter of Nora.

27   Alison Oram (1996) *Women Teachers and Feminist Politics, 1900-1939*, Manchester University Press.

28   Clem Lewis (1981) "The Invisible Man Behind those Plants of Death", *Birmingham Evening Mail*, 8 September.

29   *Midwich Cuckoos*, Michael Joseph, 1977 printing, p.19.

30   Letter to Grace, 12 July 1942. Held in the Liverpool archive.

31   Katie Roiphe (2007) *Uncommon Arrangements: Seven Portraits of Married Life in London Literary circles 1910-1939*, The Dial Press.

32   Many of Jack's birthday and anniversary poems to Grace are held in the University of Liverpool archive, but most are undated.

33   Maxwell, ibid, p.21.

34   Notes by Sister Bede, held in the University of Liverpool archive, and private communications from David Sykes. *The Chrysalids* quote is taken from p.192, Penguin 1961 edition.

4

Pulp Fiction

For Jack, the Penn Club was a safe haven in a life that was otherwise drifting. Although an adult, like many former pupils he had barely moved on from Bedales.

Part of the problem was that he had just enough money from his mother's inheritance to allow himself to fail. But all along, through his various half-hearted careers, he had written occasional stories. After giving up on advertising, he decided to write full-time. His brother Viv later wrote:[1]

> Only one who has worked against the stone wall of non-ac-ceptance can know the immense determination needed to keep on working never doubting clouds would break. He lived on an allowance from Mother who had a remarkable tolerance and love for us.
>
> In those days between the wars living was cheap in London and there was no problem for cigarettes were 11d for 20 and my brother always smoked about 40.

At only 23 he had his first success as an author, but was dissatisfied with his own efforts. He never listed his first novel amongst his works in later life, but the setting in a seaside boarding house and the sparky heroines mark it as his work as much as the name John B Harris.[2]

The Curse of the Burdens was published in 1927 in Aldine's mystery series, sold alongside Aldine Racing Novels, Boxing Novels and Football Novels. Others in the Mystery series were *Black Honey, The Broken Cigarettes, The Peer and His Plunder* and *The Man who Lost an Hour*.

It is 64 pages of close type, printed on the cheapest paper and sold for fourpence. The only known copy is in the British Library. The best that can be said about the plot is 'confusing'.

The story centres on Dick Burden and his fiancée Letty Kingsbury. She has recently come from India with her father. They are prevented from marrying by Dick's poverty, although the recent death of his cousin Robert has moved him closer to a baronetcy. Robert's death is one of a long series of unnatural ends in the family. They were cursed by a monk when Henry VIII's dissolution of the monasteries gave them their family seat of Shotlander Priory.

A bewildering number of relatives and detectives shuttle between London, the seaside town of Easthill, Shotlander Priory and country inns in two villages. Dick's older brother drowns, the priory burns down and Dick disappears.

In the final scenes, Dick is discovered trapped in a hidden passage beneath the estate. A shell-shocked soldier is revealed as the arsonist. Dick's enemies are killed in a struggle involving two guns and a chair. Dick and Letty are thus free to marry and build a curse-free home with the insurance money from the fire.

It's a messy read. The author seems to repeatedly add characters to keep interest high, then runs out of commissioned pages and desperately tries to tie up all the loose ends. It's not surprising Jack never referred to it again. But although it is far from polished or original, amongst the stereotypes and melodrama are some distinctively John Wyndham touches. One is the sense of religion as a kind of insanity: the shell-shocked soldier had become a religious maniac determined to work out the curse. And though the country house library and secret passage are detective novel staples, there's a real sense of place about the out-of-season seaside town.

> He looked round the room and the drab reality of life came home to him. This ugly furniture – those dull, uninteresting people – this dreary boarding house that called itself a private hotel!
>
> This was the real world after all. And he wondered what the old ladies who were sitting by the fire would say if he suddenly cried out:
>
> 'You had better be careful. A murderer is living in this place with you.'
>
> He could imagine one of them replying:
>
> 'Dear me – how dreadful – fancy that! I always told you,

Amelia' – yes, the other one would probably be called Amelia
– 'that the society in these places is dreadfully mixed.'

He laughed out loud at this imaginary conversation, and
everyone turned and looked at him in shocked amazement.

The only escape from the zombified residents of the boarding
house is to the barely less depressing pier:

> In late spring, in the summer, in early autumn there was about
> as much privacy on the pier at Easthill-on-Sea as one would
> hope to find in Piccadilly Circus . . .
>
> In the winter, however, when the sea was grey, and either
> sullen or angry, and the sou'-westerly gales blew, and the rain
> came down in torrents, the pier was deserted by all the res-
> idents except the untiring anglers, and it was a place where
> lovers might meet with as little fear of interruption as in a
> country lane. And there were innumerable shelters from the
> wind and rain – shelters of glass and wood, facing all ways,
> so that one could find protection from every wind that blew.

If this is a picture of Jack's purgatorial holidays with his mother
and her boarding house acquaintances, it's no wonder the youthful,
international atmosphere of the Penn Club was so attractive.

It was at the Penn Club, a couple of years after his detective story
was published, that he came across a new kind of writing. An American visitor left a copy of *Amazing Stories*, a pulp magazine, in the club
library. They weren't common in Britain, but out-of-date copies were
shipped as ballast and sold in Woolworths for 3d each. Jack sought
more out and was hooked.

Pulp magazines – named for the low-quality, uncoated paper – were
common in America, with titles like *Argosy*, *All Story Weekly*, *Weird
Tales* and the saucier *Snappy Stories*.

The first science fiction magazine publisher was Hugo Gernsback,
editor of *Science and Invention* and *Radio News*. He wanted to develop his
titles beyond a hobbyist base while widening readers' minds about the
possibilities of science.[3]

He coined the term 'scientifiction' and printed stories within his titles. These were so popular, he launched the first dedicated magazine,
Amazing Stories, in April 1926, with bold covers by artist Frank R Paul.

Most of the stories were reprints, with H G Wells featuring in all the first 29 issues. It was a winning combination – *Amazing Stories* had a circulation of 100,000 within months.

Paul's covers were both popular and damaging. The magazine was meant to be at least partly educational and aimed at young people, but the lurid covers suggested they were harmful trash. Gernsback experimented in 1928 with a formal design of cog and pen instead – three times as many unsold copies came back. The sensational artwork with zip-suited girls and tentacled monsters were confirmed as part of the science fiction package. It was a decision that was to contribute to the ghettoization of science fiction to this day.

Gernsback spent money as fast as he could earn it: he loved to experiment with inventions, and liked smart suits and comfort. The result was that *Amazing Stories* was taken over by administrators. His response was to launch *Science Wonder Stories* in 1929, followed six weeks later by *Air Wonder Stories*. To avoid the trademarked 'scientifiction', now owned by his creditors, he coined a new phrase 'science fiction'.

He launched a competition for a slogan for his new magazine, with a tempting prize of a hundred gold dollars.

Lying on a beach in Eastbourne, Jack told Viv he was going to enter. Jack's slogan was 'Future Flying Fiction', and it beat 3,860 other entries. It was never used as the magazine merged into *Wonder Stories*, but it was a heartening success, and not only for the winner.[4]

Although British author H G Wells is known as the father of the genre, good science fiction was hard to find in interwar Britain. Jack was not the only person searching for out-of-date pulps.

Leslie Flood, who would be part of the team that started *New Worlds* magazine with Jack after the war, also spotted the competition announcement in *Wonder Stories*. It was to be a long time before he would find out the winner:[5]

> Discovering the result some years later in, I think, the September 1930 issue of *Wonder Stories* seized upon from the bargain-bin of a chain store, was akin to finding a message in a bottle cast adrift by some distant Robinson Crusoe, and I well remember the surge of jingoistic pride in noting that the winner was an Englishman, John Beynon Harris.

Jack had to shoehorn the money out of Gernsback (who was a notoriously late and poor payer) but he was not put off. He was sure he could write better than some of the featured authors.

He began by collecting rejection letters. One of his first, in December 1931, may have reconfirmed him in his dislike for Roman Catholicism. Harry Bates, editor of *Astounding Stories* and *Strange Tales*, wrote:[6]

> Your story, 'The Cathedral Crypt,' was a good one, and with a genuine jolt of horror at the end, but we would never dare use it. Cathedrals involve the Roman Catholic Church, and the action of your story would imply unthinkable things to many people.

Bates was later known for the story that became the film *The Day the Earth Stood Still*. He was not always so kind. A month later he wrote:

> Your latest story, 'The House at Hardease,' is a thousand miles off. It is too slow, far too slow. Almost nothing happens. It is extremely gabby. You carry the whole story in dialogue. I should guess, offhand, that you have three or four times as much dialogue as other writers of the weird tale use in their published stories. And the whole thing lacked the mood, the feeling of the supernatural and the weird. This mood should start with the first paragraph. Witness Poe.

But Jack kept plugging away. He soon had two stories published, "Worlds to Barter" (*Wonder Stories*, 1931) and "The Lost Machine" (*Amazing Stories*, 1932).

"Worlds to Barter" leant heavily on H G Wells' *The Time Machine*, but added anomalies and puzzles about time travel that would be a hallmark of his later work. It provoked a great deal of debate on the letters page. After the war he would play with these ideas in a series of love stories, perhaps the most charming being "Chronoclasm" (*Star Science Fiction*, February 1953)

"The Lost Machine", with its friendly, sentient, self-repairing hero, was more original, both in theme and treatment. Several of Jack's key obsessions appeared here for the first time: artificial intelligence, the superior adaptations of insects and the loneliness of a perceptive individual amongst a dull-witted herd.

Illustrated by MOREY

"*A second later there came a stunning explosion. . . . The cause of the disaster must always remain a mystery. . . . I only know that when I looked up the vessel was nowhere to be seen . . . only a rain of metal parts dropping to earth all about me.*"

41

Illustration for "The Lost Machine" by Leo Morey, in *Amazing Stories,* April 1932

As editor Mike Ashley pointed out, this is one of the earliest stories in the pulps to write from the point of view of a robot, and an alien robot at that. As in his very first published story in his school magazine, "Vivisection", the other may be strange, without being a monster. This empathy with the alien would recur again and again in his fiction, from the doomed insects of the short story "Meteor" to the abused wife of "Dumb Martian" and even the enemy psychics in *The Midwich Cuckoos*.

It was this human treatment of the subject, rather than the subject itself, that made his work stand out. Mike Ashley wrote: "He was much more sympathetic to his characters, especially aliens, and I think this portrayed a more British attitude unlike most American writers who wrote with a more active frontier spirit." [7]

Jack himself recognised that it was this that satisfied a deep human need. One early editor asked him if he could write stories about aeroplanes. He replied: "Nobody can write stories about aeroplanes. Stories are about people." [8]

The science fiction market had grown rapidly at the start of the 1930s, but the quality dropped. In formulaic stories, heroes monotonously pursued villainous aliens to rescue damsels from other dimensions.

Jack disliked it, labelling it the "hold-him-cowboy-you-can't-do-this-to-me-kiss-bang with rays for shooters" style, [9] although he followed the pattern at times. In "Wanderers of Time" (*Wonder Stories*, 1933), the anti-heroine has her dress ripped off by an alien machine early on; she spends the rest of the story in her underwear. Jack later wrote about the breed of space opera writers: [10]

> It was clear to the newcomers that [science fiction] needed hotting up. Bigger is better, and faster is better. For proper thrill and excitement, therefore, wars must be intergalactic, with thousands of ships mounting hundreds of rays; speed must be reckoned in light-years per second, worlds be propelled from one system to another. And what about the sex angle? Hey, bring on the dancing girls!
>
> In the ensuing orgy whole universes were vaporized, non-interacting super-men slugged their way around space more like supermaniacs. Impermeably space-suited heroes

Cover art featuring "Wanderers of Time" by Frank R Paul. The real heroine, pictured, keeps her clothes on throughout. Jack described her as dark-haired and wearing a knee-length russet tunic, but Paul has made her blonde, and re-clothed her in this scarlet zipper-suit.

(Illustration by Paul)

The surviving Batrachs fought with each other to escape through the narrow doorway. A bellow of rage came from Angus as the men rushed forward.

166

Another Frank R Paul illustration for "Exiles on Asperus", *Wonder Stories Quarterly*, 1933.

cavorted through the cosmos with curvaceous cuties inevitably clad in bathing suits – and all interest departed from the stories. The contemptuous cracks in other periodicals were well deserved as the form which had shown such promise was reduced to moronic levels – from which, in some instances, it has never recovered.

The editor of *Wonder Stories*, former engineer David Lasser, wanted something else. He wrote to his regular contributors a letter which defined what John Wyndham was later to call "logical fantasy":[11]

Science fiction should deal realistically with the effect upon people, individually and in groups, of a scientific invention or discovery. The flow of the story should be reasonable, although dramatic; the situation should be convincing, the atmosphere conveyed vividly and the characters should be really human. In other words, allow yourself one fundamental assumption – that a certain machine or discovery is possible – and then show what would be its logical and dramatic consequences upon the world; also, what would be the effect upon the group of characters that you pick to carry your theme.

Lasser was also willing to allow freer debate in his letters pages. He let his writers explore themes such as sex, feminism and religion. Jack responded with two of the most original stories to feature in the magazine, exploring "mankind's Achilles' heel".

In "Exiles on Asperus" (*Wonder Stories Quarterly*, 1933), a classic space adventure twists to show how a perverted religion is used to adapt humans to slavery. The huge bat-like aliens use aversion therapy, similar to that in Huxley's *Brave New World,* published a year earlier. They train a 'new breed' of men to pride themselves on spending all their lives in the darkness of their caves, slaving for their masters. It was one of his first stories about how future humans could evolve, the most famous being *The Chrysalids*.

"The Venus Adventure" (*Wonder Stories,* May 1932) shows man's religion corrupting an innocent race early in their development. A hundred years in the future, technological development on Earth has allowed babies to be incubated from conception, freeing women from the dangers of pregnancy and childbirth. A revivalist preacher is angered by this unnatural practice, despite his own mother having died giving birth to him.

The preacher convinces a wealthy industrialist that Earth is doomed by men's sins. They flee in a space ship Ark, crashing on Venus. There, they split into two factions. The religious followers literally put the fear of god into the innocent Venusians; while the rocket ship's builders and scientists start a new civilisation.

When a second ship, the Pyra, follows many years later, the crew find themselves caught in a war between the two sides.

"The Venus Adventure" is unusual for its treatment of women. At the time of writing, Jack was friends with Grace but they had not yet become lovers. He was already revolving in his mind the problem of how women combine relationships and careers, a problem he would return to again in *Trouble with Lichen*.

In "The Venus Adventure", of the seven Pyra crew members, three are women: two chemists and a photographer. One of them hires an incubator before jetting off to Venus with her husband. The moral is clear: religion – and religious men – are women's oppressors, while science is their liberator.

The idea of women taking a useful part in a space adventure was so unusual that in one serial, an editor 'corrected' the heroine's name Joan to John. "Stowaway to Mars" was a spin-off from Jack's earlier short story, "The Lost Machine". The machine had met Joan, a scientist's daughter, and she had learnt a little of its language.

In the longer story, Joan hides aboard the first Mars-bound rocket ship in order to meet more of the machines. While the men waste time in ridiculous territorial flag-waving, Joan meets the original Martian race, explores their dying cities and learns to understand the evolution of machines.

She falls in love with one of the Martian men and becomes pregnant with his child. It was serialised with Joan in the lead in the British magazine *The Passing Show* in 1936, then published as a book, retitled *Planet Plane*, in the same year. A year later, it was sold as a serial under a third title *The Space Machine* in *Modern Wonder*. Jack was amused to see Joan turned into a boy in the first episode.

He said: "I watched with interest to see how they would get out of

Illustration for "The Space Machine" by Chester, in *Modern Wonder*, 1937. Joan, in the spacesuit, has become John.

the difficulties looming ahead. Apparently that had not occurred to them. In the end I got a rush appeal for a final instalment."[12]

Planet Plane sold about 2,400 copies before being remaindered in 1939. This made Jack about £40 – four months' bed and board at the Penn Club.

The idea of Venus and Mars being habitable planets with breathable atmospheres seems ridiculous now, but it was based on the science and observations of the time. It was assumed that Mars had cooled earlier than Earth, being further from the Sun, and so might have an older, more advanced civilisation. By the same logic, it was assumed Venus would be behind us in evolutionary terms.

It had scrawled a series of queer lines in the dust.

420

Frank R Paul's vision of the last of mankind, trapped in a zoo on Venus, in "The Man from Beyond", *Wonder Stories*, 1934.

Jack had two other successes around this time: a detective novel, *Foul Play Suspected*; and *The Secret People*, both published in 1935. Neither was a huge success, but at least they were attractive hardbacks – Jack enjoyed bookbinding himself, creating anthologies of his favourite magazines. Reviewers praised the originality of *The Secret People*, and it was serialised in the British magazine *The Passing Show*.[13]

The Secret People are a race of albino pygmies, who have imprisoned hundreds of unlucky wanderers underground. They are discovered by a wealthy pair of travellers who crash in the Sahara.

Like "Exiles on Asperus", it shows the way religion can be used to control people. Though some sequences tip from fantastic to ridiculous, it's still an exciting read. The heroine is typical of Wyndham's later brave, active and unconventional women. She sees nothing wrong in taking a hotel acquaintance as a temporary 'playmate', happy to enjoy his attention with little emotional involvement.

Three novels in two years should have made him a name to watch, but they are three such different readerships that they didn't help build his reputation. He generally used the name John Beynon Harris in the US, and John Beynon in Britain which also confused matters.

Throughout the pre-war period, his ideas were often ahead of the field. Particularly significant was "Spheres of Hell" (*Wonder Stories*, 1933), later republished as "The Puff-Ball Menace", mentioned in Chapter Two. He pre-empted *Planet of the Apes* by 30 years with "The Man From Beyond" (*Wonder Stories*, 1934). The last human lies on Venus for centuries in suspended animation while life evolves around him and Earth grows old and dies. He is awoken by the descendants of his pets, now scientists who exhibit him as a curiosity. "The Moon Devils" (*Wonder Stories*, 1934, also known as "The Last Lunarians") and "Sleepers of Mars" (*Tales of Wonder*, 1938, a sequel to *Stowaway to Mars*) also use suspended animation.

Though he wrote some space opera and gadgetry, his work is often lifted from the ordinary by both his human treatment of the subject and a political consciousness. One example is "Trojan Beam" (*Fantasy*, 1939) about a new magnetic weapon developed by the Chinese in their fight against the Japanese. The interest lies only partly in the technical wizardry. The double-crossing British agent is the real focus as he learns more about the subtleties of turning an enemy against itself.

In all, he had 17 short stories published in the 1930s. Most were science fiction. He completed two further detective novels but couldn't find a publisher for either.

Wonder Stories usually paid at half a cent a word, so "Wanderers of Time" was worth about $110. "The Man from Beyond" was worth about $50, or £10 by 1930s exchange rates, so more profitable per word than his full-length novels. Getting the money was another matter. Jack resorted to a debt collecting agency to get $545 out of Gernsback for eight stories printed between 1932 and 1934.[14]

It was common for him to sell the same stories to several magazines under different titles. He also used many variants of his name: John B Harris, John Beynon, John Beynon Harris, Johnston Harris and even Wyndham Parkes. Occasionally he would have two stories in the same magazine, using two different names.[15]

He was frequently rejected but rarely put off – he would re-type the title page and re-send stories later. This sometimes worked, especially if a magazine had a new editor. Though his many aliases enabled him to make a little more money, they may have prevented him from building the reputation he deserved.

In Britain, he remained almost unknown as the American pulps were little sold, but he was well respected by the circle of enthusiasts who formed the British Interplanetary Society and the short-lived Science Fiction Association. The heart of the SFA was a tiny flat on Gray's Inn, inhabited by writers Arthur C Clarke, William F Temple and Maurice Hanson.

Jack kept a scrapbook of cuttings about scientific advances, organised by theme. He attended the debates of the new British Interplanetary Society, founded in 1933, which drew up plans to send a manned rocket to Mars before the war. Arthur C Clarke was one of the early members.[16]

Temple, who would later be famous for *The Four-Sided Triangle*, invited him to speak at the Science Fiction Association's convention in 1939, writing: "The trio which inhabits this flat greatly appreciated your enjoyable yarn "The Trojan Beam". We envy your smooth, accomplished style, which we ourselves cannot seem to hit nohow."[17]

But though he enjoyed their company, he always kept a slight distance. Sam Youd, who later found fame as John Christopher, began writing as a teenager in the late 1930s. He soon became a major part of the science fiction circle and a good friend of Jack. He remembered him as a good listener rather than the life and soul of the party: "He never discussed his personal life, he never talked about his parents, his background, he was a detached sort of person. He liked being on the edge of things, part of the group, but not necessarily wanting to say too much."[18]

The first attempt at a British science fiction magazine, *Scoops*, awkwardly tried to straddle both adult and boys' interests and failed within a few months in 1934. A new British quarterly, *Tales of Wonder*, tried the market again in 1937. It was edited by Walter Gillings, also a member of the SFA. The first issue included Jack's "Perfect Creature" about a classic mad scientist. Gillings was struggling to find original material, so Jack wrote him a lengthy short story for the second issue, "Sleepers of Mars", the sequel to *Stowaway to Mars*. Arthur C Clarke debuted in the magazine a few months later. Their success inspired another British magazine, *Fantasy*, but both were doomed to failure by the paper shortages of the looming war.

By the late 30s, Jack was losing his wide-eyed enthusiasm for the wonders of science. He no longer believed in a straightforward dichotomy of the old beliefs of religion versus the new miracles of invention. As war approached, his vision darkened. "Judson's Annihilator", published in the first issue of *Fantasy* in 1938 for £30, portrays a well-meaning young scientist who invents an invisible screen that destroys everything that passes through it. He can see positive uses for it, but nonetheless agrees to adapt it for the first people to show an interest – the military.

Written two years before the Blitz, it describes the massed flights of Nazi planes crossing the channel, searching for lights in the blackout. The story was reprinted in October 1939 in the US in *Amazing Stories*. In a "Meet the Author" page, Jack discussed the adoption of ever more powerful weapons. He said the military were instinctively conservative and disliked war. They shouldn't be blamed for the escalation of violence – it was the scientists who made their use inevitable.[19]

Who is one of the chief drawers of royalties when the soldiers get blown up? The scientist. Who is it who should be the priest of progress, but is content to behave with the irresponsibility of a half-wit? That same chap again who blandly and quite unashamedly tries to shuffle the blame and evade the issue – 'Why blame me? I only sold the child a gun; somebody else ought to have stopped him shooting his mother.' ...

The scientists' brains have built the twentieth century; their morals will blow it to bits. As workers and intellectuals they inspire respectful awe; but as citizens of the world – well, they just are not.

When I began to plan this story I found that there was no need to use that hoary old standby, the mad scientist, and I wondered why anyone ever did when the reputedly sane scientists are quite efficiently getting on with the job of world destruction before our eyes.

"Judson's Annihilator" was to be one of the last things Jack wrote for years. While Chamberlain dithered and all of Britain waited for the declaration of war, Jack found it impossible to work, as he wrote in May 1939 to Otis Adelbert Kline, his American agent: [20]

> I wish that I were able to send you more stuff, but fear that I have nothing much on hand. This is the most damned unsatisfactory atmosphere to try to work in even on pulp stuff. One wastes too much time cursing Mr Chamberlain and wondering what mess the old fool's headed for next, and that combined with speculation as to whether next week or next month London will stand where it did is pretty unsettling. Even at this moment I can hear them testing the air raid warning sirens – though what you're supposed to do when you hear them doesn't seem to have been thought of.

Grace was already involved in volunteering. She spent her Easter break working at Central House, Bloomsbury on refugee work, to give a holiday to staff who hadn't had a break for a year.

That summer, she travelled to Biarritz, on the French side of the Spanish border. She was staying with evacuees, presumably from the Spanish Civil War. She had hoped to get a group together for learning English, but her host had a nervous breakdown leading to fights

Twelve hundred planes—gone, vanished into thin air!
105

A foreshadowing of the Blitz: illustration for "Judson's Annihilator" by Hugo Wolfe, in *Amazing Stories*, September 1939.

within the family. Teaching became impossible and after a holiday she returned to Bloomsbury.[21]

Meanwhile, Jack was sliding into depression. Having avoided the First World War that haunted his teenage years, Jack was convinced that he was fated to be conscripted into the Second. At the start of September 1939, he was on one of his regular visits to friends Biff and Eileen Barker and their daughters at Row Cottage, Steep.

In London, Grace was caught up in the first wave of evacuations as 1.5 million children left the cities in three days. Staff and pupils of Roan School for Girls were sent first to Kent.

As soon as Jack heard Chamberlain's announcement at 11.15 am on Sunday, September 3, he sat down to write the first of more than 350 letters to Grace.

References

1   Vivian Beynon Harris, *My Brother John Wyndham 1903-1969*, see note to Chapter 1.

2   *The Curse of the Burdens* was identified as a Wyndham book in: David Ketterer (2000) "Vivisection: Schoolboy John Wyndham's First Publication" *Foundation: The International Review of Science Fiction 79,* p.70-84.

3   Mike Ashley (2004) *Time Machines: The story of the science fiction pulp magazines from the beginning to 1950*, Liverpool University Press.

4   Cuttings relating to this are held in the Liverpool Archive, Wyndham 9/1 - Press-cuttings volume 1 - 1930 – 1968.

5   Leslie Flood (1975) introduction to *The Best of John Wyndham 1932-1949*, ed Angus Wells. Sphere, 1975.

6   These and many other rejection letters are held in the University of Liverpool archive, in Wyndham 11/2. The Cathedral Crypt was later published in the short-lived *Marvel Tales* in 1935, and appeared again in anthologies including the *Young Oxford Book of Nasty Endings*.

7   Mike Ashley in correspondence with the author. He generously made detailed comments on the draft of this chapter. Any remaining errors are mine.

8   John Beynon (1953), "Not So Simple", p.30 to 31, *Authentic Science Fiction* no 30, February. This is unusual in being bylined Beynon after the success of *The Day of the Triffids*.

9   John Wyndham (1951) "Will this hasten death of detective thriller?" *Trade Circular*, August 11, p.21-22.

10   John Beynon (1949) "The Flame That Went Out", *Fantasy Review* 2:9 p.8-9. This was a bi-monthly magazine aimed at British fans, mostly carrying reviews and gossip.

11   Mike Ashley (2004) ibid.

12   Q&A with Sam Moskowitz, see note to chapter 1.

13   *Aberdeen Press and Journal*, 15 May 1935, p.2; and *Hull Daily Mail*, 10 June 1935, p.7.

14   Letters from R K Messer, Administrative Clearing Corporation, New York, 4 October 1935 and 28 October 1935. Liverpool archive.

15   For example, *Fantasy* magazine of 1939 ran "Child of Power", a

forerunner of *Chocky*, by Wyndham Parkes, as well as "Derelict of Space" by John Beynon in a single issue. Particular thanks is due here to the creators of the Internet Speculative Fiction Database. They have made available their own findings plus that of earlier researchers, notably Don Day in *Index to the SF Magazines*, Norm Metcalf in a follow-on *Index*, and Steve Miller and William Contento on their online *Index*.

16   The scrapbook is now in the University of Liverpool archive. Walter Gillings wrote of Jack's attendance at the British Interplanetary Society in his introduction to "Wanderers of Time", Coronet, 1972.

17   Letter from William F Temple, writing on 25 April 1939, from 88 Gray's Inn Road. In the Liverpool Archive, Wyndham 11/2.

18   Interviewed for "The Invisible Man of Science Fiction", BBC Four, 2005.

19   John Beynon (1939) "Meet the Authors", *Amazing Stories*, October 1939, p.146, ed Raymond A Palmer.

20   Letter to Otis Kline, 8 May 1939. Liverpool archive.

21   Taken from letters between Grace's family, held by her niece Hilary Wilson.

Part Two

1939 - 1945

Row Cottage.
Sept 3rd 1939.

Darling,

The announcement came a few
minutes ago. I was wrong. I never thought
it would. But what is, somehow, most
wrong about it is that we did not hear it
together.

I don't know where you are at present
but I shall post this as soon as I learn
your address. I hope that you are safe
and as comfortable as circumstances allow.

As for me : well, I don't know yet.

Just in case, darling, sweet – thank you,
thank you, darling, sweet. It has meant more
than I ever knew.

Love, darling, from Jack.

102

Row Cottage, Steep,
3 September, 1939

Darling,

The announcement came a few minutes ago. I was wrong. I never thought it would. But what is, somehow, most wrong about it is that we did not hear it together.

I don't know where you are at present but I shall post this as soon as I learn your address. I hope that you are safe and as comfortable as circumstances allow.

As for me: well, I don't know yet.

Just in case, darling, sweet - thank you, thank you, darling, sweet. It has meant more than I ever knew.

Love, darling, from

Jack.

5

Jack's Blitz, Grace's Exile

Prime Minister Neville Chamberlain's announcement of the outbreak of war led to immediate large-scale evacuation of women and children from London, which was why Jack didn't know Grace's address for several days.

Jack, then 36, had grown up through the Great War thinking he was to join his many older classmates in the trenches. Two young men he knew had shot themselves on call-up. He believed that, having escaped then, he was fated to be conscripted now. He had been fretting for months: now he sunk further into hopelessness and depression.

Having written to Grace, he went to Eastbourne to see his mother and brother. Viv had had a bout of pneumonia and was there to convalesce. The brothers lay on the beach and talked but Viv couldn't stay. As a retained fireman, he had to return to Derbyshire to take up duties. Jack went back to the Penn Club to await news of Grace.

Her school had been evacuated to various villages in East Sussex. She ended up at Bexhill-on-Sea. She taught mostly in a nearby parish hall, but twice a week had a two mile walk to teach at a school in the afternoon.

For several months of the phoney war, while the German armies flooded across Europe, Jack endured a tense wait. More than 240,000 single men aged between 20 and 22 had been conscripted in the spring of 1939. On the day war broke out, the Government had passed a wide-reaching measure requiring all men aged 18 to 41 to register for service.

However, registration was a long, drawn-out process by age group and Jack was at the top of the range. It would be two years before

40-year-olds would be required to register. Viv, aged 33 at the start of the war, escaped on health grounds, though his membership of the Auxiliary Fire Service probably helped. The AFS was part of the Civil Defence Service. Firemen were so badly needed at home that some were taken out of the Army.

Viv was doing exceptionally well. His training in learning scripts helped when it came to the fire service exams. He memorised the textbooks and scored 100% in all the papers, gaining rapid promotion to leading fireman and instructor.[1]

Gertrude's Eastbourne hotel was now under the flight path of German bombers, and likely to be invaded. Restrictions on visitors meant many hotels closed and were taken over by the armed services. Gertrude moved further down the coast to Sidmouth, Devon.

For a time, Jack and Grace managed occasional meetings. In June 1940, just after Britain's humiliating evacuation from Dunkirk, he visited her at Bexhill-on-Sea. She was staying in a tiny turret room in a boarding house

Together they went to Fairlight, a few miles down the coast, and walked back along the cliffs into Hastings for dinner in an Edwardian-style restaurant. Although Jack was filled with forebodings about the days to come, it was a last snatched moment of happiness. Back in London, he wrote to her:[2]

17th June 1940

Darling Sweet,

So it was not as we thought, or as we hoped – has anything been so since this began? – but I'm glad we thought it for it made you smile a little.

No one can say what comes next, but, darling, I think if I knew a bomb was to drop on me tonight I would not be really unhappy now. You have given me so much – that which, as you said, matters most of all. It is still so lovely, sweet. I'd rather it ended now than that it should fade.

Put your hand on your heart sometimes, my lovely, and tell yourself that it is mine.

There is so much that I shall never forget.

Saturday, how lovely.

An era had shut up its houses and gone away – perhaps for ever. But we had that little much longer. How cruel the macrocosm, sweet, but how sweet the microcosm.

Oh, my darling

J.

For years to come, through the Blitz and in the horrors of France, he would remember this holiday for both his happiness and the terrible sense of his fate waiting in the wings. Ever after he would be drawn back to the walk on the cliffs, their last dinner and the sound of the radio in Grace's turret room:[3]

> . . . listening to Europe folding up with a sense not so much of history on the move as of everything coming to bits as it rolled downhill . . .
>
> The shutters were going up one by one, the town was packing, waiting and thinning. The little empty bungalows at Fairlight had such a dropped toy air that one couldn't be annoyed with them anymore. The RAF didn't know what to do with its rifles, and there were flashes over the dark sea.
>
> As long as I live, my Lovely, I shall remember that last walk along the cliffs. The warmth, the unpeopled peace, the smooth sea, you, My Sweet; but beyond us, unrealisable but heavy, the knowledge of chaos across the water and the future in a thick fog where anything might be hiding. Darling, you had such patience with my circular speculations.

It is a moment, and a confused blend of emotions, that would be repeated through his disaster novels. In *The Kraken Wakes*, Phyllis and Mike listen to the radio stations of Europe relaying news, without being able to understand what is happening within their own country. In *The Day of the Triffids*, Josella and Bill sit and smoke above the beach on another perfect June day, looking down at the empty seaside town below. The once-despised bungalows are rapidly sliding into decay; across the water, a blank of ruin and chaos. The only certainty of the future is unending work and difficulties. Yet the countryside is still beautiful; and love is still sweet.

The next time Jack would see Fairlight would be from the deck of a ship. Like Eastborne, East Sussex was now too dangerous for evacuees. Grace's school was to be moved to South Wales. The Roan Girls School was to be taught at the Old Grammar School in Ammanford. Grace boarded at Bryn Derw, a cottage in Llandybie two miles away, cycling over rough lanes every day.[4]

Meetings became rare and difficult. Bombing began in London in August 1940, with concentrated attacks by the Luftwaffe on London from 7 September.

Jack was on firewatching duties at the Penn Club. He got a job as a temporary civil servant in the Ministry of Information, working as a censor. It was the first steady job he had had for years and he found he quite enjoyed it: "It's so much easier to have someone say 'do this' than to have to invent one's own job."[5]

He may have hoped that doing war work at home would make him more likely to be exempted later. As there was no immediate danger of call up to the army, his depression lifted.

On the anniversary of the declaration of war, he wrote to Grace: "This is a different mood, Sweet, to the one I was in when I wrote to you last 3rd of September. In fact the hopeless feeling of the days about then is difficult even to imagine now - indeed, I don't want to try."

He began writing several postcards and letters a week to Grace, Viv and his mother "to reassure them of my continued existence". Many letters would stop and start several times as Jack wrote another page or two during an air raid, then pocketed it to complete later. He usually addressed Grace as 'Sweet' or 'Sweetie'. Amongst all his confusion of names, he signed himself simply J. Grace kept these letters: more than 350 during the course of the war.

Reading them is an extraordinary experience. The earlier letters are on an elegant pale grey paper, headed John Beynon Harris, with the Penn Club address - this paper ran out later in the war. Page after page is covered in flawless, effortless prose with barely a word crossed out. Written by lamplight in shelters and basements, against the noise of bombardments, gramophones and gossip, the letters speak as clearly as if he was in the room.

A decade later, renowned author, editor and critic Edmund Crispin would describe his writing as having "a sort of hyaline simplicity, perfect timing, miraculous avoidance of cliché and a gentle, sophisticated astringent humour." It is art that conceals art, and is as evident in his letters as in his fiction.

They are sometimes loving, sometimes despairing, often witty. He mocks the speeches he has heard on the radio, passes on gossip about friends' love affairs and describes the changing face of London and Londoners. Some are playful: Jack would send a letter entirely in appalling Latin, medieval English or a pastiche of Jane Austen.

> Dear Madam
>
> On the topick of the current conflict I have little news.
>
> To confuse intermission with cessation would be no more than injudiciously to second inclination. I do not think that the publick mind is at present disposed to such a folly: though had it been so the persistence until near last midnight of barbarous aerial noises had proved an efficious corrective.
>
> The radiations have informed me that few explosive machines descended in this city, certainly none was heard by your sincere admirer and affect. humble servant.
>
> Jno H.

In these early months of the bombing, Jack seems torn between his desire to reassure Grace of his safety and his need to share with her what was happening to him. When describing personal danger, he could be almost lighthearted. The first serious alarm after two weeks of heavy bombing was a ruptured gas main and a time bomb only yards from the club door. His account of their rapid evacuation mentions several residents, and gives an idea of the type of people living at the Penn at that time.

Margaret Robson, who raised the alarm, was a middle-aged lady from Devon, no relation to the wardens Reggie and Mary Robson, who had three adult sons in the services. Quentin Shannon, an Irish economics lecturer, had been called up to the Board of Trade. Molly Raymer, then aged 24, was running the library at the Royal College of Veterinary Surgeons. She later joined the Navy and worked for an outstation of Bletchley Park. Jean Shaddick was her friend and colleague. Denys Parfitt was a young accountant living at the club. Jean and Denys later married. Bob English was a marine engineer, temporarily ashore. Leslie and Enid Struthers were English teachers who had returned from running a school in Czechoslovakia. Leslie had translated Hegel's *Metaphysics* into English.

Jack's account of their flight was deliberately underplayed:[6]

Hello Sweet

At the moment I write with no particular address. We got turned out at 4am this morning. It happened with the lack of dignity where I am concerned which might be expected. About 3.45 Margaret Robson turned up and said there was a smell of gas. So I supposed I'd better go round.

After hunting for the leak in the canteen around the coffee machine, in the approved manner with a match, I couldn't find anything so gave it up. Then I thought I'd go to the gents. While I was there there was a whizz and a kerrump and then another whizz sounding unpleasantly close to one whose movements were temporarily hampered, but it didn't go off. A later whizz turned out to be Margaret Robson rushing downstairs with the news that there was a bust gas main and also a time bomb on the corner. All out in 10 minutes.

Well we charged round and roused the place and got 'em all out in about 15. Most of them were reasonably prepared and clad but some, such as your fat cousin [Basil], emerged in dressing gown and pyjamas and carrying an eiderdown – how many days he and they may have to spend with only this equipment for the battle of life, is uncertain.

Most of them had trailed away southward by the time we rounded up the stragglers. I dumped my things in a shelter in Bloomsbury Square and made a circuit of the adjacent shelters and trenches checking up on people – quite forgetting that the raid was still on.

Then I found Robson and we arranged that he and Mrs should get a room at the Bonnington and make it headquarters for information. Then Shannon and I went off telling all the various groups to disperse as they could manage later but keep in touch with him. Joe Sewell we found wandering about in Bloomsbury Square garden, he having somehow contrived to lose the entire membership, and greeting us with the enthusiasm of a shipwrecked sailor . . .

In the end there was a bunch of about ten. Three of them knew where they were going. The rest were vague. I suggested Molly Raymer's office in Red Lion Square and that seemed to meet with approval, so off we trooped, laden with refugee baggage. Seven of us, Molly, Mrs Struthers, Jean, Den, Joe, Bob English and me. We managed to wash and shave there, dumped our stuff and went off to the Strand Palace which was the nearest place for breakfast.

The idea at present is that we meet there about 5.30. If the bomb has been removed we go back to the Club, if not, we sleep in the basement there tonight . . .

Anyway, with luck the bomb may be removed. Last news was of a party of Royal Engineers seen trundling up Bedford Place.

After breakfast Mrs Struthers and I set out to come here (the Prudential) with Struthers. There were fire engines diving down Savoy Hill, we couldn't get along the Strand because of something burning there, so we tried to cross Lincoln's Inn, but there was a bad fire there too. Holborn was closed and with a number of new fires. In the end we had to go right up to Theobald's Road to get round.

There was a tremendous number of incendiaries dropped last night, one kept on coming across the remains of their tail fins in the road. And naturally there were many small fires as well as the serious ones.

Later 6pm in fact

It seems that the bomb hit the road by the lamppost opposite the club and had burrowed under. So we are spending the night at Molly's place of work.

Robson is collecting letters from the post-office on behalf of the club. So there may be one of yours waiting for me.

Love to you sweet,

J.

Jack was on duty on the roof a few weeks later when the club came even closer to destruction. An incendiary bomb fell on the flat lead roof. He tried desperately to shovel it off, but it rapidly burnt through the roof. Looking through the hole, he could see it on a table in an empty bedroom below. He raised the alarm and with several others ferried up buckets of water and stirrup pumps. They managed to put out the blaze before it spread beyond the room.[7]

Writing to Grace, he could only joke and reassure so far. His mood leaked out when describing the changes in London. Watching the city he knew disappear, his greatest feeling was of unreality. After one heavy night of bombing on 7 October, he delayed going into work until the dust had settled and any unexploded bombs had been taken care of:[8]

> ... nothing more was audible, so about 9 I set out. I'd just got to that pump, do you remember it? By the bottom of Bedford Row, when I heard 'em coming so nipped into a street shelter. There was a crash – three in fact – and a woman who had come in after me began to get hysterical. When I'd found a Warden to hand her over to, I went on across Grays Inn. There was a crowd at the corner of Grays Inn Road and the inevitable glass all over the place – I think, somehow, that the sounds of the glass crunching under foot and being swept away are the dreariest noises in all this noisy business – but didn't learn until afterwards what had happened.
>
> A bomb fell on Barham and Marriage, the grocers just round in Holborn and wrecked a bus with the blast. I began to get worried – just the rush-hour, you see. Struthers and Mrs Struthers had started before me and I guessed (rightly it seems) that they'd go that way to see the Holborn ruins. But they had got beyond the spot and sheltered in a doorway. Uncle [a colleague] turned up after a bit and he was in a bus three behind the one hit and looking a little shaky.
>
> Another man had been in the bus in front; his glove and paper had been torn out of his hand, but he wasn't touched. Others came along looking a little green. But not all. I don't know any of them, but it killed four of our people and injured 18.
>
> Why do I write these things in as much detail? I don't know quite. It's not a desire to harrow. More than anything, I think, to convince myself that these fantastic things are happening in these prosaic spots.
>
> And yet I can't convince myself. The quiet Bedford Row and the pump at the end, the place which for some reason or

other we used to find so often when we did an evening stroll, is not the place where I scooted into the shelter this morning. The present one is an imitation of it. It is not two quiet dingy houses we used to see that now have lain in splintery ruin for a fortnight close by, it is a kind of stage set. The woman getting hysterical in the shelter: she couldn't really have been frightened. The whole thing's too silly, too unreal, too idiotic for fright – though one does take reasonable precautions as far as possible, just as one would from unsafe cliffs of dangerous traffic.

Nor, oddly, am I me. It is not I who cross Lincoln's Inn Fields noticing empty window frames, cocking an eye warily at the sky, keeping an ear ready for the sound of a plane. No, I don't know quite who it is, mind you, but it isn't I. No, I am the chap who strolls across a real Lincoln's Inn Fields with his arm under his darling's and his hand on hers in a quiet dusk.

All of which, as you may readily understand, gives things a kind of confused aspect.

It is the less real, Sweetheart, for your not being here. I'm glad of that. You would give these things reality. As it is they are a dream – just a dream not a proper nightmare: they've none of that quality – an interlude (maybe a finale) but they've nothing to do with the play. No, that's wrong, a finale has something to do with the play. But even if it is a finale, what does that matter? In the madhouse values are lost – and it's a big madhouse now.

No, I think if you were here I might be frightened. As it is, to hell with their bombs.

As the autumn wore on, the feeling of unreality persisted. The aspect he found strangest was not the noise, but the silence. Walking across Hampstead Heath on a Sunday morning, he found it deserted. The entire city was sleeping off a week of broken nights and working days. At night, few ventured out between raids:[9]

At about 11 I took a look outside. There were white streaks across the sky. A few twinkles of shell-burst far to the south, but not a sound to be heard. It must be many centuries since London lay in such a silence as followed for an hour or two. No planes, no guns, but no traffic and no people either. Just complete silence. Quieter even than the country because there there are always sounds of some kind . . .

This curious hiatus feeling persists. If I thought that any of this were real life I should miss you far more than I do. But outside the times when I ache for the warmth of you it doesn't seem surprising that you aren't here because, so to speak, you never were. I write not so much to you in Wales as to you in 1939 when the lights were on. I feel that this confusion of time with distances gives me a sense that I'm living much more in a queer place than in a queer time. It's all very rum.

In Wales, Grace was feeling very cut off. She missed the convivial, like-minded company of the Penn and was alarmed by rumours. Jack told her the club gossip: the drawing room window was bricked up and mattresses put down: "the sleeping arrangements have all gone very communal, and if the overhead traffic – which is going on at the moment – gets any heavier they'll have to be more communal still, in the basement."[10] Jack counteracted rumours by telling her what was happening to her favourite buildings and how ordinary Londoners were coping:[11]

People are surprising: They don't crowd but they pause a little to look at something unusually spectacular like half a bed-room with the bed ready to be slept in. And they are apologetic to the policeman who has been put to the trouble of requesting them, courteously, to move on. In fact, a curious wave of politeness seems to have come over them. There is a lot of cheerfulness too. You'd think the people who queue up for the shelters to open in the evenings would look pretty dreary, well the odd thing is that they don't. As figures they should be pathetic with their bundles and pillows but when you look at their faces they are usually quite cheerful.

In some parts they're too darned casual. In Harrow, for instance, there had grown up a practice perturbing to the ARP [air raid precaution wardens] by which family arrived, laid out their rugs, put the children to sleep and then calmly went off to the pictures. The ARP were protesting that they were not bloody nursemaids.

He kept the most disturbing details of the raids out of his letters to Grace. He described the broken windows, but not the broken bodies. He knew better than to write anything that might draw the attention of censors. He wrote nothing about looting, or the assaults that happened under cover of the blackout. This darker side of wartime London appears later in *The Day of the Triffids* as Bill walks through silenced streets:[12]

> A cat on the pavement was engaged in sniffing something which might have been a bundle of rags, but was not. I clapped my hands at it. It glared at me, and then slunk off.
> A man came round a corner. He had a gloating expression on his face, and was perseveringly rolling a large cheese along the middle of the road. When he heard my step he halted his cheese, and sat on it, brandishing his stick fiercely.

Apart from his letters and poems to Grace, Jack wrote almost nothing during the war. Broken nights and firewatching combined with the censoring job to make him "dull as a turnip", though he stored his experiences up in notes.

Working as a censor at the Prudential building, High Holborn, was steady but boring. Even the raids – sometimes six or seven in a day – were soon more of a nuisance than an anxiety. The staff went to sit in the stuffy basement on backless concrete benches. Jack would fill in the time writing to Grace or his family.

Back upstairs, his table of four was dominated by 'Uncle', also known as 'The Tortoise', an older man who efficiently gamed the system to do as little as possible. Jack got through 80 to 100 letters a day, Uncle managed more: "He has his methods. One is that of selecting small envelopes simple to close again, another is by getting hold of a bunch of similar envelopes and then expressing surprise that they all contain the same circular letter, which makes things nice and easy for him."[13]

Nevertheless, Jack and the others liked him for lightening their days. The rest of the crowd were less amusing, but Jack was adept at camouflage. In many ways it was a perfect job for him: he had been censoring himself his entire life. He wrote to Grace:[14]

The Censorship business is done by an odd collection of persons. The women are for the most part distinctly upper middle class, but the men make me think mostly of 'poor whites'. They are not notable for much as a body except a vicious and querulous anti-semitism and they express it in a way which convinces one more than ever that it is almost invariably a hallmark of the really small-minded and unsuccessful.

It's queer to me this all male surrounding. Most of them at 50 and 60 are still making exactly the same jokes and seeing the same double meanings as they knew at their prep schools. In general I feel as if I had somehow got back into a manner of life – or rather an outlook on life which really ceased about 30 or 40 years ago.

In deference to your advice, darling, I am carefully not appearing too peculiar and manage to get on in this alien atmosphere quite comfortably – much in the same way, in fact, as I managed to avoid ostracism at Blundell's [his public school prior to Bedales]. It's really quite easily done. The point where I slip up worst is when I'm looking for a subtle 3rd meaning in a remark, under the impression that nobody could think the obvious 2nd meaning funny any longer. However, I'm learning.

Does that sound all very priggish?

It's not meant to be anything but a display of astonishment at an early adolescence being prolonged beyond anything one could have thought possible. Why they haven't died of boredom after 20, 30, 40 years of the same badinage I cannot think.

This, of course, is the point where one says 'it takes all kinds . . .' But the funny thing is how many of them are exactly the same kind . . .

Uncle is still going strong but still rather wistful at being what he calls a 'label-licker' at his age. Nevertheless he's really extremely glad to have any kind of a job. Our table still remains cheerful and gets shushed, but we get through just as much as the others so we're not in trouble yet.

Jack worked in various sections, brushing up his French in order to be able to translate. He practised this on Grace, apparently feeling freer in French to speak of love than in English: "Demain, ma belle, j'ai Monday off which will j'espere, help to clear the tete . . . je conclus, ma doucelle avec un mille baisers (cinq cent aux yeux cinq cent aux levres). Je t'embrasse avec toute ma force, ma petite Cherie adore."[15]

In the trade department, he learnt about everything from the gauges of the Argentinian railways to the slang of many different classes. He made notes of these, listing the most common phrases by officers, privates and different classes. This was a kind of jargon bingo, an attempt to stave off boredom, but he was also learning to imitate voices. He would make good use of this in his later work.

He was particularly scathing about the religious cards: "their bad printing and childish personifications". These confirmed his worst fears about the mindlessness of religion. In one note, he wrote: "When I find myself taking an emotive interest in religion I shall know that the decline has come."[16]

Safe in the Penn Club, he had been living in a bubble of liberal intellectualism and writing for a narrow audience of fellow geeks. The war forced him into contact with people other than left-wing journalists and pacifists. Afterwards, his writing would reflect a wider England because he knew it so much better.

Censoring work was, of course, itself censored. Staff were not meant to reveal what they had learnt to outsiders, but occasionally Jack told Grace a little more:[17]

> It's seldom one gets anything outside such a dreary routine of ill-expression and hackneyed letters – unless they're just news ones – among the private mail. When one does, it stands out. There was one today. The outer envelope contained a note from a Madame – well, call it Clek – written in French, asking that the inner should be forwarded to Lt Clek. Inside were three snapshots of a girl and a 10 page letter in French dated from Unoccupied France in July – no, early August. It ended up with quite a number of lip-prints.
>
> First reaction was: "What! All this! This is the Trade Dept, I'll transfer it to private." Then I thought, "Oh, well, I can just skim through it."
>
> Sweet, have you ever seen a real love letter? There are supposed to be some classical examples. I've seen them in anthologies. They're piffle my sweet.

It just isn't right that this letter should have been intended for one man alone. It was a classic – on a foundation as old as melodrama.

Lt Clek, a Czech, is in France. He falls in love with and intends to marry Mlle X. In the French debacle he gets away to England. They have been living together, she is known to everyone except her parents as Madame Clek. She has heard nothing of him since he escaped.

She writes four pages with a lovely and lyrical simplicity, an honesty and adoration which would make any professional writer just wither.

On the fifth page she mentions that she is going to have a baby. And then, again with an ingenuous simplicity and there-fore amazing charm, just why, and why it will be born next March.

It makes her cry a little. She wants him to be with her when it is born. But how, in all this, can they be married – or even meet? Somehow they must manage it, because by French law the child can never have his name if they aren't married be-fore its birth. If nothing can be managed she will have to have it in hospital like 'les filles des rues'.

I tell you, the honesty and tenderness of the thing where one false word would have destroyed it, made me go prickly behind the eyes.

There was something at the end about people who were living for one reason or another under other people's names, so I had to take it to the man in charge of our group. He said, "I think we'd better up and see MI 12 about it."

When we got there, MI 12 (Military Intelligence) were all very hearty and male. Very much taken by the lip-prints and the snapshots. One of them started in a man of the world way to read the letter. He smirked a bit over the beginning which made me feel rather annoyed with him. Then he forgot all about us, so we sat down and had a cigarette. When he'd finished he looked up, then he looked at the snapshots again.

"I suppose we ought to have a submission on this," he said. "But we won't. Get it done up and send it on quick."

So we went off leaving him looking at his desk with an odd expression.

I think he must have been feeling as I did – sort of humbled
by the impact of sincerity, faith and love.

Beyond that, as I sealed it up I felt as if I were burying a
literary treasure.

Jack's job meant that for the first time in many years, he no longer
had the freedom to come and go as he liked. Visits to Steep were abandoned. Biff and Eileen had been separated by the war. Biff joined the
Home Guard and managed the Bedales estate and farm. Eileen took
the girls, Tess and Jean, to America to stay with relations in 1940. They
remained there for four years. It was a miserable time – their relations
didn't really want them and Eileen struggled to support them.[18]

When Jack did manage to arrange a few days off in late October,
he felt obliged to spend it visiting his mother, taking urgent supplies
of whisky and marmalade. This at least gave him a chance to sleep in
a bed again. He told Grace: "I enjoyed the quiet of Sidmouth for a
change, but wouldn't like it for long. Besides being unoccupied I found
myself more than usually troubled with glimpses and visions. A smile
and lovely white teeth, shining eyes in a head on a pillow, a hand softly
straying – oh, my Sweet."[19]

Grace was anxious to come and visit Jack, he was equally anxious
that she didn't:[20]

Quite definitely darling, I think it is very foolish of anyone to
come here who has not got to come . . . It might not be the
right thing to write to a Sweetle – but you wouldn't come if I
weren't here, which makes me responsible for anything which
might happen to you. If there were a shelter a deux and quiet
and deep maybe it might be worth it. But all you would get is
a few bad nights in considerable company with nowhere even
to talk privately.

Many times they tried to make arrangements to see each other, but
the Censorings worked seven days a week. Jack's shift patterns and
Grace's holidays rarely coincided. In term time, she was now head of
English, in longer holidays she was sometimes left responsible for the
entire school party[21].

As a substitute, they wrote to each other two or three times a week,
often letters of several pages. She would send little presents of eggs,

easier to get in the countryside. On one occasion she managed to send three bottles of sherry wrapped in straw.

In exchange, he went to great lengths to buy her clothes to keep her warm: he was worried about her health particularly after she had to begin firewatching at night. Swansea, 16 miles away, was a target for German bombers. Soon Grace had to take turns sleeping on a camp bed in the parish hall or sitting up in the cold:[22]

> A climate that requires two mackintoshes verges pretty closely upon the inclement. I know Wales has a reputation to keep up, but that does seem to be overdoing it a bit – that is assuming that you are not wearing two because each leaks in a different place. Anyway, mind you wear as many as are needed to keep you dry and warm – it can't be much fun cycling to and fro every day in deluges, my poor Sweet . . . Keep warm, well, dry, my darling. Keep lovely, my lovely. Good night. J.

He spent several days off trawling the shops for boots, refusing many pairs as unsuitable and then realising they were selling out as fast as he was rejecting them. He was overjoyed when he managed to buy a pair of sealskin gloves from a friend who had returned from Iceland. He was only at a loss when she asked for stockings: "Sweetle, against my grain as it is to be a cartoon male, I must say I found myself somewhat at sea in Harrods stocking department." She was always appreciative, but these were his biggest hit:

> 12 November 1940
>
> 'Well, Darling,' he said, feeling a little bowled over (if, that is, there are degrees of bowling), 'I feel a little bowled over.'
>
> Previously I had an idea that stockings were well, just stockings – bought a certain tentativity and a dash of temerity; dispatched with wavering hopes for the best – I now half-see quite a number of different aspects. Anyway, I think that seldom can so small a present have had so rousing a reception. I feel – oh, no, I said that before.
>
> And since the bowling letter there is another this evening. All nicely decked out in headings, too. Well, then, I shall have a go at heads, also:

WEEKEND

This, my Sweet, is a matter that has me baffled. However, if we are to see anything of one another, I don't see how it can happen anywhere but here. (As I think I told you I can't get the week-end off. The best I can manage is my rest day of one week on the Saturday, and my rest day of the next on the Sunday – at least I think that can be managed. So if I have to turn up at 9 the next day, Monday, half Sunday would be wasted in getting back. Yet if the Blitz begins to show new bursts of vigour I don't think you ought to come into it – And how, my Lovely, anybody is to tell what anything will be like in a month's time, I just don't know. It is in a moment like this that I damn the Censorship and its workings.

All that I can suggest, Sweetle, is that you arrange to come, pending developments. If it is no worse than now, risk it. If it is like it was a month ago, don't.

It isn't just the risk. One notices clearly that the whole thing is much more worrying for people coming fresh to it than for those who have been following it along . . . I wouldn't forgive myself if you were to go back tired out instead of rested.

So Darling, there it is.

Turning to another head, viz:

BOOTS

We are, Sweet Madam, giving this matter our best attention.

CORRESPONDENCE

Letters such as yours of the 10th inst. set up awful disturbing sensations. Their warmth when I read them by day, Lovely, increases the chill by night. I don't know that there is much to be done about this – except that I like feeling warm by day

CLUB

There was a committee last night. Loss on the year, £55. Damn good. And but for the time bomb we would have been just on the right side. Robson had somewhat gloomily reckoned on much more loss and is therefore cheered.

Turner still isn't back, though he comes up once a week to do Home Guard at the University Building. (How that is supposed to frighten bombs away is a mystery known only to the Home Guards). He and his girl friend, Miss Cragg, were the only removals due to the time bomb, but things did drop off a little while we were without gas and water.

Yesterday's deluge found out several of the smaller shrapnel holes in the roof – I have a fine show of ewers and what not on the top of my wardrobe.

6.40 – they wail for their demon lover. Wind's getting up a bit, probably a shortish raid tonight. Here's hoping.

My Sweetle, my Lovely, so many things I want to say . . . No good.

Can you feel my hand on your lovely breast? I'm kissing your eyes.

J.

References

1   Viv wrote about his wartime experiences in his memorandum book, now in the University of Liverpool archive.

2   All letters from Jack quoted here are held in the University of Liverpool archive.

3   Letter 6 April 1941. Jack had been listening to news that Hitler had commenced bombing Belgrade in Operation Retribution.

4   Notes on Grace's war history kindly supplied by Hilary Wilson, drawn from letters between Grace's sister-in-law Alice and her brother Peter.

5   Letter to Grace, 21 September 1940.

6   Letter to Grace, 25 September 1940.

7   David Maxwell, *The Penn Club Story*, p.26.

8   Letter to Grace, 8 October 1940.

9   Letter to Grace, 21 and 22 October.

10   Letter to Grace, 15 September 1940.

11   Letter to Grace, 20 September 1940.

12   *The Day of the Triffids*, 1981 edition, p.153.

13   Letter to Grace, 5 October 1940.

14   Letter to Grace, 21 September 1940.

15   Letter to Grace, 14 November 1940.

16   These notes are held at the University of Liverpool archive along with drafts of poetry.

17   Letter to Grace, 7 November 1940.

18   Notes by Marion Tess Barker, kept at the University of Liverpool archives with the Wyndham collection.

19   Letter to Grace, 28 October 1940.

20   Letter to Grace, 12 October 1940.

21   Letter from the headmistress to Grace's prospective employers, 11 May 1943, held by the Wilson family.

22   Letter to Grace, 18 November 1940.

6

The Long Haul

The end of the year saw no let-up in the heavy bombing, and national morale was dropping. Jack was working over Christmas. A few days off before had been spent seeing his mother in Sidmouth. Returning to London, he was depressed. He opened Grace's presents early – a pocket-case and some honey sweets – and wrote to her:[1]

> I feel morbid, my Sweetle. The siren has just announced that some more people are to die this evening. It doesn't seem at all necessary or sensible. I fear, too, that something pretty nasty may happen before I see you again – not just because the papers have suggested it; they were bound to do that, but because it is in the air that there is something brewing, because, too, it is appropriate to that vicious schoolboy mind. I hope that, selfishly, it may not happen here – I want to love you again, my Sweet.

Six days later, on December 29, German aircraft attacked the City of London, dropping 10,000 firebombs. At one point, 300 were dropped every minute. The widespread blaze became known as the Second Great Fire of London. Over the next few months, the Germans shifted attention to seaports. Major inland missions were reserved for moonlit nights. Jack was firewatching on the roof of the Penn during one of the heaviest raids on 8 March, when 130 tonnes of high explosives and 30,000 incendiary bombs were dropped on London:

> 9 March 1941
> Dearest Sweet,
> This time I'm trying an earlier start: Teutonic repetition being what it is.

I resented the pest's arrival last night more than usual. I was just about to tell you I had the loveliest letter you have sent me. I was no more sure then, though, than I am now that it was really I to whom it was written. It is difficult to understand, that week-end doesn't have any particular time or place, yet clearly it must have existence since we both know about it. I am taking my part of it, wrapping it up very softly and carefully, going to have a look at it now and then on occasions when I need encouragement – and even then I am not sure whether I shall quite believe it, my sweet. This, darling, and, I feel convinced, much more able things I was going to tell you last night. But then the voice that had missed breathing o'er Eden by a week started up and bayed at the half-moon.

The first five minutes or so left no doubt than it was going to be busy. First a drove of heavies droning high up and then a flock of less heavies bolting along like anything.

Joe came up on to the roof and then Shannon. Things started banging. Never in the best Blitz days have I heard quite such a variety of noises. In fact there can't have been a lot in the armoury that we didn't hear. Doubles came down, a larger proportion of timers, a few screamers (the first I've heard). Some really hefty guns started up to the South-East (I think, on reflection, Lincoln's Inn Fields way) and every time they cannoned the roof shook. Smaller guns in all directions. A mobile gun squeaked into Russell Square and let off suddenly and made us jump.

There were strange and baffling whizzes seeming not to come from anywhere in particular. Some flares dropped away to the East. A group of incendiaries plonked around in Bloomsbury Square. Shannon leaning over the parapet had a bawling conversation with a warden in the street about a couple which had landed on the Liverpool Victoria. Chaps were hurling sandbags at one just at the SE corner of Bedford Place. Wardens were piping away thinly but manfully on whistles. Up above somebody was spasmodically letting off bursts of machine-gun fire – at balloons one supposed – and the sky was twinkling all over with shell bursts, and just to add variety bits of shell came whirring down with a whine like a pheasant.

Then there was a great glare in the sky, a little south of East. No mistaking a direct hit on a plane. We waited seconds for the noise. It came with a great crack and a reverberation that rolled round and round the sky.

Two bunches of four flares each suddenly started up directly overhead. Shannon threw his head back and happily yelled: "Put that light out". Local Home Guards seemed to think it was an order for they all began potting at them with rifles as they drifted northwards – much determination (particularly by some gentleman at the far end of Bedford Place who kept it up when they were far out of range until people began to shout him down) but little result.

It seemed quite dark when all that illumination had drifted down. There was a big outburst of noise citywards but we were baffled to know whether it was bombs or new bigger guns, or both. Several showers of incendiaries fell in different parts but none took hold. A plane buzzed hell for leather southwards leaving a trail of five or six explosions which we reckoned to be along the line of Great Portland Street.

Another plane got a direct hit, and blew up. It was almost in the same direction as the first. But nearer, and even noisier. Soon after that things began to quieten down quite a lot. It was a case of only two or three planes at a time and then only single planes with occasional bursts of gunnery until about midnight it petered out altogether.

There were a lot of streets roped off this morning and there was an unexploded bomb in no 1 of our 3 buildings, but that was taken away about 10 o'clock.

The nastiest piece of trouble, as you may have deduced from the papers was at the Café de Paris (under the Rialto Cinema in Coventry Street). I had a bit of a jolt when I heard that a Spanish restaurant had gone, and in Dean Street, but it turned out to be another, right up at the Oxford Street end. Except for those and a small shelter I believe the casualties would have been low, probably because of this large proportion of delayed action bombs.

I see that there is nothing about the destroyed planes in the reports, but if we saw two I imagine there must have been several more and a good many seriously damaged.

The Imperial and the Bedford and the Royal have distribut-
ed the Lofoten Islanders among them. Healthy, husky looking
youths in sea boots and vivid pullovers just as the wireless
described them. Traffic and double decker buses seem to im-
press them most. Last night they were celebrating – knocking
it back in true Norwegian style.

Darling, I'm so glad it was last week-end you came – if you
really did – and not this interruptions one.

Since I started writing they have come back as one expected,
but it's a rainy, cloudy night so I shouldn't think they'll stay
very long.

Goodnight my lovely Sweet

J.

The Cafe de Paris was known as the gayest and safest nightclub in
London, being 20ft underground, but two bombs fell down a ventilation shaft. The blast was magnified in the confined space, killing 34
people and seriously wounding many more. Looters were seen cutting
the fingers off bodies to get at the rings. It was the worst incident in
a night of heavy bombing. Buckingham Palace was hit on the same
night.

But unbeknownst to Jack, the tide of the war was already starting to
turn. The Lofoten Islanders who moved into the hotels surrounding
the Penn had come to London following a raid by British commandos
five days earlier. Their Norwegian islands were an important centre of
glycerine and fish oil production for the Germans. The commandos
had returned with 228 German prisoners, 314 loyal Norwegian volun-
teers and a number of collaborators. They also brought back a set of
rotor wheels and code books for an Enigma code machine. This gave
the British the ability to break German codes and was to be one of the
most important Allied intelligence gains.

Meanwhile, British civilians were facing more sacrifices. One was
the registration of women aged 18 to 60. They had to give their occu-
pations and be interviewed for a range of war jobs. It was an obvious
preparatory step towards conscription of women, which had never
happened before. This was unlikely to be a problem for Grace, as she
was already working full time and firewatching as a volunteer.

But Jack and Grace were both interested in how well-to-do young women leaving their homes would impact on the established class structure. Would this lead to a more equal society, or would the classes be replicated, with better-off girls given the equivalents of officers' roles, while the less-educated were given drudge jobs? Jack wrote:[2] "The registration of girls is going to cause a bit of fluttering in the suburbs isn't it? If it's really applied I shouldn't be surprised if it doesn't do socially more old order changing than any steps so far." Jack also discussed it with Viv, who was still working as a firefighter in Matlock. Jack reported back to Grace:[3]

> Matlock, it seems, is seething with indignation over the registration of women, at least the female part is. The men are gently amused and not very sympathetic – it was rather a white-feather minded place when it was a case of only men being called. The attitude of the youths whose girls persuaded them into the army is not considered locally to be in the best of taste.
>
>   However, I feel that it will be little short of a miracle if the class distinction doesn't weigh pretty heavily.

Grace registered later in the year when her age group was called, but one of the Penn Club residents avoided it, claiming ignorance. Jack wrote to Grace:

> One is just wondering at the moment what percentage of women have registered, and what they will choose to do about those who have not. My own bet is that in a few weeks' time there will be an announcement tending to show that a) the times were awkward for many women, b) quite a lot of them didn't understand, and c) that another day for registration will be appointed to 'enable' those who were unable to register at the proper time to make up for it. This possibly preceded by a few token fines.

But their friends' shock at the registration of women was as nothing to the impact on the Bloomsbury communists of Russia changing sides.

The intensive bombing of London had eased off in mid-1941 as Nazi preparations for the invasion of the Soviet Union began. The Soviet Union had signed a non-aggression pact with Germany in

1939, but on 22 June 1941 Hitler broke the pact. About three million German troops invaded Soviet-held Poland and the Soviet Union. Several of the Penn Club regulars were communists or fellow travellers. Stalin's alliance with Hitler had been difficult for them – now the Comrades were Britain's allies, presenting a different set of dilemmas. Their natural antipathy to the British establishment was at odds with their loyalty to Stalin.

Although Grace had travelled to Russia, she and Jack were not communists. Jack was a liberal, and Grace a socialist. Jack had sympathy with the ideals of communism but had little time for propaganda of any kind and had been irritated by some of the Penn Club regulars' sermonising before. When Russia allied itself with the British establishment, Jack enjoyed seeing how they would square this circle:

> 22 June 1941
>
> Darling, now what? Millions of once Communist Germans set to fight against the once Little Father; millions of once Communist Frenchmen backing them up. Thousands of men once chased, persecuted and imprisoned for shouting Rote Front [Red Front] now off to slaughter and be slaughtered by the Comrades. Neither side much interested or worried by casualty lists.
>
> I wonder if this war has now really begun. Obviously Hitler considers he can bring them to terms in between three and four months. Perhaps he can do it. (Everyone has said 'Huh!' scornfully to this when I've suggested it. But then they've said that before). Anyway, the point is he thinks he can do it and get it settled before the summer finishes – maybe he even thinks he'll have time for another smack at us in the Autumn.
>
> Well, are the Comrades tough or will they just make a bit of a show and then crumple?
>
> Again it's a gamble. If it doesn't come off quickly Hitler stands to lose a lot of his best troops and best machines. If it is over by, say, the end of September he'll be able to make up his losses during the winter, ready for the Spring . . .
>
> What about our local and (particularly since the war began) excessively fatheaded Comrades? They will probably be much too clever to be taken in by mere facts. One might think that they would be all for greater armament to assist Russia – one

might, but what on Earth would be the good of being a Comrade if you went quietly doing the same work as the mentally inferior dupes of capitalism? No, one of the really important things about being a Communist is that you must keep on thinking differently from the Community – the complete reflection of the Old School Tieist.

So cheap a jibe, Sweet. Yes, I know it, I know it's cheap. But what has been so sickening for so long is that such a magnificent conception suffers from such fools. Holier than thous enhancing their own importance by scenting out parochial villanies with the aid of a Detectives Handbook and Guide and the twisted subtleties of an ingenious schoolboy.

Interval for supper and Churchill's speech. A touchy matter, that speech. How not to frighten Americans who still support a 1923 Bolshie Bogey.

Have just rung up Howell[4] and put to him this question of how to keep the Party a Party. He says it's simple: just take on the 'Tribune' line: 'Sack the sabotaging bosses and increase the war effort'. Not a bad idea, either.

Well, darling, a what-do-you-call-it to these jottings.

Goodnight my sweet Sweet. Sleep well.

Love J.

I wonder if I can go to the workings in a red tie tomorrow?

Jack enjoyed teasing Grace about her political affiliations and love of Russia – she had never forgotten her trip there and kept much Russian memorabilia for the rest of her life. Jack addressed her as Tovaritch (Comrade) Gracushka: "You will be driving one of 300 tractors in a line, polishing it with a loving and politically educated touch every evening and retiring to your collective bed".

But whilst Grace might take a joke, some of their friends found it hard to handle. One was Dr Molly Barrow, who had been officially commended for her gallant work during air raids. She also campaigned for state nurseries in Birmingham, where she was then living with her husband George, a solicitor. Jack told Grace:[5]

About the first person I saw after I had posted my last letter to you was George Barrow. I duly inquired after Molly, and whether she had had further honourable mention.

"No," said George, "there's been nothing since the policeman."

He seemed surprised that the fame of the policeman hadn't spread to London. It seems that even in the teeth of the paper shortage the Birmingham papers enjoyed it in a large way.

Somebody got knocked over near their house and Molly went forth in her medical capacity. The man was lying on the pavement with a broken leg and he, two policemen and an interested crowd of Irish factory workers were all waiting for the ambulance. They waited quite a time, and the crowd, for lack of anything else to pass the time, started ragging the policemen. After a while it occurred to the subjects that the law was being mocked and that it was necessary for it to assert its dignity. This, one of its representatives did by pouncing upon one of the smallest and most inoffensive members of the crowd and arresting him.

One gathers that Molly's sense of justice was violated, and a deep suspicion of policemen, held ever since 'we' became Moscow, was confirmed. Protests being unavailing, she smote him decisively on the jaw. An excellent blow, one understands, and its effect by no means minimized by her thoughtfully placing one foot behind the man as she hit him.

He was off duty for three weeks.

In the police court a good time was had by all, all one morning. Two guineas and costs.

George became something of a local hero for a week or so a) for having a wife who could lay policemen out cold, b) for intactly surviving the association so long.

I can see Molly's expression as she did it. What I should like to have seen was the awed admiration which must have gripped the crowd. One imagines she is more popular in the practice than ever.

For the next two years, Jack and Grace's correspondence settled into a regular pattern. Jack grew more used to the horrors of the bombing and the boredom of work. He wrote to maintain a contact with her, to tell her news of friends and raids, and to arrange their occasional meetings. Miles apart, they listened to the same radio programmes and discussed the likely political outcomes. He sent her books, magazines and a copy of the Beveridge Report on the future welfare state so they could discuss it by letter.[6]

He may also have wanted the enjoyment of writing in itself: throughout these years he wrote hardly any fiction. His only published work in these years was "Meteor" (*Amazing Stories*, March 1941), written before the Blitz. This hiatus in his work was unusual both for him personally – he had been churning out work for 15 years – and in terms of the writers of the day.

Other authors were turning out short stories about the war as it progressed. The short story form lent itself to being written quickly "in the heat of the moment, responding with utter immediacy to a mere facet of a huge situation as it unfolds". Short stories as political or social commentary were usual at the time.[7]

One of many Second World War writers was Alun Lewis, who wrote excellent accounts of the lives of ordinary soldiers, with barely a delay between the events described and the fictional version. Jack read Lewis' work, admired it, and sent it on to Grace.[8] Jack was writing accounts of the Blitz in his letters which mirrored the German invasion he had imagined in "Judson's Annihilator" only two years' earlier. So why didn't he render these into fiction?

Reading novels made him long to write another book, but disturbed nights and long working days kept him in a mental fog. He complained he was "as mentally active as a poached egg".[9]

There may have been another reason for his lack of output. Everyone's lives changed during the war, but for Jack, the change was extreme. Naturally private, he now lived, worked and slept in noisy, crowded rooms. There was no retreat to his attic room, no peace in the sanctuary of the Downs.

Long interested in social order, he now saw it vanishing and transmuting before his eyes. He needed time to come to terms with these changes. Ultimately, they would appear, dross turned to gold, in *The Day of the Triffids*. In the meantime, the mental effort needed to get through every day was exhausting him. Nevertheless, he was constantly evaluating the war itself:[10]

Dear Sweet,
Many is the time when I think: now I'll write a nice intelli-

gent letter on the sociological effect of this and the psychological impact of that – but it goes on being one of those things that never happens.

And for why? Mostly, I think because there is no viewpoint, no means of studying a scene: so that gradually one gets more and more out of touch with whatever lines of thought may be going on – like an MP.

I say _may_ be going on advisedly because I'm not at all sure that they are at all. The impact of concentrated, if not very good, propaganda on us who had learned to get a fairly good picture of things by comparing various views of known bias has left me still at sea (excusing the mixture).

Only of late has it begun – and that dimly – to show itself to me how necessary concepts are. Postulates enough to erect something on. Without them hopes become astrology, thinking, being impossible, is replaced by superstitious credulity – a kind of super manured bed which grows ecstatic blooms and nightmares under coloured lights.

All decent revealing light is blacked out. The best one can do is wander around in this quite artificial twilight and take a slosh at a few of the more obviously monstrous growths by way of trying to avoid being quite grown in.

Before the war one had a sense of being a creature which inhabited the earth – an individual with a path to choose. Now one travels in the manner of a parasite upon some creature which chooses its path in a fashion which one's position among the fur makes it impossible to guess.

There is no understanding of the mentality at work because there is no mental contact. No significance of movements because one is utterly ignorant of the physical possibilities and limitations.

No savage put into a city could be much more baffled about how and why than I feel in moments of honesty.

We keep the superficial day to day habits by inertia – now knowing whether they have point or not. Primitive man did just that – wandering, sometimes afraid, but mostly just blankly gawping at the things he lacked the basic concepts to explain.

And I heartily dislike it.

Somehow I seem to feel that reason as we used to try to use it can be no more – at least not for a very long time. That unreason is pushing it out, and will be preferred. It seems to hang over ready to take charge, and one wonder is that may not be how the unstable feel about a madness they fear.

There will be a generation brought up in mental fetters – how long can it continue without a chance of recovery. Just how many years of war will it take to produce a range of age which burns its books because it is less trouble and less un-comfortable to have a simple faith.

I begin to feel now that whatever comes of this you, my Sweet, and I have had our day. The rest of our lives we may have to live comfortably or uncomfortably, but I begin to fear that for our generation there is at best the prospect of being paying guests, as long as we behave ourselves, among people whom we don't, and will not want to, understand.

This, Darling, is not a conservative groan for the world that has gone – far be it . . . It is more an apprehension that the culture of the mind for war which has now gone on for nearly 3 years will soon do irreparable damage, and that win or lose we shall be in for a mystic age.

I must say Sweetle when I started I had no idea I was head-ing into all that. I'm too lazy to tear it up and start again, Darling, so if you have bothered to wade through it, I should just forget it.

I propose now to have a pint.

Goodnight, my lovely Sweet,

J.

As the war dragged on, the usual hours for the Censorings length-ened. Jack was occasionally put in charge of several tables of censors, though he didn't enjoy this. The department expanded, at one point 10,000 people were employed. It moved from the Prudential building to the Senate House, also known as the University Tower. This was one of the most significant buildings in wartime London. At 18 sto-reys high, its stepped art deco pyramid outline was visible across the city. Jack and Grace could see it from their bedroom windows. It was long a matter of wonder that it didn't suffer more damage. In fact, bombers left it untouched as it provided such a handy landmark.[11]

George Orwell's wife Eileen also worked there for the Censorship Department. Orwell would transform it into the Ministry of Truth in *1984*. For Jack, it also became a beacon of a new world order as the rallying point for the new sighted community in *The Day of the Triffids*.

Jack was on the seventh floor, which was exposed to all the weather. The broken glass of the windows had been replaced with Windolite, a kind of plastic sheet reinforced with netting.[12]

> We've been having a lot of climate here lately. Tearing wind, rain horizontal – I suppose that's what you mean when you say it was a bit 'showery' on Saturday. In the office on Sunday it seemed like a drum factory. All the Windolite panes down one side of the building would conk in (like a tin lid) when the blast hit them, and sound like a bomb a few yards away, then they'd all conk back again, then the other side of the building would get it. Fearful uproar all day long. One had a sort of feeling that it was very wonderful of the building to keep on an even keel.

As well as increased work, pressure from the family also mounted. Viv's health had remained fragile. He had another bad attack of flu, exactly two years after his pneumonia. Jack could get little information from Lila:[13]

> She said "No, it wasn't pneumonia", but she said it in an in-definite sort of way – as if she had never heard of pneumonia, anyway – which left me very worried. Well, then I had to inform Mother why Viv had not been able to write. And I had to keep Lila's name out of it because if I had once mentioned the source of my information the whole thing would have been suspect, and probably Mother would evolve some theory that Lila had made him ill for a dark purpose of her own. So what with one thing and another, and being worried at my own sketchy information it was all very trying.

Viv took months to recover and was signed off work as a fireman by his local doctor. However, in December 1941, the Medical Board designated him Grade 1, and he returned to work, now full-time instead of retained. This meant he lost his stripe and ceased to be a leading fireman, which in turn meant grim hours and physical exhaustion. After some extra training he managed to get his stripe back, but mentally, the strain of being out in bombing raids and seeing carnage was building up.[14]

Gertrude was also becoming more needy. She had left Eastbourne in 1940 for Sidmouth. In early 1942, she had to leave Sidmouth due to 18 hotels in the town being taken over the by the RAF. She moved to Tunbridge Wells, then Croydon.

She couldn't find anywhere she liked. Smedley's Hydro had been taken over as a military hospital. Elsewhere, the shortage of staff meant a drop in the level of service she was used to. The food was poor due to rationing, and her circle of acquaintances had dissipated. Even active older people often felt their age during the war as the focus was so much on the young, and Gertrude was then 73.

She became morbid and depressed. Grace sent eggs and Jack did his best to settle her in her new rooms, but nothing made a difference. Jack wrote:[15]

> The moment I saw her yesterday I knew something was up. And that was a prelude to one of those emotional, hysterical businesses, and I was scared stiff because they used, at Matlock, to prelude these 'attacks' of hers, and I didn't know what could be done with or for her if she went off like that in a strange place.
>
> She's determined that she hates the place, loathes her room, and can't stand any of the people. So she's determined to leave directly Whitsun is over. She's been writing to various places, but of course the trouble is to get in anywhere nowadays – also to find out whether the places are suitable or not. And, further, that this continual moving is bad for her.
>
> For one thing she is feeling lonely and that there's nobody to take the least interest if she were to be ill – then, the next moment she's saying she couldn't put up with having someone always with her – so where are we? (even supposing someone suitable could be found).
>
> Frankly, I just don't know what to do about it. I have a nasty feeling that either the food or the company, if not the place itself will seem to her insupportable wherever she goes – which means she will work herself up, and then collapse.

There was never any suggestion that Gertrude was physically ill – she would live well into her eighties. It's hard not to think that her "hysterical businesses" and "attacks" were a blend of self-indulgence and manipulation – a practised, effective means of getting attention plus her own way. Her emotionalism may also have had its roots in boredom, leading to introspection and self-obsession. She was a fanatical bridge player but had almost nothing else to do – no job, no family to care for or house to run. In hundreds of letters, Jack never breathed a word against her, but his later books would tell a different story.

On top of longer working hours and a demanding family, the threat of call up had not receded. More men were still needed - his friend Bill Sykes had joined the Royal Army Ordnance Corps. In June 1942, Jack received a notice telling him to prepare for call up into the Home Guard. He volunteered for the Censorings Home Guard unit, as he didn't want to end up being posted to somewhere further away. Joining a uniformed service could not be a straightforward decision for Jack.

The attitude in the club was complex. Many residents and visitors were pacifists or conscientious objectors. One member, Joe Bradshaw, went to prison for refusing to firewatch: a pretty extreme position even by Quaker standards. Grace's cousin, Penn treasurer Basil Burton, had been imprisoned as a conscientious objector in the Great War.

Occasionally members of the services did stay at the Penn. One was Commander Cooke, retired Royal Navy, who had been recalled to the Admiralty for the duration. Molly Raymer, a younger resident, said she was never made to feel judged for her decision to join the Navy. Though the Friends disagreed with those who went into uniform, she said: "They respected our right to our convictions as we respected their right to theirs. No bad feelings, no arguments, not many places could have had that reputation, it says a great deal for the Club." [16]

Jack told Grace of his reception when he first put on uniform:[17]

> I appeared in Home Guard outfit this morning, to be greeted with modified raspberries by most of the dining room. The Commander heard the comments, and for the first time I saw him with a very icy Service look in his eye. It would, of course, be a perishing hot day – that was trying, but my boots were worse than the rest of the outfit. I feared that – there's

something about my ankle bones. They stick out too much.

Meanwhile, Grace was also sick of being cut off in the country-side. She was seeking to return to London but was unsure what to do. She considered teaching at a boys' school, or joining the new British Institute of Public Opinion. Jack was concerned that she might find herself out of work at the end of the war when the men returned, as had happened to many women after the First World War. This was less likely if she remained teaching girls.

For the meantime, she remained in Wales, with occasional visits to London as bright spots in a long, tedious exile. On one occasion they saw Disney's *Fantasia* together, on another *In Which We Serve*. Grace wrote to her brother: "I saw the Noel Coward film but otherwise spent the time looking for books I need – extremely difficult to get the most obvious classics now. Of course, it's a treat for one to be among kindred people if only for a weekend."[18]

Jack's life became more sociable again as the bombing raids decreased and people were able to venture out. He went to regular dinners with friends Howell and Becky Davies and heard the gossip from the BBC, where Howell was writing scripts. He was popular as a shoulder to cry on for female friends in the grip of the hectic love affairs of the war, such as writer Molly Borer. Coming home one evening, he was astonished by just how hectic:[19]

> I found myself coming back from Piccadilly at about 11.15. Not having been around there for a long time at that hour, I was a bit country cousin. I met another chap I knew, on Piccadilly station. When I remarked on the amount of drunken girlhood surrounding us – because it really was rather noticeable – he looked at me surprisedly and said where do you live? It's always like this. So I felt that I had come out into the great evil world you read about in the Daily Mirror. There were astonishing numbers of poor little flippets looking extremely ill. Somehow it hadn't occurred to me that with cinemas ending early, and a blackout on there just isn't anywhere to go but a pub. Their American pals teach them to mix beer and whisky, and there it is. It was a very pathetic trainload, not noisy, mostly sentimental drunk.

He was invited to the marriage of Percy and Phyllis Halliday, long-standing friends. He had been best man a couple of years earlier for Jean and Denys Parfitt at the same venue, a Church of England church at Woburn Square. Nonetheless, he was shocked by the service which he described as a "more ample affair than Jean's":[20]

> To my unaccustomed ear it sounded (save for the language) singularly like something out of the advice page of the Daily Mirror embroidered with some casuistic and some downright phoney arguments and instances – apart from flat misstatements of fact – in order to drag it into the province of the priesthood.
>
> In a way I felt quite shocked to perceive the unblushing blatancy of the way the institution had been grabbed. I kept on thinking – of course one knows that the church tries to grab every main turning point of life, but this is scandalous, it's so terribly clumsy. It's like listening to a lie which is so badly told that you even want to help the speaker out of the mess. I think what was upsetting me most was that in my simple way I have taken it for granted that the Church is an expert propagandist, now I'm all at sea because this stuff was simply terrible. Further, though it paid some slight passing lip-service to love and kindness and happiness the rest of it had about as much human warmth as a tenancy agreement – where again my simple outlook was fogged because I had thought that that was supposed to be the department in which it scored over the registry office.
>
> Well, one keeps on learning.
>
> A not unsimilar line of thought had occurred to old Robson, who, with his customary tact, was moved to begin a debate on it as we waited in the church for the crowd in the porch to clear. I believe he took the point up with the clergyman later, at the reception. Anyway, next time I saw him he had elicited that we had been listening to the revised version, loudly wondering what the original could be like . . .
>
> In the evening Arthur Halliday (Percy's brother), took a party to dinner at the Coq d'Or. I was there, I fancy, because somebody said – "My God, we're all uneven. Must find another man" and they cast about for somebody much the same

age and not a teetotaller. It was quite a nice party. As you may recall, Sweetle, I am not a teetotaller – but I must in honesty admit that either I am out of training or they were all in unusual form. I did have some breakfast this morning, but I had unfortunately lost it before I set out for the workings.

However, it really was quite a good party.

By the summer of 1943, they had been apart for four years, and Grace decided to come back to London regardless of the risk. Whilst she looked for another job, they started to arrange a summer holiday at Devil's Bridge, a beauty spot in central Wales.

On his 40th birthday, he wrote to thank her for her present and tell her he had made progress on the holiday plans:[21]

So here I sit – on a milestone labelled 'II score'. Very queer. I don't feel a bit like two score. That surprises the internal me which cannot give up expecting some kind of change. It shouldn't do of course, because nobody within sight behaves as if he were more than about 22 – his only change being that he wears his various false fronts for different proportions of his day than he did when he was actually 22 – but still, it does.

Perhaps I am older than I feel. If I weren't I might not find this time of concentration on bigger and better bangs so adolescently tedious. Apart from such externalities, though, I think I feel younger, and I'm sure I feel happier than I did ten years ago. For that, there's just one reason, my Darling Sweet.

I was wondering the other day, too, what 40 would have been like without the last 8 years. I felt it would have been something very depressing – and somehow self-belittling: it isn't now, my Sweet. You've made it just a number. Darling, there's so much I'll never thank you for.

I do hope Devil's Bridge hasn't gone and changed its mind, or found it's booked twice over or something. One can't help feeling, times being what they are, that complete smoothness is an unattainable ideal. I'm liable to get cramp from keeping my fingers crossed.

Oh, concerning that map. Don't you bother. I've managed to get one without any trouble whatever. Isn't that the way of things – the everyday is rationed or extinct – the improbable arrives on a platter.

But only a few days later, Jack had bad news: "It looks now as if the blow has fallen. They graded me 1 medically. Sent me to an interview with the RAF who said it was afraid it had nothing for me, and then passed me on to the Army Interviewer. He wound up by saying that I could expect to be called in 3 to 6 weeks. So there it seems to stand."[22]

Jack could almost certainly have escaped service if he had claimed to be a conscientious objector. His age, war work and, above all, his longstanding residency in a Quaker club would all have been on his side. In the First World War 'conchies' had received a very hard time, but they were more leniently treated in the Second. He may well have been able to remain working as a censor and in the Home Guard.

It's not clear why he didn't. Certainly, he loathed fascism and had a great deal of personal courage, as shown by his high-risk climbing exploits. But fatalism also played a part. He believed all men had to fight at some time, and still had a strong feeling that he had somehow cheated fate in the First World War. This debt had to be paid.

They pressed ahead with plans for the trip in August. It was another holiday that would live long in memory, although for Jack the news about his likely call-up was a new anxiety. He would later berate himself for wasting their time together in gloomy forebodings.

Ironically, Grace had good news – she was offered a job teaching at an emergency secondary school in London. She returned to London on 1 October 1943.

On 30 November 1943, eight weeks after Grace's return, Jack was enlisted in the army and posted to one of the many primary training camps in Northern Ireland. In January, he was transferred to the Royal Corps of Signals and posted to the barracks at Catterick, North Yorkshire, for training as a cipher operator. In March 1944 he was posted to 11 Armoured Division Signals and granted the paid acting rank of Lance Corporal. No letters survive from this time until D-Day. There are just three poems, one a Valentine, the others written in May 1944 to commemorate the ninth anniversary of their becoming lovers.

So many things so little mean unshared,
And were it not for you they had meant less
So at each scene for which you might have cared
At every little thing which I could guess
You'd love, then, phantomly, you came.
Because of you the colours lived and glowed,
Eoan skies were beautifully aflame
The air was sweet, and latticed branches showed
Their patterning. Because of you the moon
Hung beautiful. You showed me little streams
All lacey edged with ice. By night or noon
You made my sleeping and my wakened dreams.

  Because of you the lovely things were mine
  Oh be, still be, my Sweet, my Valentine.

Nine years abloom with dear and precious things.
Each crimpéd petal burst its bud to spread
Its scent more sweetly on successive Springs.
Upon their honey from your lips I've fed.
Sipping a mead with subtle drug imbued
To tinct new nerves, to sooth a secret sore,
To show a world more love and living hued
And yield a treasury of lovely lore.
Soft on the scarlet cushion of my heart
You lie. And yet so deep that bed is pressed
Its pristine shape not time nor any art
Could now restore. There must you rest

  So close have you immingled with my stuff:
  Nine years, my Lovely Sweet, is not enough.

Now will I weave the gossamer that I dream,
Contrive a pattern of ethereal thread.
Make me a coverlet which shall bespread
My loneliness, to warm me and to gleam
When all is dark. An iridescent skein
Of lovely memories with promise weft
Asprinkle with beloved flowers reft
From time, unwithered ever to remain.
With you, my Sweet, the sweetness sweeter grows:
The dear familiar you paradox
And mint afresh; bedeck with pretty frocks
And more endear: the known in new enclose.

  So, Darling, shall my woven threads combine,
  Sweet past with precious present to entwine.

G for 15 May 1944, J.

References

1   Letter to Grace, 23 December.

2   Letter to Grace, 16 March 1941.

3   Letter to Grace, 23 March 1941.

4   Howell Davies was an author and editor. He wrote science fiction novels and scripts for the BBC. He lived with his wife Becky in Pond Square, Highgate. Later in the Blitz, Jack decided to keep a change of clothes there in case the Penn Club was bombed out.

5   Letter to Grace, 20 December 1941. The case described here was reported in the Birmingham Mail, October 9, 1941.

6   Letter to Grace, 5 December 1942.

7   Philip Hensher (2015) *General Introduction to the Penguin Book of the British Short Story*, Penguin.

8   Letter to Grace, 22 June 1942.

9   Letter to Grace, 13 June 1941.

10   Letter to Grace, 25 April 1942.

11   Neil Pollard, *In John Wyndham's Footsteps*. Unpublished at time of writing.

12   Letter to Grace, 2 Feb 1943.

13   Letter to Grace, 10 August 1941.

14   Letter to Grace, 20 December 1941.

15   Letter to Grace, 14 May 1942.

16   David Maxwell, *The Penn Club Story*, p.27.

17   Letter to Grace, 22 June 1942.

18   Letter to Percy Josiah Wilson, 4 November 1942. Held by Hilary Wilson.

19   Letter to Grace, 2 February 1943.

20   Letter to Grace, 28 March 1943.

21   Letter to Grace, 10 July 1943.

22   Letter to Grace, 23 July 1943.

7

Somewhere in France

Five days after D-Day, Jack wrote to Grace. He knew he was leaving for France but could not tell her because of the censors. She knew what his letter meant. Thousands of women received letters like it that week, heavy with unspoken words.

11 June 1944

My Dear Sweet,

I know you will have been writing to me, but there's a delay, so I'm longing to see your writing again. I expect I shall soon.

Again nothing I can tell you, Darling.

But how glad I am you were able to come at Whit, and how dear it was of you to come. Another of the things I am never going to forget.

Give my best wishes to the Robsons and anyone else in the Club, will you.

Once more I'd like to write so much and can write so little. My heart is very full: there's so much of you in it, My Sweet.

My love to my Lovely Darling,

J.

Early on the morning of the 15 June, Jack came up from below to stand on the deck of the ship before breakfast. It was a beautiful day: "one kept on feeling that it must be some kind of summer cruise. Sun, lovely cloudscapes, the water a wonderful blue-green. Seemed so much more like a colour travel film than real life."[1] It was then he looked across the water and saw Fairlight, the little town they had visited when Grace's school was first evacuated to nearby Bexhill.[2]

It was just four years ago that we walked back from there into Hastings – almost to the day it must have been. And those

Top: John Wyndham Parkes Lucas Beynon Harris.

Bottom: His father, George Harris. Picture probably taken on his becoming a barrister, in his early forties, shortly after Jack's birth.

Top: 'A cross between a Roman senator and Jesus Christ': Badley of Bedales.

Bottom left: Jack at Bedales, taken from a school picture in 1920 aged 17.

Bottom right: Viv at Bedales in 1920, aged 14.

Top: Jack, pictures taken on leaving Bedales.

Centre and bottom: a ski-ing holiday in the early 1920s. Pictures taken from Jack's own album. Centre picture is labelled Mary, self and Clarissa. Bottom picture is unlabelled.

Top: Grace Wilson, front row, far left, at a fancy dress party, aged 18.

Bottom: Grace outside the Penn Club, aged about 28.

Grace, by Jack, contact strips and selected enlargements from his own and Grace's albums. Although they were lovers most of their lives, there are no pictures of them together. Jack was a keen photographer but disliked having his picture taken.

Top: Viv, probably taken
as a publicity still during
his short-lived acting
career in the 1920s.

Bottom: Two
photographs by Jack of
his mother Gertrude,
from his own album.

Top: Viv, taken by Jack, from his own album. Viv would always follow Jack on his terrifying climbs, however frightened he was.

Centre: Jack, taken by Viv.

Bottom: Lila Grettan, Viv's long-term partner. Taken by Jack.

Top: Arthur T Sykes, known as Bill, who was at Bedales with Jack. He and his wife Leslie often welcomed Jack to their home at the Red House, Cockshott Lane, Steep.

Bottom left: Harry 'Biff' Barker, Jack's closest friend, with his older daughter Jean in 1934.

Bottom right: Biff's wife Eileen with their younger daughter Tess in the gardens of Row Cottage, where Jack spent many summers.

Top and centre: Two pictures of Leslie Sykes from Jack's album. He made a rather grainy enlargement of the top picture, which is obviously a detail from another photograph. She was the inspiration for the strikingly beautiful, fiercely intelligent Sealander woman in 'The Chrysalids'.

Bottom: Jack with Leslie and her friend Dilys Jones outside the Bee House, in the grounds of the Red House, Steep, c1935.

Top and bottom: Jack and Grace reading in the garden of the Penn Club, c1935.

Opposite: The 15th anniversary of the Penn Club in 1935 was celebrated with a reunion dinner. Grace is on the back row, right, half hidden behind another woman. Jack is on the left, cupping his face in his hand. Basil Burton, Grace's cousin and club treasurer, is the tall figure dominating the back row.

Top: Grace went prematurely grey but kept her masses of hair in the same elaborate style.

Bottom: Senate House, visible from Jack and Grace's bedroom window, was used by the censorship office during the war. Jack worked there, as did George Orwell's wife. Jack would use it as the meeting place for the sighted in *The Day of the Triffids*. George Orwell made it the Ministry of Truth in *1984*.

Top: Jack in army uniform, cigarette in hand as usual, at a training camp in Catterick, North Yorkshire in 1944. He gave it to Grace with "Moi" written on the back. He is already looking older than in the self-portrait taken in 1938 (front cover), which he used for the back of his 1950s bestsellers.

Bottom: No. 7 squadron, Junior Leaders course, 1944, Royal Signals. Jack is middle row, third from left.

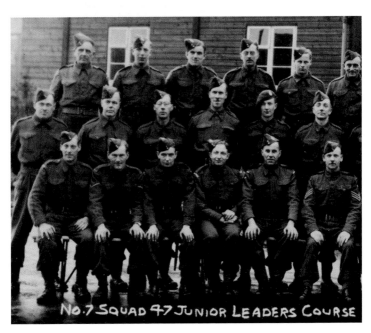

NO.7 SQUAD 47 JUNIOR LEADERS COURSE

The 1957 World Science Fiction Convention, London. Top: Belle Dietz (seated), Frank Dietz, Jack, Sam Moskowitz (in background), Ted Carnell, Arthur C. Clarke, Robert and Barbara Silverberg.

Bottom: Jack presents a Hugo award to Ted Carnell for New Worlds as the Best British Professional Magazine, watched by Bobbie Wild, an editor of the British fanzine Vector.

Top: Oakridge Cottage, Steep, 1963.

Bottom: Grace sunbathing in the garden, taken by Jack.

Top: Jack outside
Oakridge Cottage,
Steep.

Bottom: The last
picture taken of Jack, in
Leslie Flood's London
science fiction shop, on
28 January 1969. He
was 65.

14684047 L/cpl JBHarris.
'J' Troop R. Signals,
att. H.Q. 159 Inf. Bde.
A.P.O. England.
11th June 1944.

My Dear Sweet,

I know you will have been writing to me, but there's a delay, so I'm longing to see your writing again. I expect I shall soon.

Again nothing I can tell you, Darling.

But how glad I am you were able to come at Whit, and how dear it was of you to come. Another of the things I am never going to forget.

Give my best wishes to the Robsons & anyone else in the Club, will you.

Once more I'd like to write so much & can write so little. My heart is very full; there's so much of you in it My Sweet.

My love to my Lovely Darling,
J.

Jack's letter held in the University of Liverpool archive. The squiggle in the bottom left corner is the censor's signature.

four years just dropped away so easily as I looked, that I felt happy just to see it. And there was Hastings, further on, and later Bexhill, and I missed my breakfast because I couldn't leave any of it alone. You know my goodbyes, Sweet. I just hung on while they slowly took it all away from me.

I was feeling then that I'd probably never see it again unless I were wounded instead of killed – and I hoped it wouldn't be the kind of wound to stop me walking along the cliffs again. I hoped I'd be wounded pretty quickly.

The arrival in France on Juno Beach put a swift end to this dream-like state. Jack was working as a cipher operator out of a lorry in a team of five: Jack as lance corporal, a driver, a sergeant major and two corporals. They were attached to the 11th Armoured Division of almost 15,000 men and 343 tanks. The 11th was working with Canadian forces on the Eastern end of the strip of coast held by the Allies. At their end, the strip was only five miles deep. The troops had not been able to move further south because of two German Panzer (tank) divisions at Caen, who made a fanatical defence of the town.

That morning the Times reported:[3]

> Grim fighting is in progress in Normandy. Nowhere is it fiercer than in the eastern sector of the bridgehead, where the Germans, threatened by a pincer movement aimed at the conquest of Caen, are counter-attacking in strength and with toughness.
>
> In the area between Tilly-sur-Seulles and Caen armoured battles are growing in intensity, but so far the allied line is holding firm against repeated counter attacks ... The 2nd and 21st Panzer, the Hitler Youth, and the 12th SS divisions have been identified.

It was this fight that Jack was to join. The surrounding terrain – the bocage of Normandy – was hilly, often wooded country with twisting roads bordered by banks topped with hedges. It had a claustrophobic atmosphere and favoured German defence.[4]

He wrote immediately to Grace, to let her know he had arrived safely: "My Sweet, In spite of the above familiar address, I am, I understand, allowed to reveal that the term England, above, includes somewhere in France. And if that phrase doesn't take one back a bit, what does?"[5]

Over the next ten days, Grace's letters reached him, but his didn't reach her, frightening her dreadfully. They were probably delayed due to the necessity of sending everything through censorship. He kept sending brief notes, hoping they would eventually get through. These were cheerful letters, describing the countryside as being like southern England and telling her about the dehydrated meat and porridge in their rations: "Only personal news is that I've had a tooth out: that one that broke. The boiled sweets found it out. A most dextrous and satisfactory performance by a very pleasant Canadian dentist."[6]

As a cipher operator, he probably had a clearer idea of what was coming that most of the men. The day before the division joined a major offensive against Caen, he wrote again to Grace, knowing he would not be able to write for some days at best:[7]

> Just a little note to tell you that there's an ache where my heart used to be before you took it.
>
> So far, Darling, my letters don't seem to reach you, but yours reach me and I love them. I will write when I can, but don't worry over the gaps: everything is bound to be a bit involved and erratic in the circumstances – and when you come to think of it it's pretty wonderful that mails come through at all in all this immense business.
>
> Much as I dislike old adages in general, I do think we can apply the 'no news is good news' to this situation, so bear that in mind, my Sweet.
>
> What I have been unable these last six months to explain about myself, I find that Master Shakespeare has, as so often, experienced and explained already. I can't quote, but you will find it in the last line or two of one of the Sonnets where he weeps for the fear of loss.[8]
>
> No more words for now, just
>
> All my love for my Lovely, my Sweet,
>
> J.

Early the next morning, Operation Epsom began, involving several British divisions. Jack's division crept forward behind a rolling artillery barrage. British radio broadcast the sound. Jack wrote:[9]

What you don't get on a broadcast, however, is the duration: when several hundreds of guns start up and then keep it up for 2 or 3 hours you wonder that anything can live among the tons and tons of stuff they fling over, but that's where the slit trenches come in, and as far as I can gather if the fire is concentrated on open positions it is less destructive than one could believe from hearing it in action but has, and no wonder, a stunning and dazing effect . . .

One of the impressive things . . . is the passage of a German raider. You hear a noise in the distance. It has a different quality from the ordinary artillery noise because it is composite. It seems to fall towards you like a high-speed thunderstorm. As it comes you can hear the parts of it getting clearer, sorting out in to Borfors, Oerlikens, Brens etc. It gets close. Then you are in the middle of it and all sorts of things on every hand that you hadn't even suspected were there open up at once and then, if the raider is still miraculously able to fly, the noise rolls away in a diminuendo to the other side.

At noon, the 11th Armoured division was ordered to rush the bridges over the Odon river. German holdouts attacked them and prevented any advance. By the end of the day, they had lost 21 tanks. They captured bridges in two villages the next day. Over the next five days, British and Canadian troops broke through elaborate German defences and advanced six miles. But they had captured only part of the town of Caen. It cost them 4,000 casualties, including 257 men killed from Jack's division.

Jack could tell Grace little because of the censorship, but he described one bout of enemy fire. It may have been the moment caught by an army photographer, the explosion of an ammunition lorry hit by a mortar bomb. Just as in the Blitz, a life-threatening attack becomes a gentle comedy in his hands:[10]

There came a peculiar sound outside my experience. Obviously something rushing through the air and equally obviously from its volume, not the kind of thing to be ignored. We took a look at one another and retired quickly to the nearest trench. Then things began going off all round in an unpleasant manner. My first encounter with a flight of mortar bombs.

When that clutch was over I looked up. There was a lot of smoke near George's trench. He was all right, though somewhat put out. (Poor George, it was extremely painful bad luck to fracture that rib just at the beginning of a series of dives for cover.) Two wagons in different directions were on fire and it seemed to be time we moved because it appeared unlikely that the thing would finish with one salvo of mortar shells so we collected our stuff.

Just when we were nicely in the open wondering whether our truck could be starting now or not we heard another bunch coming. All the local slit trenches seemed to be occupied so I dropped flat where I was – narrowly escaping death at the feet of George who was charging along like a rogue elephant.

After that lot, I looked around once more. Nothing seemed to have been touched that time. But there was some kind of dispute going on locally. George, of course. He had flung himself into a small slit trench on top of the two earlier occupants. What with their displeasure, his rib, and the general mix up, they were having difficulty in sorting themselves out. It seemed to me better to get near some empty trenches, so I did. Got, in fact, into one. I lay there with a cigarette for a bit trying to discover what was happening, for by this time both wagons were well alight, things in them were exploding, and fragments whizzing about. In fact whenever I shoved my head up something banged or whizzed, and I couldn't for the life of me make out whether it was all the wagons' contribution or whether there were still bombs falling.

After a time I got tired of it and emerged, hoping it wasn't bombs – it didn't seem to be. Soon after that we removed ourselves to less exhilarating parts – though not less noisy, still, we did have the consolation of knowing that the shells whizzing over our heads were almost invariably our own.

His division was granted a few days' rest to regroup. They moved beyond the shore to a belt of countryside which had been so quickly over-run it had not suffered badly from the fighting. A film show was set up in a nearby field. The men could sleep in tents instead of trenches. Jack found a few plums in an orchard and wrote letters while listening to someone's gramophone "conditionally supposing that you are the only girl in the world". He told Grace:[11]

> The last few days I've been pottering – constructing an intended guitar out of a piece of fencing and a biscuit tin – only owing to difficulties with unsuitable wire it has had to turn into a ukulele. Making a stove from another biscuit tin. An elegant washstand from sticks and a box lid and doing my mending and washing so that there hasn't been a great deal of time over, somehow.
>
> Every now and then, though, I've looked into Wilkinson's 'More Diversions' – it is a good anthology, and occasionally I read an E V Lucas essay.
>
> Now I must stop. At any moment there will be a cry of "Come and get it" so I must be ready to set out with mug and tins. Maybe it'll be a tin of steak and kidney pudding.
>
> I'm longing to hear more about how things are going on.
>
> All my love, Sweet,
>
> J.

The rest was brief. A few days later, the division took part in the ill-fated Operation Goodwood, an attempt to capture the rest of Caen. It has been described as the largest tank battle the British Army has ever fought. Even now, it is not known how many casualties there were during three intense days of fighting: certainly thousands were injured and several hundred men killed amongst the allies. The 11th Armoured division lost about half their tanks.

They again failed to capture Caen, but advanced several miles and tied up the Germans while the US Army launched further attacks further west. Jack and the 11th Armoured withdrew for a brief rest.

Jack had kept up his lighthearted façade as much for his own benefit as for Grace's, but now it started to crack. For one, he missed Grace and their life together terribly. For another, living in constant company, often battered by noise, was a strain on a naturally solitary soul. But there were deeper reasons.

For a man of great personal integrity, joining the army had set up a terrible tension within him. He had been in uniform for two years, but in the Home Guard his job had been defence. Now he was part of an invading force, seeing daily the bodies of the men he had helped to kill. He believed in the fight against fascism, but he had lived long enough to know there was always another war. Now he was a part of that destructive force and he feared he was permanently tainted.

The only way to deal with the pressure was a rigid divorce between the two parts of his personality. Jack hadn't been able to write to Grace for almost three weeks. Now, after six weeks in France, the tension started to show.[12]

Sweetle Darling,

I've wanted to write you a love letter or a little verse, and I can't do it, my Sweet. You'll have to go on reading me into these arid letters which look so impersonal that I sometimes hate to send them. What else can there be? This that writes them and sends them is not me. It's a kind of abridged version – abridged of all but the extravert part. The introvert must be kept away – he is dangerous and bloody unhappy and hasn't any place here. I don't think I dare loosen him even to say what I want to to you. So you can see me feeling quite well and looking after the extravert in order to keep a habitation going. But it isn't really alive.

Nine weeks now since Whitsun, Sweetle. Though I try not to count for either it takes me further or it means nothing – nothing real. Rather I would take out my pictures, few of them with dates and see four and five years ago as close as nine weeks ago. But with the weeks grows an ache, Darling. Not an ache for leave to see you – I almost think that would be worse now than no leave; an ache to be back with you and for all this to be over.

Often, Sweetle, you have thought my remarks on this kind of life rather cheap, and I thinking them over and admitting to myself my inexperience of what I was talking about, felt a little ashamed. I am not ashamed now. They were cheap: they could not fail to be cheap; the target is too easy. My little perspicacities as I thought them, were nothing but the most obvious truisms. No, it is not of the remarks I am ashamed. I had sometimes wondered what was meant by the facile phrase 'a sense of shame': I think I know now and it is something which gnaws and nags. I used a phrase once about changing which I think you thought cheap. It wasn't – at least, its motive wasn't – it was the expression of something very painful. If I ever wondered what sense it was that violation brought to the mind, I shouldn't wonder any more. For eight months now I've felt like something unclean and horrible. I thought it would pass. It doesn't. All that consoles me is that the stench of uncleanness doesn't seem perceptible enough externally to drive everyone away. Consoles me in prospect, that is, for there is the hope that I may some day get clean again.

That's one of the reasons against looking inside. It mustn't be stirred. First casualty, you see – failure even to expose to honest criticism – loss of integrity and with it, loss of any self respect.

I don't know, my Sweet, whether all that makes sense to you. It doesn't matter much if it doesn't. But what I have to feel and have to know is that there are people and particularly you who can regard me as a tolerable human being and give me ease from this sense of guilt until the time comes when I can recover what is left of myself and look at it honestly again.

What has all this been? An attempt to express? A whine? A self excuse? I can't even examine it honestly enough to say. But if you have borne with it, you find now my gratitude and

All my love, my Sweet,

J.

Over the next weeks, the pace sped up. Allied forces moved further and faster into France, pushing the Germans ahead of them. The 11th Armoured was one of 18 divisions who succeeded in trapping about 80,000 German troops in the area around the town of Falaise. The scenes inside were horrendous. At least 10,000 Germans were killed. About 40,000 were taken prisoner, the rest escaped leaving equipment behind. It was a decisive end to the Battle of Normandy.

General Dwight D. Eisenhower later wrote: "The battlefield at Falaise was unquestionably one of the greatest 'killing fields' of any of the war areas. Forty-eight hours after the closing of the gap I was conducted through it on foot, to encounter scenes that could be described only by Dante. It was literally possible to walk for hundreds of yards at a time, stepping on nothing but dead and decaying flesh." [13]

In the hot August weather, conditions quickly became rancid. Pilots reported being able to smell the stench from hundreds of feet above it. Clearing the area of corpses – soldiers, civilians and animals – was low priority. In one village, Jack saw a bulldozer being used to bury the dead. The Allies pressed on.

Jack could not reconcile the ideals of war with the reality of it. He believed neither in pacifism, nor in fighting. As was usual with him, the religious justification was the most sickening. He wrote:[14]

> One faces only two roads: and both lead in the wrong direction. I can see no third. And I have no inclination to bury my head in the sand of any organized religion. They can, for some, supply drugs; but in the giving of answers they are no more capable than anyone else. Meanwhile one goes on living in a world which is a cross between a preparatory school and a lunatic asylum.
>
> Whenever we get somewhere near the front and I see the padre about, I feel that there is something utterly crazy on hand. Things have no links of reason. It is all full of the kind of missequiturs one finds in a deranged mind. It would be funny if it didn't exude the strong smell of routine death and wasn't so easily accepted by the majority.
>
> I have a feeling now that I know whence arose the idea of purgatory.
>
> Here is a world of lies and life of fake. Windows full of goods which are not for sale, plaster facades, catchpenny maxims, pretence, attitudinizing, pomposity, unacknowledged mistakes, pettinesses, meannesses and sham ascendencies. That is, without the glasses of glamour and the whisperings of propaganda, the idea aimed at – ideal for what, God knows: a state conceived in the abstract as being efficient: a comfortable inflator for indifferent little egos.

Yet in the midst of this, he could still escape inside his head. Incredible as it seems, he used the inevitable delays of war to try writing sonnets. He later said: "You can't carry a lot of paper on a campaign and they are more interesting than crosswords."[15] One of these survives, a love poem sent to Grace in August 1944: "To a Lady on Her Birthday". 'Waniand' is Middle English for a waning moon.

No pretty treasuries are here, my Sweet,
No chain, nor brooch, nor bracelet to delect,
No sighing silk nor velvets to entreat
You to adorn them. What I would confect
Of that I see is now within my gift
Or else should Venus in a ring be set,
A dress length from Aurora's sky be rift
Apollo's beams enmeshed á Juliet,
The pillow for your head be summer's cloud,
Sundappled orchard floor become your shawl,
Your bosom be with waniand endowed.
A heart I'd string on dewdrops, but of all
    That were the hardest gift: my heart's not mine,
    And should I give thee what's already thine?

Soon they were on the move again, entering Belgium. Here people welcomed them, tanks were draped with flowers, girls blew kisses. Jack's mood improved a little. He wrote: "It's curious to know that at present one is part of one of those black arrows on a map – a little ahead, perhaps, of a Times arrow, not quite as advanced as a Telegraph one, and certainly feeling narrower than a Daily Express one."[16] His division liberated Amiens on 1 September, and Antwerp three days later. After a week's rest, Jack was transferred to the Guards Armoured Division.

Within a few days, they spearheaded Operation Market Garden, the nine-day attempt to take Arnhem later filmed as *A Bridge Too Far*. It was the last great defeat for the British Army, yet became considered as one of the greatest examples of courage and endurance. The worst casualties were suffered by the paratroopers: the 1st Airborne Division lost three-quarters of its men. It was widely reported thanks to two BBC reporters and three other journalists who were with the British forces. Jack does not seem to have been on the front line but wrote to Grace about seeing the remnants of the troops returning:[17]

> The Arnhem reports affected us much as they affected you. Viv tells me that even the thick Derbyshire heads absorbed enough to make them very seriously quiet. It was good. Good that men should have been with them who were able to put across with such reality what was happening and what had

happened.

I happened to see some of them coming back in lorries after the withdrawal. We just looked. You couldn't wave or cheer. They were too tired.

It was some time before Jack found out that one of the men who did not return was the son of the Penn Club wardens, the Robsons. He was taken prisoner. Within three weeks, two of their other sons were killed.

After the failure of Arnhem, it was clear that the war could not be finished by Christmas. The pace slowed down. Jack had little to do in October but "show a clean rifle" in a parade once a day. For a few weeks he was billeted in a house with the luxury of a bed in Wijchen, Holland.[18] He was given a couple of days leave in Brussels at the end of the month and enjoyed looking round the shops, although not much was on offer. He bought an anthology of Belgian and French prose and verse, but said he failed to behave in the proper 'on leave' manner:[19]

> In fact, I behaved in my usual pottering manner with breaks for ices or beers. It seems to be assumed that most of the lads will automatically spend the nights with their girl friends. Some of them do. Trouble is, of course, that those they pick up with are most likely to be those who have lost business with the departure of the Germans. Nine years of specialization leave me with an ache, and there's only a specialized cure for it. It would have been a more interesting place for your company, Darling.

Settled in Holland, Jack was experiencing fewer horrors and was again trying to keep a lid on his emotions. Reading his letters, it's painful to hear him trying to keep up a flow of normality. He thanks her for sending copies of the *New Statesman* and *The New Yorker*, for checking his clothes for moths and answering his letters. He tells her of the rusted railway tracks, "no better tribute to the RAF"; finding a Victorian album with Doré engravings in an abandoned house; and a Vichy-produced propaganda magazine called *Maman* got up to look like *Vogue*. He passes on news from Viv and reminisces about the moonlit nights in London that won't come again now the neon lights are back on. He even tried translating a French play, though he later lost this somewhere in Germany.

Jack was always interested in the details of women's clothes, and he amused himself by sending Grace his observations of the crowds that watched them advance:[20]

> You know, Sweet, I really haven't got a thing to tell you, but I thought I might give a fashion note. Hats, particularly best clothes hats such as you put on when you walk out with your boy friend to watch the invasion go by, tend to a lot of brim in front and not much anywhere else. And yet should we call it brim, for it goes almost vertically upwards – with a little encouragement I can well see it developing in a season or two in the kind of apotheosized Salvation Army bonnet which gives such pseudo-demure charm to the Belle of New York (anyway, demureness is not a noticeable commodity hereabouts).
>
> Shoes, Darling – and I'm sure you'll be glad to hear this – are not, definitely not, worth wasting your time coming over here to see. Designs are, generally speaking, inferior to ours. Wooden soles are more in evidence, but they haven't dealt with them as well as we – their trouble being, I suspect, that they have not been used to designing for a low heel. The prices are much the same. (You wouldn't be interested in the male shoe, of course, but en passant I may say that it is not utterly unfashionable to wear bedroom slippers on a bicycle.)
>
> And that, my Sweet, is just about all I can tell you on this subject. I don't think I've been very observant – must remedy it in future. But I was tempted to get you a highly decorated pair of clogs though deterred by the considerations that a) they aren't being worn even in Bloomsbury and b) you'd probably have nowhere to keep them if you didn't wear them. Difficult, really.

But he couldn't always pretend. Despite his attempts to wall off his other self, the cracks keep showing:[21]

> Oh, while I think of it, Darling, it seems to me that a pair of gloves might be useful before long. I think there was a pair in that kitbag I sent back. Could you sometime dig them out and send them along – there's no hurry.

No, I can't go on with that.

Seventeen weeks ago, my Sweetle, seventeen weeks last Sunday since Whitsun. I want you so much and, oh, I am so weary of this. Not tired, weary. Sick of keeping up the extraversion: sick of trying to be interested in things I'm not interested in: sick of knowing nothing of the things I am interested in. And bored. I thought I'd enough resources to avoid that . . . most of the time I can but not all . . .

There have been times when one thought, it <u>is</u> worth it – the people are glad we've come: they really are. There wouldn't be the flowers and the cheers, and the fruit and the flags if they weren't.

And then the whole thing is dust and ashes . . . the three Frenchwomen laughing and cheering: the dead German a few feet away. It's all like that. Always the cheers are because more are dead – Yes, I know the answers. Guernica, Rotterdam, Lublin.[22] There isn't any other way. But where does this way lead?

There are groups of little white crosses along the roadsides. Back by the Somme there were regimented stone crosses and stone memorials. Behind them the crosses stretch back and back for hundreds of years. Each cross being the symbol of a needless torture, each a symbol of a fight for a better world according to someone's lights. The symbol no less muddled than the aim. And what does it amount to? – A dreary succession of killings in bigger and better ways.

There run two parallel thoughts. One is that this must be gone through, deplorable as it is, in order that things shall be better. The other, that there are always being wars and it is the business of every self respecting man to be involved in one or two as evidence of his manhood – it doesn't matter much what they are about. I should have said converging thoughts for it is here they meet. The result has brought them to the same place. It has brought them, in fact, to the same place that no thought would have done. What is one to draw from that – that thought is no use? Or that any line of thought which countenances killing leads to the same end – whatever the motive?

Perhaps killing and being killed is not such a serious thing as we Westerners [are] inclined to think it. I don't know. But even so, this is a remarkably wasteful and frivolous way for reputedly adult nations to behave. And, coming round the circle, wearisome and tedious.

Darling, I don't think I know what I'm talking about, so don't try to make much sense of all that.

Just take it that my exile is irking. And that I ache for you, Sweetle. It seems too long already – and no telling how much longer it must be.

You've more than ever of my love, Sweetle.

The more he saw of the war and its aftermath, the more fearful he was for the future. He would fictionalise this breakdown of society in his future novels. Seeing where brutality had taken over made him realise how paper-thin the line was that separated civilization from savagery. The feeling that he was unclean persisted: was he turning into someone Grace could not love? He feared not just for the world, but for himself:[23]

> We came across little that was outside the usual beastliness of wars. But just tonight they have been talking here of atrocities in France, Belgium and Holland which are as bad in all but scale as those in Russia. The men who committed them aren't sane: they can't be. With them the hold that the centuries of toil to civilize had built up has been shaken off completely. They make me afraid as a madman makes one afraid – they force an unwilling recognition of the narrowness which divides the clean from the obscene. You feel this is so like a normal man in nearly everything it does and that so little difference in the rest has made it a monstrosity. And, worse, it seems as though it could so easily unbalance and contaminate anyone with whom it should come into contact. I understand better now, I think, the kind of fear which led good men to persecute witches.
>
> And, once more, what is to be done? Many of these sadists have been overtaken and killed. But there are many among the prisoners and others who have escaped. What of them?
>
> Of the ordinary brutalities of war one can often say that the men who commit them do it under pressure of fear or uncontrollable nervous excitement, and with those stimuli

removed, will relapse into comparatively normal citizenship. But these evils have a different aspect. One has an awful feeling that something is loose in these men that they will go back and foster in others. – And, as far as I am concerned – a weary inability to see that anything can be done about it.

Sometimes, my Sweet, I feel that when this stage is over, all I shall want is to hide my head in your lap and shut out all the world that is to follow.

What is the good of humanity having got this far without having developed any counter to brutality but brutality?

He lived only partly in Holland, and partly in the Penn Club of his imagination. He liked his colleagues well enough, but he found the all-male company tiresome and there was no-one he could talk to except Grace. Sometimes he tried to keep himself an inanimate block, to no avail:[24]

I can't help slipping out and saying now what are they all doing? It's, say Sunday lunch-time. Sweetle will have spent most of the morning with an attention divided between the Observer and the north-lounge fire. It was probably beef for lunch, and the room was pretty full. It's not much of a day. Go upstairs this afternoon and – oh dear, then the empty ache again. God, how I wish – we all wish – this business would fold up.

If we feel like that, how must the Germans, their plates piled with dust and ashes, feel? Perhaps it won't be so very long.

All that I'm really conscious of at the moment is that I want my Sweet and with her my own life back, for she has

All my love

J.

At other times, he gave up and indulged in an entirely imaginary life that left him unsure what was real and what wasn't:[25]

I'm frightfully muddled, too. I've had lots of conversations with you lately, Sweetle, and I've written bits to you – but I can't tell you what was spoken to you in the dark and what went into a letter. It's all I can do to sort out the things you've said from the things you might have said. It seems probable that when we do meet again you'll be thinking me a little

unhinged from references to things we've done which you
don't recall – you'll have to make allowances.

You do and say some very sweet things – but I miss the funny little things – our expeditions tend to be rather serious and
rather sentimental. We don't break much fresh ground, either:
a marked inclination to occur at Kew or Hampstead Heath.
Though we sometimes go to Fairlight or Devil's Bridge . . .

Do you know when the last time was that I really saw Fairlight? It was early on the morning of June the 15th. I came on
deck before breakfast and there was Fairlight. People were
arguing and calling it everything between Dover and the Isle
of Wight. I didn't need to: I could almost see the magpies . . .

I feel like starting on a long list of 'don't you remember?'
– but once started, where to stop? Besides, I'd better not.
You've had enough of my rather revolting moods to put up
with in the last year, poor Sweet – but nice Sweet.

And to think that a few weeks ago you said that I was un-
complaining! Still, to make up for it I'll be wonderfully un-
complaining when I come back.

Think I ought to stop now. This evening I'll go out to dinner with you and then on to Studio 2 [a cinema]. First we've
got to make up our minds where to have dinner. That always
takes a while. So you'll understand I have to stop this now.

Grace did all she could. She arranged for a newsagent to send him
200 cigarettes a week (the arrival or non-arrival of these is a recurring
feature of his letters). She reassured him and distracted him with gossip from the club. She sent him books and magazines, and spent her
coupons on warm clothes for him. Unfortunately, this brought back
his old fears that she might not be warm enough:[26]

Are you properly clad? – that is, I mean needfully clad to keep
the winter out. If not – and by the newspaper's account it is
already the kind of winter that snaps at the legs – I recall a
pair of flannel trousers, virgin ones, which might be put to
good use (blue with white spots – I know that sounds a bit
fierce, but they're kind of pinhead spots). Probably they're in
that tin box. So should later temperatures snap at legs uncou-
poned on my account, pray remember them. I'd hate you to
have snapped legs.

In particular, he was worried about her health. She had a recurrent pain in her stomach. The hospitals were stretched by the war and she couldn't get a diagnosis. She told him it was better and he should forget about it, but he refused: "Must stop now Darling. But, as a final warning, I don't intend to forget your tummy, as you instruct. And please, my Sweet, don't neglect the business because it is better for the present. Please."[27]

A week later he was still fretting: "Sweet, that pain of yours worries me. Do, do, for goodness sake, do all you can about it. I don't want to be alarmist, but one has heard far too often of women who have gone on putting up with pain to a stage where it had grown inoperable."

He was also worried about her safety. Grace was living through a repeat of the Blitz in London. Hitler was now using V1 and V2 rocket missiles. It was Grace's turn to sleep on mattresses in the drawing room. One rocket landed in Russell Square, shaking the club. Gertrude was also in London at Lancaster Gate. After several hotels, she had spent time with her sister in Leamington but was soon longing for an independent existence again.

Jack saw pictures of the V2 rockets and was astonished by their size:[28]

> I was thinking the other day (anent a story that young Gillings still wants me to produce) that were I, five or six years ago, to have sat down and written a story in which the leaders of a hostile nation sat down and accepted the invention of a) a bomb that would fly and b) a long range rocket, and then said: 'With these we will wreck the enemy. We will send over so many that his cities will be ruined, his services chaotic and his people battered into demanding peace. Let the production of these weapons begin.' If I had done it what would it have been? – Just another of Harris's crack-brained, far-fetched stories. Might amuse a few schoolboys . . .
>
> As Mr Wells said explanatorily a few years ago – the world has become so fantastic as to make the writing of fantastic stories impossible by reason of their comparative dullness.

Viv distracted him for a while by sending him the White Paper on Social Insurance, laying out the Government's intentions for unemployment and sickness benefit. Discussing politics with Grace and Viv by letter made him wonder about the inevitable election at the end of the war:[29]

> Just at the moment there is a drive on B2626 going on (that, as you'll remember is the voting form.) To all appearances there is worry about it in some circles resulting in exhortations to sign it and now a poster in the mess. The only reactions I've found so far are three behind me in the queue who agreed with one who said 'Hah! Trying to soft soap us now are they!' Presumably apathy has been pretty widespread.
>
> It's scarcely surprising. Most of the lads know nothing of politics at all. It's a long time since the last election: and look at what the last few elections have been! One or two inquire earnestly the difference between parties as if they were hearing of such things for almost the first time. Others announce that they will vote Labour because – as far as I can see, Labour sounds hefty while the word 'Conservative' conveys cigars and Rolls Royces for the few. Anything in between is unknown. Communism doesn't seem to be taken seriously save by a few talkative advocates who know little or nothing of it. Policies are greek.
>
> In general there is suspicion of it all. It is something 'they' do. It isn't really believed that if you do vote it can actually make any difference to anything. It's just a bit more of 'their' eyewash. Distrust of democratic methods ever succeeding seems to have been thoroughly impressed.
>
> That's small wonder of course. For formative years of their lives these lads have been caught in in a system where the lowest common denominator is the standard, and initiative is a nuisance if not a danger and where authority is a kind of extension of parentalism. Then somebody suddenly ups and says – it's your country, it's up to you to decide how it shall be run after the war, it's your duty to vote.
>
> They're used to suddenly learning that something is their duty, but a kind of voluntary duty such as form B2626 is a bit baffling. (Duty, generally speaking being something you get punished for not doing). As for it being their country to be run by their decisions – well, that just doesn't click. Decisions

are things other people have always made. First their parents, for a time their bosses, and then the army.

And, beyond that, what are these things they must decide about? For many the problems and possibilities which exist in normal life have receded from view outside, and not very really or very urgently outside, the monastic paternity which has ordered them for years.

Here, of course, is the stuff of fascism. There will be an interval, but after that, there will be plenty who will want an authority who can do any worrying for them – in the way they are used to having it done.

Well, we shall see. Yes, darling, there will be, I'm afraid, some pretty unpleasant things we shall see.

He spent Christmas appropriately enough in a vast, Catholic theological college in Boxtel, Holland, decorated with saints, crucifixions and the pin-up girls of the previous American occupants. A few days later, he had good news. He was to be granted a few days' home leave on 18 January. As well as his mother and Grace, he would see Viv for the first time since the beginning of the war five years earlier.

Viv had had a tough time. As the war progressed, he was working 48 hours on, 24 off, with most of the 24 spent catching up on sleep. Like Jack, he had been thrown out of the Bedales bubble. He later wrote: "I can't say that until the war came that I had been exposed to the terrors or the mess of human accident and death. Really, looking back, I can see that I lived in an artistic world where I was pretty much insulated from reality. So I had to steel myself pretty quickly . . . especially as I was in charge of a crew of seven."[30]

Viv was asked to lead a special squad to deal with damaged bombers that were failing to make it home. The Derbyshire area had been littered with wrecks, and it was thought lives could be saved if fire crews could get to them faster. It was a perilous job to find their way in the pitch dark over moors pockmarked with old lead mine shafts.

One night they received an alert that a crippled Lancaster was heading their way. They drove as far as they could on rough roads, stopping regularly to listen for the plane. They heard it come down, and followed a trail of debris to the site of the crash:

"There she is," shouted my Number One. "What a mess."

Actually it could have been worse for it had tobogganed to a halt on the soft heath and peat . . . There was no sign of a fire but in a wind of that strength even the tiniest spark could be fanned into a flame. So we tried to get into the plane but as it had turned there was no way in.

Shining my light upwards I could see a figure above in the Rear-Gunner's position. As we couldn't reach it, I sent two of my crew back across the moor for an extension ladder. When it came my Number One went up . . .

"Is he alive?" I shouted up.

"Don't know," replied my Number One. "He looks queer. I'll try to get him out."

He reached in and though I didn't realise it then these were the last minutes of life as I had known it up to then.

"Careful!" I cautioned.

"Oh, God!" exclaimed Number One. "Oh _____ hell!"

Something fell at my feet. I turned my lamp on it and for one fearful minute I looked down at the head of the Rear-Gunner. It had, as they say in Derbyshire "come away in me 'and." There are always elements of humour in horror and war.

I suppose if this had been fiction we should have all reeled away into the darkness to be horribly sick but we had already seen too much for that. We had seen burnt bodies, broken bodies and bodies that needed to be cleaned up with a brush and shovel. But for some reason, in the long term, this had some element that we couldn't push to the back of our minds and slam the door. Each time we rushed across the moor in the wake of a faulty aeroplane the apprehension of what we would find grew stronger and stronger until at last we felt we couldn't go on. We asked to be relieved but we were told we were the only trained experienced crew, this was war and we must stick it.

So one morning I woke up and I couldn't face it. Neither could I make my body face it. I called in my doctor. Knowing me he gave me a certificate at once. But the officer at the station had it in for me. I was put under escort and hauled off to the local fire service where they agreed with my doctor's assessment and gave me a certificate.

I had become a stuttering wreck with all my self-confidence shot away. I never went back and after 14 weeks I was discharged as unfit.

It would be years before Viv was fit to work again. Just before Jack returned on leave, he told Grace: "He still has his ups and downs I'm afraid. They put him back on dope for a week or two now and then. One thing I think will be good and that is that with this 35 age limit he ought to be free from further badgering by Uncle Ernie [Ernest Bevin, Minister of Labour] and his loathsome hirelings, bad cess to 'em".[31]

References

1   Letter to Grace, 18 June 1944.

2   Letter to Grace, 16 October 1944.

3   *The Times*, 'German Positions Bombarded', Thursday June 15, 1944, p.4.

4   HP Wilmott, Robin Cross, Charles Messenger (2004) *World War II*, Dorling Kindersley.

5   Letter to Grace, 16 June 1944.

6   Letter to Grace, 18 June 1944.

7   Letter to Grace, 25 June 1944.

8   Sonnet 64, 'When I have seen by Time's fell hand defaced'.

9   Letter to Grace, 9 July 1944.

10   Letter to Grace, 9 July 1944.

11   Letter to Grace, 9 July 1944. Wilkinson's anthologies were known for bringing comfort during the war. They were printed on tissue-thin paper in small type with hard covers, so could slip into a rucksack without getting damaged. *More Diversions* contained poems and short extracts from texts from the 1100s to the present day, so could be dipped into at any moment. They were loosely themed from birth to death. Highlights included extracts from Dorothy Wordsworth's diaries about William's tiredness and sleep.

12   Letter to Grace, 29 July 1944.

13   Dwight D Eisenhower (1948) *Crusade in Europe*, New York: Doubleday.

14   Letter to Grace, 10 August 1944.

15   In interview with Sam Moskowitz, see note to chapter 1.

16   Letter to Grace, 31 August 1944.

17   Letter to Grace, 3 October 1944.

18   Jack did not name towns in his letters to Grace. Place names in this chapter come from unpublished research by Ken Smith, who was kind enough to share this with me.

19   Letter to Grace, 22 October 1944.

20   Letter to Grace, 18 September 1944.

21   Letter to Grace, 28 September 1944.

22   Guernica: Nazi Germany bombed the Basque town in 1937 on behalf of Franco during the Spanish Civil War. It was the first use of the Blitzkrieg technique. Rotterdam was bombed by the Luftwaffe in May 1940. Lublin, in Poland, was captured by the Germans in September 1939. The city had a large Jewish population and a Talmudic college. The soldiers burned the library and set up a concentration camp which was liberated by the Red Army in July 1944. Only 230 Lublin Jews survived the Holocaust.

23   12 October 1944.

24   Letter to Grace, 10 October 1944.

25   Letter to Grace, 16 October 1944.

26   Letter to Grace, 15 November 1944.

27   Letter to Grace, 3 October 1944.

28   Letter to Grace, 3 December 1944.

29   Letter to Grace, 15 November 1944.

30   Viv wrote about his war experiences in a memorandum book now in the University of Liverpool archive, VBH 2/1

31   Letter to Grace, 14 October 1944.

8

The Final Push

After 11 days home leave, Jack set off back to Europe. Despite the cold and the knowledge of what awaited him, he was less miserable than he had been seven months earlier. His greatest fear had been that he was tainted by his experiences, and that the change was so great Grace would not want him anymore. The few days they spent together reassured him that his old life would be waiting for him.

Jack kissed Grace goodbye in the middle of a bitterly cold Saturday night on the steps of the Penn Club, a tender farewell unfortunately interrupted by the arrival of her cousin Basil.

Jack wrote immediately to let her know he had arrived. He rarely complained about the conditions, but his description of the journey back paints a vivid picture of what it was to be a small cog in the machine of this massive logistical exercise.

> 30 January 1945
> Dear Sweetle
>
> I've just written you a silly extravert note by the ordinary route to let you know I'm here. It should race this.
>
> It doesn't feel at all pleasant to be back. And yet it's better than before I went away. I know that we are still us. And somehow, my Sweet, there seems to be a little bit of you here with me now that wasn't before. You're much nearer and, if possible, dearer than before. Thank you, Sweetle, for a lovely leave – all I could wish were that there had been a bit more of it for us, and less had had to be spent elsewhere.
>
> Well, now you'll want to know about getting back. (I'm sorry the figure in the darkness had to be Basil – I thought it was just a passer-by: can you live it down?)
>
> I trailed along without seeing any others similarly bound

until I reached the top of Great Portland St. There I joined a thinly wending throng. At the barracks it became the inevitable queue. We got the passes stamped and changed our money. I took some of each, just in case – and a little French, too, for NAAFI purposes.[1] Then I sat in the NAAFI. There were large and impressive fires in each room there. But either ventilation or lost windows saw to it that one got colder and colder.

We went off in various parties according to the colours of tickets we held. Mine being the last I did manage to get near the fire for half an hour or so and thaw. About three we made for Gt Portland St Station and then to Victoria. (While I hope you were sleeping peacefully.)

On the boat I found a convenient piece of deck under cover and not too cold. It was a long time before we sailed and I think I dozed a bit. The ship's loud speakers gave out notices about lifebelts. I smoked one of the Players No3. (Sweetie still sleeping: about 3 hrs before she need have breakfast). The ship rolled a little, but not enough to cause many to disappear. 9 o'clock news on the speakers. (Perhaps she's hearing it too. She'll be getting up soon: hope she'll say good morning to the daffodils.)

Off the boat and strait on to the train: unexpectedly expeditious this. Visibility about ten yards owing to driving snowstorm. We set off. Very nice work. But no! Train after ¾ of hr or so, stops. All out. We find ourselves at Calais: where we thought we were before.

A camp. Big hut with benches. One or two stoves closely surrounded. (She'll have had her breakfast: read her Observer, too. Pottering I expect. Perhaps putting away what I left about.)

Time has trailed along to 12.30. Take my detestable mess tins for dinner. 24 hours ago . . . Oh I don't believe I thanked her – and it was a nice dinner, too.)

Back to hut. Wrap in a blanket and lie down on the floor. Sleep for an hour or so. Wake up terribly cold. Draught comes up through gaping floor boards as well as through broken windows. (Wonder if she's been having Sunday afternoon nap, too. 24 hours ago . . . Oh no, mustn't. Makes my eyes prick. Oh, my Sweetle.)

Go off to find some tea at YMCA Canteen. Feet painfully come to life again. Hot tea is reviving. Read about Anthony Eden. (Of course she was right about bringing the New Yorkers.)

Think I'll go to cinema after tea. No good. Full up. Wander into Calais. Not nearly so wrecked as I had thought. Town YMCA has a queue. Usual kind, full of the perpetual tuneless, conflicting but always shrill whistling. Wander back. Warmer for the walk anyway.

About the time Sweetle is having supper we wander off to train. Hard class – like she had in Russia. Journey seems to go on for a long time (actually about 12 hours – by which time she will be leaving for the morning's work) doze a bit now and then.

Hang around in a cold room at distributing camp. Build a secluded corner with palliases and get about an hour's sleep. Find out that there's a wagon going straight to corps which will save spending another night on the journey. Get on it about the time Sweetle is finishing her lunch.

Wagon goes less straight than we had hoped. It has a cover but is open at the back. For five hours one gets steadily colder in it. But it arrives at last and I land here exactly 45 hours from saying goodbye to Sweetle on doorstep. (Bother Basil – I am so sorry Sweet.)

Luckily (in a way) it's a place I've been before, so it's not so difficult to dig out my bedding and get it into place. (I didn't curse the kit bag. It was a most useful seat at various stages of the journey.)

It's not an interesting place. Not knowing a word of the lingo is so offshutting. The ex-theological college or whatever we are in, is ill found. The heating is occasional, the water supply frozen up. The cookhouse is in the same building which is an advantage. There has been some kind of row about the feeding. One of the results of this is a greatly improved method of washing plates. One bath for washing and a couple of rinse.

It has taken the cooks about 2 days to counter this improvement by the simple dodge of not changing the water. Lunch's plate comes out of the rinse therefore with a film of breakfast's grease.

Now I light the last but one of the No3's and wonder what more I shall tell you.

Nothing of here I think. It's dull and mostly sordid.

Darling, it was all so much better than I hoped. I felt that in 7 months something must have altered. Why should it – and how? I don't know. But it hasn't. And it's really been worth all your bullying.

What? – Oh yes, I don't care whether you knew it or not, but you did. How many times in those months have I sat down before some practically uneatable mess and gone ploughing through it simply because you kept on jogging away at my elbow and reminding me I'd got to go on being well? And – oh, well lots of other things, too.

And now you'll go on doing it – and I shall go on being obedient, and more willingly.

You've made me greedy, My Sweet. And very happy. I ought to be miserable. I'm irritable. But I'm not miserable – and that is because as I said you've sent something of you along with me this time. I'm going to hold it in me until I can bring it back home to you, and with it

All my love, my Sweet,

J.

If Jack had returned to filthy conditions, they were about to get worse. The ground had been frozen solid – thus the struggle with the water supply he mentions above. A sudden thaw meant conditions were reduced to mud. Jack complained that it was everywhere, including in his blankets. But the thaw meant a serious problem for the Allies.

Ahead was the next stage of the war: the push into Germany. Jack was part of the XXX Corps, which was meant to invade from Holland through the Reichswald Forest as part of Operation Veritable. Their front was between the rivers Maas and Rhine. This is a flood plain. As it turned to mud, it became a nightmare for lorries and tanks.

The operation began on 7 February with the biggest British barrage of artillery in history. Men were deafened for hours by the guns. On the next day, 50,000 men with 500 tanks attacked through the forest.

The advance was short lived. On 9 February, the Germans released water from the Roer dam. They jammed the sluices open, sending water surging down the valley and flowing on for many days. The flood prevented the Americans moving forward. The German forces could concentrate their attack on the Canadians and British.

But the floods had also damaged German defences and minefields. Some of their units found themselves isolated on islands, where they could be picked off one by one. XXX Corps used amphibious vehicles to move through the flooded areas. Casualties were heavy on both sides.

Jack could tell Grace nothing of this, though he said he was now in a bivouac tent which didn't leak much: "No weather for camping, this." He does not seem to have been right in the front line of the heaviest fighting, but followed through in the wake of the invading force. After a few days, he cautiously began prowling about in the abandoned German trenches.[2]

> What millions of tons of earth the Germans must have moved (or forced others to move) and by hand, too, all over Europe. Further into the forest the dugouts were mostly finished and many had been lived in for some time. They'd made themselves comfortable with mattresses and one supposes a stove did something to keep the damp at bay. The only one I found that wasn't dripping from the roof was a comfortable affair where the inhabitants had laid tiles above their log and earth roof and given a good overlap all round.
>
> There were not a great many graves. Now and again one would come upon a dead one. I always had a feeling they weren't really dead – the forest is an eerie place even without them. Nastiest moment was when I went into one dugout and found one lying in bed with a bandage on his head.
>
> Technique in this matter varies – I suppose in accordance with the officer in charge. Sometimes there would be formal graves, topped by crosses with the identity discs on them, helmet, mess tin and broken rifles thrust muzzle down in the earth. Elsewhere no one had bothered. One lay within five yards of a dugout which one of our battalions had used for a time as a headquarters. Nothing had been done save to put a cloth over his face.

Ammunition lies about in great quantities. Naturally it doesn't do to leave the weapons ready for anyone to use. The idea is to hand them in for safety. That's all right if you only find one or two rifles, but more becomes burdensome. My custom was to break them and take the bolt away. Machine guns are even more troublesome. I found two one day and couldn't lug them for miles. In the end I took away what looked like a pretty strategic part and left the covers open for the rain to get at them.

For Jack, the work of a cipher operator continued to be extremely busy, with one night in three on duty creating a cumulative sleep deprivation. He could only write occasional scrappy letters; he felt too confused to think straight.[3]

There's been little to show that all this and Bedford Place exist in the same world. Just one thing jerked me back the other day – a fine show of snowdrops behind a ruined house – but even those are out of date, for you've gone on to crocuses . . .

In a town where the fighting has been hard, destruction of what is left appears to be wanton. The rifle butt in the middle of a mirror, the furniture tipped out of windows, paint and ink poured everywhere. I've no idea how one feels when one has fought hard to get into a place – perhaps this is the psychological result of it: continued destruction for its own sake – sweeps all the stuff from the shelves, stove in the door, fire shots into stacks of plate glass, go for a printing machine with a hammer, break all the bottles in a surgery.

One's own reaction to it all is hard to gauge. Every now and then there is a shock when you find some valuable object shattered or ruined, but for the most part you feel curious, and unexpected indifference.

You aren't consciously saying to yourself – this is the only way they'll understand: perhaps they'll begin to understand now what they keep on letting loose on other people, yet something like that thought must be at the back of the mind to account for indifference in the face of such appalling waste and ruin.

As they moved further into Germany, the weather improved and better billets were found. In one town, he found a house with a coal-fired stove, and rigged a car bulb to a battery for lighting. Looting also became a game for many. For Jack, this was on a very low-level:[4]

> As for my doings, I regret to have to make a confession. It's not a thing I thought I'd be doing. It is in fact an occupation for which I've always had a slight contempt. Shame covers my actions in a modified way. I have in fact, taken to stamp-collecting. It wasn't altogether intentional. It arose through Viv asking for some stamps, and somehow without quite realising it, I found I was putting some aside for myself. It does have advantages here. Gives one something to potter with and takes up the minimum of room – that of course being highly important.
>
> So should you at any time receive mysterious boxes or packets to be put away safely for me, that's probably what they'll contain. It certainly has a historically interesting side: the Germans have used them to a noteworthy extent for propaganda and celebrations. All the same, I can't help feeling it's a pretty grim state of affairs.

But in April, there was an opportunity too good to be missed. The company found themselves billeted in an abandoned textile factory, in Zeven, north of Bremen. It covered several acres and had been run with compulsory foreign labour. There were floors full of rolls of cloth. Clothes rationing at home was acute, and all the men decided to take what they could and send presents back to their wives and girlfriends.[5]

> We passed one of the several floored buildings with large 'Out of Bounds' notices on the doors. I wondered about the notices: I've more than a suspicion that they sometimes occur when someone has his eye on one or two things inside.
>
> People were wandering round investigating this and that and helping themselves – except one chap who was sitting miserably on a box and looking at the packed shelves.
>
> "There's too much of it," he said, unhappily, "I don't know where to begin."
>
> But if he was admitting it, others weren't. They were swooping on things with cries of triumph, only to abandon them a

moment later when they found something more interesting. The disorder in the place was naturally increasing. I went to have a look at some of the Company's files. Quite interesting. I hope the security people look, but there'll be too much of that kind of thing for them to have time for more firms' files.

During the evening word went round that someone had got the printing machinery going. This seemed to be worth looking at. The first thing I encountered as I got out of the door was the familiar sight of the Regimental Sergeant Major. This time he was haring upstairs with a determined expression. There was not the hurried exodus from the upper floor that one expected. Not at all: the RSM had heard of the printing, and was determined to have some headed paper for himself.

It was a good scene. Chaps were cutting the firm's heading off paper with an enormous guillotine, others were sitting down all over the place with frames on their knees, intently and determinedly fiddling with type. The printing machine was banging away. There was a confusion about type and type sizes. Much lamenting, cursing and groans over the results. It took some of them a couple of hours to get their headings set up, but they did it and proudly handled their frames as if they were baskets of favourite eggs. The area round the machine was about ankle deep in misprints and everyone was having a roaring time.

The next afternoon as I came off duty there were a number of persons to be seen carrying parcels. They were ill-wrapped and most of their owners had expressions of exaggerated innocence as though they would be surprised to be told that they had parcels under their arms. On the storehouse doors the notices had vanished. Upstairs were rolls of rayon all over the place.

Some were proclaiming this a piece of good stuff: others fingered a bit and then hustled off the roll into a corner hoping no one else had noticed their particular finds. On a large screen someone had chalked 'Great Buckshee Bargain Sale' 'Come one – Come all'. All over the huge room chaps were intently discussing qualities. Cutting or tearing pieces off the rolls. "Good stuff this," says one. "But what for?" demands another. "Oh, sheets!" "Naow, but she could make a good tennis dress out of it." (This referring to the harshest rayon I've ever seen – nearly like hessian). "Wouldn't 'alf like to take a roll of that 'ome." "My old woman'd go crackers over that." "Look at this stuff for civvy shirts, by god."

In point of fact, if there ever was any good stuff in the place it had vanished before we came. I don't think there was. The level was very much as supplied to Marks and Spencers. Still with nightdress (or any other useful material) in mind I wandered round. I couldn't find anything you'd be seen dead in. But all around the collecting was going on. What the wives are going to think of some of the stuff if they ever get it, I can well imagine. It's going to be a nice point whether they'll wear it out of compassion for the senders. What would you do in the circumstances if you got a present of yards and yards of obvious coat lining because your husband thought you'd like it for evening dresses? It must be difficult, too, when the value of the material is judged in proportion to its shininess.

After a tour I sat down and watched. A few were being selective, but a kind of collecting mania had descended on most. With both arms full of a pile of ill folded lengths, they staggered along tripping over bolts of cloth, getting their boots entangled in yards of it, bumping into others, cursing rifles which would fall off shoulders and slowly making their way to the packing room below. Word had certainly gone round, not only with us, but apparently round the district. A bunch of Military Police arrived, loaded up a Jeep and went off. Officers and their batmen sought useful lengths . . . The cooks staggered out with huge rolls of coarse creamy rayon (we've had tablecloths ever since and when they get too dirty another piece comes off one of the rolls).

The whole place was as busy as an antheap, everyone fearfully intent upon his search and his finds. The more one watched it the funnier it got. How they hoped to carry or send away a quarter of the stuff, nobody knew, and they weren't bothering about that at the moment.

Back at the billet, the stationery store was almost in a similar state. The first thing I came across was our Sergeant Major and the Padre more or less hand in hand picking up useful trifles. In the printing room activity was still immense. Somebody had got the electric guillotine going and was chopping a huge ledger in half to see that it was working properly. Some minor printing machines had gone into action, each surrounded by an intent crowd. Some others looked a bit odd because someone had opened an interesting looking package on a high shelf and gold powder had cascaded out.

The offices are now all rolling in staplers, typewriters, ribbons, carbons, telephone extensions, writing paper and notebooks, pencils, pens, flasks of ink, boxes of clips and all the rest of it.

Sweetle, this has turned out longer than I expected. I'll try the ethics of looting etc next time.

Looting was not always so joyously communal. When it was freelance, it could be more dangerous. Jack very rarely told Grace about being in danger, but after the war he wrote to a friend about a frightening experience:[6]

I remember I once met a Canadian soldier. We were both prowling around a shell-shocked house in search of what there might be – bottles in my case. He took a long slow look at me, then he drawled to his pal upstairs: "Say, Bud. There's a Limey here. He's got a wrist-watch – but he <u>hasn't got a gun</u>!" He had, and I had only a nasty kind of double-edged trench knife. We had a tableau for a bit, and then he just lost interest. Never understood why, but it <u>is</u> nasty looking down gun-barrels, even for a short time.

The official attitude to this was hazy. The unspoken policy was to turn a blind eye in German territory, but not Holland. Many loaded themselves up with anything they could carry, discarding earlier finds to make room for later prizes. Others wouldn't take so much as a needle, feeling obscurely that they didn't want to be in any kind of debt to their enemies. Jack himself felt he simply didn't want any reminders of the war: "I have seen some books I coveted for their illustrations, but they were too cumbersome – besides, well, I should have hated them afterwards."[7] He described a conversation with the army chaplain which didn't raise official religion any higher in his estimation:[8]

I'd just got the tent fixed and, after a look at the sky, dug a

hurried gutter round it . . . As I was putting the final touches to the back a voice said: "May I shelter here?" so I said,
"Do, Brother. Walk right in," I turned round to find it was
the Padre. We set on bundles of bedding and regarded the
downpour. A bit disconsolate he was. It seems that in common with others he was lamenting his limited means of trans-
port. This time because, also in common with others, he had
heard of a store of records in a nearby town. On reaching the
place he found himself faced by complete sets of Beethoven
Symphonies, Brandenburg Concertos, Bach Chorales, etc etc.
He leapt in and loaded himself with an assortment of these
including Albert Schweizer organing and some Chopin, but
there was such a lot he wanted and couldn't carry.

From this he got on to looting in general. It seems that if
you pinch people's watches, radios, cameras etc, that is looting
and to be deplored. But things in stores, factories and ware-
houses are the legitimate spoil of war and fair game. There is
a keenness of perception and evaluation here which I must
confess had hitherto escaped me. Anyway, he announced his
intention of going back for more some time and of comman-
deering a radiogram for the edification of the unit. However,
things move fast: I see by a notice that he is giving his first
concert of this liberated music tonight. Evidently someone
had a radiogram about him already. I'd meant to go, but I
think I shall go on writing to you instead.

Sweetle, I have almost a feeling that before this reaches you,
it may all be officially over. Last night Hitler's reported death
and, since I began this letter, the surrender of the German
Armies in Italy . . .

Another news flash . . . Berlin's captured. What an excellent
thing it was the Russians. Good old Joe. There can't be much
left to capture now. Still it's not all over yet: there are guns
rumbling away in the distance . . .

It sure has been a day of events. Now I'm beginning to want
to know when I can call it a day and come home.

Must stop, Sweetle. Got to work early in the morning.

All my love, my Lovely Sweet,

J.

PS And now Goebbels – what consternation in Valhalla!

A few days later, Jack wrote again. Although the war was ending, he struggled to appreciate it. He had heard that his company would be moving to the German coast for three or four months' reorganisation, then there was likely to be an administrative presence in Germany for 30 to 50 years.[9]

Jack was frustrated and longing for home and Grace: "18 months or more of exile and boredom in military charades, oh God."[10]

His presence in the army at the age of almost 42 was an anomaly: only a few months after he had been called up, the age of conscription was lowered again. But as his age group had been called up so late, it was likely to be late being released, while others who had been due for call up had escaped altogether. The end of the war made little difference.

8 May 1945

My Sweet

Churchill has just spoken. We ought to have heard the end together – but we didn't, just as we didn't hear the official beginning. Things fall into odd patterns. First your exile and my blitz, then your blitz and now my exile.

I don't expect you're liking this particular day any more than I am. Out here it seems utterly pointless: had I been with you, oh, how different.

Somehow, it's very puzzling now it has come. It is both sooner and more definite than we expected. Looking back to that little beach head last June it's amazing. Now what? . . .

Darling the irritation and fretting I feel at the moment is over-riding everything. During the fighting it was bad enough, but to be kept out here away from you to perform tedious military clowning for an indefinite time is sickening.

Yes, I know that's very little of me. I ought to be whooping with joy and getting drunk: or, alternatively, thinking that now the western world can begin to apply the Four Freedoms; or personally giving thanks that I'm still in one piece. Instead, I'm grizzling – and I don't like grizzling, and, anyway, this wasn't meant to be a grizzle letter.

It was meant to tell you all sorts of things that I now find I can't express. It was to thank you, Sweetle, for being you. For keeping me going all this time. But for knowing you were there all the time, and having your letters, it would have been insupportable. I have wondered what the world would have looked like had I got a letter to say that a V1 or V2 had fallen on the house. I couldn't visualise it. It wouldn't be a world I knew any more, nor that I had any interest in getting to know.

All I've seen or done seems to have had a double meaning. One for me, and always a qualifying one saying, "She wouldn't like this: she would like this: this would interest her. This would interest me – if I could share it with my Sweet." – And I've not been able to tell you much about these things, either.

In times to come I shall think – I could have written her interesting letters, and kick myself for not doing it. I shall forget how difficult it was with an uncertain censorship overhanging, constant interruptions, in cold corners with a dim light, or against blaring wireless. So I remind myself of these things now – in the sun, leaning against a cowshed in a north German field – for even a little sunshine begins to make one forget how difficult it can be to keep warm, and already I am telling myself what dull attempts I've made to pay a debt which couldn't anyway, be paid.

I'm telling myself, too, how poorly I helped your exile compared with what you have done for me. Oh, I do owe you such an awful lot my Sweet. Is it any wonder that you've

All my love, my lovely Sweet,

J.

Perhaps I don't feel as bad as I sound. But I want you so, oh, my Sweet Darling, I want you so.

But others were not so despondent. That night, the Allies celebrated, and the next day Jack wrote to Grace again.

9 May 1945

Did I, Sweetle, write you an awful letter yesterday? I was so mixed up, somehow, and muddled and through it all was a longing for you.

In the evening the authorities made their one V day gesture – a double ration of rum (about 3 ½ tablespoonfuls). Other drinks appeared somehow, though. Bonfires started up in various parts of the fields. Behind some woods the airstrip people were shooting up flares, white, green, red. I wandered round – my hideous Reichswald mug in hand – from one to another. There were wirelesses going describing London and visiting different places by microphone. The bonfires grew more exuberant. Some distance away someone let off a couple of big guns: I wonder if that's the last of all the times I shall hear the sound of the shells echoing away into the sky?

Then I came back to our own fire. Some of them were singing. Somebody was giving a demonstration of bottle opening. Stand up the bottle and shoot the neck off with a pistol: very clever really, considering his alcoholic handicap. I didn't want to join in the orgy, so I went to bed and left the tent flaps open. It was nice to watch them all out there and see the sparks shoot up . . .

And I listened to them singing. They went on quite a long time and I got drowsy. Bert, my co-tenter, looked in and nearly wrecked the tent. He disentangled himself, said seriously: "Very sensible, John, wish I'd had the sense not to drink so much." Then he staggered off in search of another one, tripping over a guy and pulling out a strategic peg on the way, so that I had to get up and restore the place.

They sang all kinds of banal songs, but they didn't sound so banal as usual. Even 'When the lights go up again . . .' had point, 'The Siegfried Line' too, and I myself was 'A little on the lonely side'.

Bert rolled in again, fought manfully with his blankets to the further hazard of the tent, lamenting the while about what a fool he was and how he wished he'd been more sensible. He took one more swig from his mug and subsided, still mumbling regrets.

I lay listening. The bonfires were dying, a few of them were still singing as I drifted off to sleep.

References

1   The Navy, Army and Air Force Institutes ran shops and cafes for servicemen and their families.

2   Letter to Grace, 8 March 1945. At time of writing he had already left the Reichswald behind and was living in an unnamed German town.

3   Letters to Grace, 10 and 15 March, 1945.

4   Letter to Grace, 18 March 1945.

5   Letter to Grace, 22 April 1945.

6   Letter to Fred Pohl, 2 January 1954.

7   Letter to Grace, 11 May 1945.

8   Letter to Grace, 2 May 1945.

9   This was an underestimate. At time of writing, the British Army still had 2,800 soldiers on German soil.

10   Letter to Grace, 7 May 1945.

Part Three

1946 - 1969

The Penn Club, London,
12 June, 1949

Outside his window, the gleaming white pyramid of the Ministry of Truth looms over the patched-up terraces opposite, staring down at him as he sits writing at his desk. Last week, it was Senate House, part of the university, but Orwell's new novel has given it a second, sinister identity. The tower broods above him, its ghostly staff of censors and spies lurking inside. He bought the book the day it came out, read it immediately and passed it to Grace.[1]

He is writing, not typing, to avoid disturbing her. He lights another cigarette and turns in his chair to look at her lying on his bed, shoes and stockings off. The evening sun slants across slim, bare legs. Her blouse is unbuttoned, her mass of hair, already turning grey, falls unpinned across his pillow. *Nineteen Eighty-Four* lies facedown beside her. He knows she is not really sleeping, just drowsing in the heat of dusty, post-war London after a long week at work. It is too hot for her to climb out of her window onto the sliver of flat roof she uses to sunbathe.

Sharply, she sucks in air and shifts on the bed. His own stomach tightens in sympathy. These last months have been hard for them both. Her stomach pains which worried him while he was in France turned out to be a duodenal ulcer, which has never healed. She had an operation in January. She had barely recovered before a breast cancer scare meant more surgery. She surrounded herself with an iron carapace as soon as she found the lump. Only he knows how frightened she was. She is due to see her doctor again about it and her ulcer still pains her, but there can be no question of more time off work. She is the only one of them earning.

His gaze passes over Orwell's book as he returns to his latest story. Perhaps this one will find a buyer? He knows it is no masterpiece, but he has to write something that will make some money. His thoughtful, lyrical short stories have been returned by his new American agent. His last novel set in London was rejected by several publishers. Most of the magazines who used to buy his work no longer exist. Next month, he will be 46.

He can't keep writing for the British market but this new story hangs over him like a doom. If science fiction won't sell, maybe American noir will? So in his imagined New York, celebrity photographers hide out in nightclubs and bottle blondes trade dances for diamonds. He can't keep out the fantasy though, and flying saucers staffed by cloned Nazis jet off from jungle lairs.

Everything is wrong, the plot is wrong, the style is wrong, the voice is wrong. It will never sell. It has to sell.

In a box beneath his desk, another manuscript lies forgotten. It is a total departure from the rocket ships and New York detectives. It is nearly finished, most of it has been professionally re-typed.

Within its pages, the mutant spores of the puffballs have floated through the rarified atmosphere and come to earth. Their descendants stalk through the English landscape, feasting on decaying human flesh. Suicide and despair lie behind cottage doors. An indefinable, unforgettable sense of horror pervades it, born of the tensions and unease of the new nuclear world.

But it is more than a horror story. Grace strolls lightly through the nightmare, coolly assessing the future, taking charge of the hero. She dances with him in Russell Square, keeps a place for him in their farmhouse in the Downs.

And Senate House rises as a symbol of a new world order from his imagination too.

It is a masterpiece of its time, and it is more than just of its time. These messages will resonate down the decades: of red-clawed nature threatening a complacent, over-civilised world, of the dangers of science manipulated by politics.

But it lies neglected. Years in the making, it is almost finished but not quite. Still Jack hesitates.

On the desk, forgettable pages of hardboiled, wisecracking ex-cops pile up before him, while the international bestseller that will grant him immortality gathers dust at his feet.

The Day of the Triffids is still to come.

9

The Day of the Triffids

In October 1946, Jack once again sat down to write at his desk in the Penn Club. His hopes of an early discharge had come to nothing. He had only just been released from the army. He had spent the last year in Britain, in a camp near Harrogate, which allowed him to visit his mother and Viv in Matlock, Derbyshire.[2]

His testimonial on discharge read: "A keen conscientious and hard-working NCO with a very good record of service. He displays initiative and has a pleasing personality. Is of a type on whom reliance can always be placed. Honest, sober and thoroughly trustworthy."

On his return to London, prices were higher and his income was reduced, but life at the Penn Club was almost as before the war. Jack was co-opted back on to the committee and he was given his old room next to Grace. After the horrors of France and Germany, he could do just what he had wanted: bury his head in her lap and shut out all the world.

She was happy teaching again at Roan School for Girls in Greenwich, where she was promoted to head of English. As she grew older, she was known for her cool, kindly elegance, always reliable and unruffled. She was respected and admired rather than loved, and remembered by her pupils as being rather remote and self-contained. Like many teachers, she was unsentimental about children, though keenly interested in her pupils' success. One of these post-war students remembered:[3]

> She was an extremely good-looking woman with good bone structure and especially attractive white hair. She was extremely well groomed and dressed usually in expensive blouses and skirts and medium-heeled shoes, all in a 'county' style.

There was always a hint of cigarettes about her, along with good scent . . . She was not a disciplinarian: if you did not want to learn she would ignore you.

She taught the girls that if they spoke firmly and with authority to people in office they could carry off daring feats. She herself walked most days through the (private) Temple Gardens. If challenged she would firmly and brusquely say: "Wilson", and was always allowed to proceed.

Grace's diaries of the time survive, although she destroyed her earlier journals believing them immature. From 1946 her writing is of her life rather than her soul: frustrations and satisfactions at school, her still variable health and the birds that visited the garden behind her room. Her diaries paint a picture of Jack spending contented days bumbling at the club: "J has turned a very pleasant kettle into an electric one, a lovely job."[4]

It was a return to a life of quiet sociability with plenty of friends, conversation and occasional theatre trips. Sometimes Grace liked to come back from school and snooze on Jack's bed until dinner, or tiptoe next door when she couldn't sleep.

Jack still presented her with poems, posies and Valentines which she treasured along with the sealskin gloves "still noble in old age". By now they were well used to each other's weaknesses.

Jack returned to his regular visits to Steep to stay with Biff and Eileen Barker and their girls at Row Cottage, or with Bill and Leslie Sykes at the Red House. Sometimes Grace went with him but more often she stayed in London to work. She often wrote of waiting impatiently for Jack to return. He was always jumpy if returning from Viv and their mother at Matlock. She wrote in her diary: "Hairwash in the afternoon and it set so badly I had to do it again at six. I doubt if I should have bothered if J hadn't been returning on Monday. Silly after all these years."

But though modest, this comfortable life had to be paid for. While Grace's income was reliable, Jack's was not.

The luxury of time was disappearing. On discharge from the army, he was 43. His mother was in her late 70s and was beginning to need more nursing than a boarding house could provide. His private income, which had provided a cushion for his whole adult life, had to reduce to pay for her care. Viv has not fully recovered from the nervous breakdown he suffered during the war and was again recovering in Matlock. He wasn't earning at all.

Jack calculated he had two years to make a success of writing. Otherwise, he would have to give up and return to the civil service. But the market he was used to had changed.

The two British science fiction magazines, *Fantasy* and *Tales of Wonder*, had both folded. *Fantasy*'s editor T Stanhope Sprigg had joined the RAF as a pilot in 1939 after only three issues. *Tales of Wonder* editor Walter Gillings tried producing the magazine from his army camp when he was conscripted, but it closed in 1942. The American market had also shrunk to only seven titles, where there had once been 22.[5]

The problem was not just the quantity, but the quality. The early days of creative freedom were over, replaced by a shoddy reliance on action and saucy pictures.[6] The beginning of McCarthyism in the United States was having an impact on editors' willingness to publish radical ideas.

He continued writing short stories, but his work had matured and the magazines were only beginning to grow up. In addition, his American agent, Otis Kline, had died. His new agent, Margaret Christie, was less in tune with his ideas.

One of his most reflective, lyrical short stories, "Time to Rest", was written at this time. Bert is a middle-aged man stranded on Mars after the destruction of Earth. He sails his boat along the great canals, working as a travelling tinker for the gentle Martians. They are peasant survivors of an ancient race, with a Buddhist like tranquillity which helps Bert accept his fate.

It was promptly returned by Miss Christie with a note that this kind of thing would not do at all. To stand a chance it "must be completely filled with action, adjectives, drama and suspense and what-have -you." [7]

Jack believed more editorial freedom was to be found in books. He tried a spy thriller about Nazi cells in present-day London, *Project for Pistols*, aimed at the British market. He submitted it to several publishers in 1948, with no luck. He later said the book was "mistimed and topicalities out of date in a month or two in an era when it took 18 months at least to publish."[8] However, it seems likely publishers realised the British simply didn't want to hear about resurgent Nazis.

His old friend Walter Gillings, editor of the short-lived pre-war *Tales of Wonder*, began to use him as a reviewer for his science fiction newsletter *Fantasy Review*, but this wasn't well paid. In a satirical essay about the state of science fiction, he wrote of H G Wells' *The First Men in the Moon*:

> Where in the opening chapters is the zip, pep and dynamic action necessary to capture the reader's attention?
>
> Frankly, it isn't there – so, as any experienced editor will tell you, nobody will read it. This man Wells doesn't apply journalistic principles. In the whole book he shows no glimmering appreciation of the neon-lit fact that it's love makes the world go round. Pity a present-day magazine illustrator put on to this job: no bulging brassiere, no provoking panties!

Jack understood why magazines could not take risks – a large circulation needed a wider appeal. A regular publishing schedule meant they couldn't alienate readers who would desert them by the next issue.

> The magazine, though it may start out with ambitious freedom, learns to toe the party line of publishing as it grows. It becomes politely uninquisitive about anything that matters and plods a well-trodden avenue where warning signs are borrowed from the Hays Office[9]: Religion – do not disturb – penalty 20 per cent or more subscribers; Sex – do not inquire – penalty, parental Comstockery[10]; Social system – beware of FBI; International politics – proceed with caution – everybody touchy (and yesterday's friend may be tomorrow's enemy, which can be awkward); Nationalism – do not ignore – penalty for foreign triumphing, large disappointment of readers; and so on, and so on.
>
> On the whole, it is much less trouble to keep to a path which leads to a happy-ever-after in a gadgeteer's heaven . . . This is not the editor's fault . . . it is just part of the price we have to pay for the advantages of mass-production, the process which is now gradually squeezing the individual either into the right shape or out of existence.

> Fifty years ago, the world was freer . . . To a great many
> people it seemed right that minds of all types should examine
> the possibilities which science was exposing; now it no lon-
> ger seems quite so right, particularly in nuclear research and
> bio-chemistry.

By 1948, he was almost broke and his two years were up. For a time, Grace paid for his board at the Penn Club. He briefly tried advertising, where he was horrified by the blatant lies and the manipulation of women into the new 'profession' of housewife.[11]

But he was granted a reprieve by Miss Christie. She succeeded in placing a short story, "Jizzle", with *Collier's Weekly*, an American general fiction magazine in September 1948. It was the dream of all pulp fiction writers to get into the 'slicks' as they called the magazines printed on glossy coated paper. *Collier's* was one of the biggest, with a circulation of 2.5 million. Their writers included Martha Gellhorn and Ernest Hemingway; before the war Winston Churchill had been a regular contributor. They paid well, and this gave him a cushion for another few months.

He managed a couple of other short story sales to American science fiction magazines: "Technical Slip" (*The Arkham Sampler*, 1949) about a man living his life on a loop, and "Adaptation" (*Astounding Science Fiction*, 1949) about a child raised on another planet.

Meanwhile, Viv was getting stronger, and looking for something to do. Jack suggested he tried writing. He gave him an introduction to his agent at Curtis Brown, and an old manuscript of his own as a guide for punctuation. To everyone's surprise, Viv completed a light come-dy, *Trouble at Hanard*, which sold immediately. He wrote another, sold it, and signed a contract for two more. Viv later said: "It wasn't that my books were any good as anything but time-passers or laugh providers, but it upset him to find a mere amateur was getting away with it while a professional writer couldn't."[12]

With two years of struggle behind him and few prospects ahead, Jack took stock.

He wanted to write a new kind of story, or rather, an old kind, like the logical fantasies of H G Wells that had inspired him. He was more cynical now about the wonders of science, and far more politically conscious than before the war. And though the war was over, the nightmare of those days still lay buried within him.

Then, while walking at twilight in a deep country lane, a sapling swaying in a high wind seemed to be taking jabs at him. In a rare interview about the origin of the triffids, he said: [13]

> The tops of the hedges were only just distinguishable against the sky and the higher things sticking up from the hedges were rather menacing. One felt they might come over and strike down, or if they had stings, sting at one and the whole thing grew from there.

The format came from an earlier short story, "The Puffball Menace", published in 1933.[14] British gardeners have been tricked into planting poisonous spores of a modified puffball. The hero, more of an action figure than Wyndham's later narrators, dashes across country from London to find his fiancée, as Bill Masen, the hero of *The Day of the Triffids*, later would. He joins soldiers building barbed wire fences and wielding flamethrowers to slow the progress of the rolling puffballs before they can spread their seeds farther inland, just as Masen and his adopted daughter would try to hold back the triffids from their farm.

Jack combined this with another, unfinished work in which the population of a single Pacific island is saved by a blanketing fog from seeing strange green lights which affect the rest of the world.[15]

But his new idea was far more than a mash-up of reheated stories.

After years of setting stories in spaceships, *The Day of the Triffids* was the first to be firmly rooted in the world that he knew. It is partly this that makes the horror so believable. Bill Masen's final days in London are set in the streets around the Penn Club. He dances with Josella outside the Senate House, one of Grace's favourite buildings, visible from their bedroom windows. The fragile haven of their farmhouse in the Sussex Downs is close to Bedales.

Josella herself mirrors Grace: independent and unconventional. Like Grace, she is happy to be part of an unofficial but permanent 'marriage', bound by love rather than a legal ceremony.

Jack abandoned the square-jawed heroes with the exotic settings. Bill rescues Josella when he first meets her, but after that he rarely takes the lead. He is closer to Jack himself: a thoughtful observer, practical and brave, but no alpha male. Perhaps his time in the military had given Jack a distaste for the type.

Though set roughly 30 years in the future, the whole book resonates with Jack's war experiences – experiences which would have been shared with and recognised by many of his readers.

When Bill Masen wakes on a Wednesday which "starts off by sounding like Sunday", he discovers the eerily silent city that Jack described to Grace. Following heavy Saturday night bombardments, the whole population slept off a week of disrupted sleep and the streets and parks were empty. The hysterical woman's scream and the crunching of broken glass also come from his early letters of the Blitz.

Bill stands looking out at the London Jack and many others knew as a firewatcher. He sees the flames that have broken out and smoke climbing into the sky, and says goodbye to the beautiful city he had known.

On Bill and Josella's last night together in London, as they sit outside talking, someone puts a Strauss waltz on a record player: "And we danced, on the brink of an unknown future, to an echo from a vanished past."

So did Jack and Grace, and thousands of other couples, snatch final moments of happiness before separation. As he wrote in one of his first letters to her: "Saturday, how lovely. An era had shut up its houses and gone away – perhaps for ever. But we had that little much longer. How cruel the macrocosm, sweet, but how sweet the microcosm. Oh, my darling." [16]

More disturbing are the cycles of elation and depression Bill experiences as he leaves the city with Coker. They pass by an apparently sleeping rural England, while conscious that horror lurks in every cottage.

Jack experienced the same psychic dislocation when driving with the British army through the bombsites of Germany into the untouched town of Lunesburg. He wrote to Grace "I have constantly to be reminding myself that most of the towns of Germany are like that [ruined] and not like this: that the ruins are not something historically past but something geographically passed." [17]

It's this personal experience that separates *The Day of the Triffids* from his early work and gives the book its emotional veracity and power. It is commonly pigeonholed as a dystopian novel, but on a personal level it is Utopian. Driving past the endless war graves of Europe, Jack had been depressed by the relentless cycles of destruction. Within this book, he wiped the slate clean.

England – even the world – would be rebuilt on his old school's principles, outlined by the new community leader Michael Beadley, a conflation of Badley and Bedales, in his address in Senate House. The new England would be formed of linked communities of common vision, unchained from the old taboos and strictures of marriage and private homes.

Perhaps it was this personal connection that made Jack, always modest and reticent, reluctant to expose it to the world. He completed it to the point of sending it out to be professionally typed, but was so dissatisfied with the ending he told the typist to stop work.

In 1948, the future bestseller was left to gather dust.

Then, Grace's health began to suffer. The duodenal ulcer that had worried Jack while he was in France had never cleared up.

The new year saw Grace admitted to hospital for a week for an operation. On her return she wrote: "J came three times, and came to fetch me on Wednesday. I had lunch with him at the Italian restaurant opposite Kings Cross and all was very dear and calm."

But less than three months later she found a lump in her breast. Several days of fear and anxiety followed:

> Tues April 5th: I rang up Dr Turner and went to her. Now I have to be as hard as iron so as not to depress myself or other people. J has been marvellous, all that is loving and sympathetic and sensible, and I feel now that I may be over the worst of the apprehension.

> Wed April 6th: Less than two hours' sleep in spite of J's soothing kindness. But today was not too bad. It is strange and exhausting to change the whole background and foundation of one's thinking. When I got back J had washed the rug which workmen had muddied in getting at the rainwater pipe on the roof.

Thursday April 7th: I had a good night on half a sedomind and feel much calmer. The trees are coming out and everything looks very beautiful between the storms. In the evening I began to climb upwards and feel I have got on top of the worst.

Friday April 8th: A hard day, but I got everything done in case I cannot go back this term . . . It's damn funny that I started this diary just to have one year of my dull middle age to read when I am old.

She was again admitted to hospital for an emergency operation. She was relieved to be told she was "still symmetrical" – the doctors had not had to carry out a mastectomy. She was also told tests on the excised cyst were negative though a mention of radium treatment casts doubt on this. By late June, the doctors were willing to discharge her 'top half'. She was soon back at work, but her ulcer continued a problem.

Though she had many friends at the club, she had little real support apart from Jack. Their lives were strictly compartmentalised, which led to more problems. Her colleagues could not know she was 'living in sin' – she would certainly have lost her job. Jack could not accompany her on visits to her parents; they still had no idea of their real relationship. At Easter and Christmas she went to stay with them, while he went to the Barkers in Steep. Her father, a non-conformist preacher, was disapproving of her independent lifestyle. After one fraught half term visit in 1949 she wrote of him:[18]

He asked so many questions on Saturday that I felt very unhappy, seeing that he was thinking I could give up everything and go to live at Devon Road [with them]. I knew this would not work at all, but felt wretched at facing the problem in all its aspects. When I had time to do a little arithmetic in my mind on Sunday, though, I saw that it was economically quite unsound, and he must have seen that too because he was consigning me to hell-fire in the well-known style on Monday night. I have come back pretty humourless and dumb, but at least I am back with J.

The need to support Grace emotionally wasn't Jack's only problem – through 1949 he badly needed money. The success of "Jizzle" in

Collier's Weekly had not been repeated and he was selling little else – his total income from writing during the whole year was about $25. Grace wrote in her diary in June:[19]

> Darling J is sad because Miss Christie has sent stuff back, and he says this puts him where he was three years ago. I do sympathise and think he is marvellous to bear it, but I don't know how to be helpful, I wish I did.

Though Jack was doggedly persistent, he was always a modest man. The combination of stresses seemed to lead to a crisis of confidence. Jack turned his back on his own life experiences once more. He wrote several short stories, including a novelette, *Survival*, about a woman stranded on a spaceship.

He also tried another novel, ignoring the struggling British publications and aiming again at the American market. He went back to a detective format, hoping that a private eye-type intro would enable him to sneak the fantasy he really loved in later.[20]

Like most of his work, *Plan for Chaos* was based on ideas decades ahead of their time. He invented a cloned Nazi super-race thirty years before Ira Levin's *Boys from Brazil* and based them in an unnamed equatorial region. Presiding over them was a matriarch who dominated and suffocated them, one of Jack's many unsympathetic mother figures.

He may have taken inspiration from the Paraguay colony of New Germany. This was founded by Elisabeth Nietzsche, antisemitic sister of the philosopher, in 1886. The offspring of her 'pure blood' Germans still exist, now intermarried with the local population.

The hero was an American magazine photographer, but his voice was not convincingly American, and the plot demanded that he was of Swedish extraction. To try and solve both problems, Jack turned him into a transplanted Brit, trying to act as American as he could.

The result was a mess. *Plan for Chaos* starts as clichéd detective noir with hardboiled editors and diamond-studded blondes, then morphs into militaristic science fiction with flying saucers staffed by Nazis. It finishes by exploring a paralysing psychological impasse between a mother and her many children: fascinating, but with no stylistic connection to the rest. Plot holes gape throughout: who has raised this family of thousands? The ending is inconclusive, marred by cod-Australian accents: "Ain't that a fair cow!" Despite several efforts at re-writing, *Plan for Chaos* was never published in his lifetime. [21]

It was only at the end of this difficult year that Jack remembered the triffids. He re-worked the ending, though he was never completely satisfied with it. Despairing of Miss Christie, he passed it to Walter Gillings in early 1950, who was then acting for a New York agency.

Walter later recalled:[22]

> It was after an agonisingly bad patch, during which he was producing little or nothing, that he entrusted to me a nov-el-length manuscript, assuring me of his grave doubts of its worth. I didn't wait to finish the MS. Halfway through I shipped it over, confident that so long as it ended somehow, it would sell . . .
>
> After that, John Wyndham had no more arid spells to torment him, as far as I am aware. It was only later that I learned he had spent two years trying to find the ending I had not stopped to read.

Walter sent it to Frederick Pohl, a writer who had stepped in to run the Dirk Wylie agency in New York. Fred had joined to help out his oldest friend who was suffering from unhealed war wounds. When Wylie died of complications, Fred agreed to keep the agency going to help out Wylie's widow. Fred immediately spotted the potential of the manuscript, but he hoped for a mainstream appeal, and took issue with the origin of the triffids.

In the version Fred first saw, the world had advanced to set up colonies on other planets. The source of the triffids was seeds brought back from Venus. When the survivors speculated about the cause of the blinding green lights, they believed they may have been weapons controlled by these off-world colonies.

Fred disliked this nod to interplanetary travel in a book otherwise firmly set in England, and Jack agreed to change it: [23]

> Your . . . point is well taken. The origin of the triffids was written in as a kind of dangle for the science-fiction editorial mind. It doesn't belong, it did not exist before, and it shall disappear . . . I will revert to some form of terrestrial generation for them. It will, too, as you say, give a closer unity in time.

Within two weeks, Fred had sold the manuscript to American publishers Doubleday, subject to Jack making the changes agreed.

In a conscious break with the past, Jack chose another of his many names. He told Fred:[24]

> The original idea of John Wyndham was that I was using it for a different style of stuff. To begin with it was clearer, but the whole thing has slipped a bit, and now I find John Wyndham behaving pulpishly too. However, John Wyndham is not cluttered up with memories of early Wonder Stories. (John Beynon has no value as a name, in fact, I'd say the opposite – I strongly suspect that he is regarded by any science-fiction readers who have heard of him as one of the old back numbers.) So if you are agreeable, we will adopt John Wyndham and stick to it.

Jack got to work on the revisions, bringing the story closer to the current time. Like *Nineteen Eighty-Four*, published at the same time, it was set just 30-odd years in the future. In the new version, the world was not significantly different from the time of writing. The triffids were the result of genetic meddling behind the Iron Curtain.

He namechecked Trofim Lysenko, then the director of the Institute of Genetics at the USSR's Academy of Sciences. He was protected by Stalin: scientists who refused to believe his controversial theories on heredity were sentenced to death as enemies of the state.

In real life Lysenko was involved in improving crop yield. This, with his political background, gave a frightening realism to the idea of a Soviet science deliberately creating monsters for their valuable oil.

To heighten the Cold War links, the blinding green flashes and later plague came from the proliferation and weaponisation of artificial satellites then in discussion. The first, Sputnik 1, was launched six years after *The Day of the Triffids* was published. These changes reduced the element of fantasy, strengthened the political base of the novel and gave it a more immediate sense of threat.

Fred also sold some of Jack's short stories to magazines. He had tried to sell *The Day of the Triffids* as a serial as well but had no success. As the publication date of December 1950 got nearer, he told Jack to give up hope as magazines would only serialise stories before they were published as books. But on 6 November 1950, he wrote to him again.

> I've been sitting on this for three weeks, unwilling to take a chance on telling you about it until I actually had the check in my hands – but I am informed that the voucher for the piece went in today, and so I guess I might as well break the news: COLLIER'S is buying "THE DAY OF THE TRIFFIDS" as a five-part serial.
>
> Truly, I couldn't be more delighted if it were my own story; it was a last-chance offering and one that had previously seemed ruled out for any number of valid reasons. But it's a definite sale, and at a fine price. Take a deep breath . . . $12,500.00.

This equated to about £4,500. The annual average wage in Britain was about £100. Even without the book royalties, it was a success beyond Jack's wildest dreams. He replied: [25]

> Just at the moment I'm a bit shaken. I lift my hat to you with an awestruck and dithering hand. And on thinking it over, not least do I thank you for sparing me suspense and not breaking any of the news until the fait was pretty well accompli. Altogether I do thank you for, and congratulate you on, what must have been hard work, pertinacity, and undoubtedly is a triumph. (For one thing, you know and I know that TRIF-FIDS is not the proper stuff of serials – but as long as *Collier's* doesn't know that it's all right, and redounds still more to your credit.) It all leaves me a little winded . . .
>
> I had meant to write to you in any case to say that I have seen some kindly reviews of Mrs Pohl's book. I hope there are plenty, and I do hope it is doing well. How nice to have a baby and a book at the same time. Here's wishing that they may all three of them continue to thrive.

Collier's agreed to start the serial in January 1951, so Doubleday wouldn't have to delay their own publication too long. In addition, Fred managed to sell the book to a subscriber service, "The Adventure Book Club", for April 1951. This made it more acceptable for Doubleday to agree to the delay for the sake of the increased royalties.

It meant another considerable cheque for Jack.

Soon Fred was discussing a serialisation in Australia, and foreign rights for the book. For the British rights, Jack approached an old Penn Club friend, Robert Lusty (later Sir Robert). He had met his future wife Joan Brownlie at the club, but hadn't stayed in touch with Jack. By 1950, he was the deputy chairman of the publisher Michael Joseph, which generally took literary fiction.

Sir Robert later recalled Jack's diffident request:[26]

> One day in Bloomsbury Street I was told that 'a Mr Harris' was downstairs and would like to see me. In my office he handed me a manuscript. "This is a novel I've managed to write," he said. "I don't quite know what to do with it and I thought you might advise me. It is not for you," he added, as though horrified that I might think it was . . .
>
> I took the manuscript home. "Old Harris has written a novel," I told Joan, "and he sends you his love."
>
> I read it with rising interest and excitement. It was not, as its author had prophesied, quite my cup of tea, but it was wonderfully good. I invited Harris to come again to the office. "I know," I told him, "that you didn't think this was for us, but would you mind very much if we were to publish it?"

While Doubleday had wanted cuts to make it a faster-paced read, Michael Joseph wanted the heft of the original. The Michael Joseph version was about 91,000 words, while the Doubleday version was 80,000 and the *Collier's* version was only 47,000.[27]

But there was a further surprise when *Collier's* published. Somehow, they had ended up with the earlier version in which the triffids originated on Venus.

Jack generously praised the production and refrained from blaming his agent:[28]

> I succeeded in finding a copy of COLLIER'S with the first instalment of TRIFFIDS in it. They've made quite a nice job of the send off. And, boy, is reading it an education in how to edit! Immensely impressed by their skills in attaining what they want; it's a fine example of really expert slanting and tailoring to suit a specialised need.

> What did rather stagger me was to find that here we have
> to deal with the Venusian Triffid ... so now we have three
> versions: the Collier Particular, the Doubleday Abbreviated
> and the Joseph Uncut. You ought to be having fun sorting
> out who wants which. It's a consoling thought that people
> who like books customarily can't stand serials, and people
> who read serials customarily don't much know or care what's
> happening anyway, so long as it seems to keep moving.

A few months later, the American Doubleday version was published and review copies sent to the science fiction press. In Britain,
Michael Joseph pushed it as a mainstream novel. The reviews were
warm but not fantastic. Most recognised the quality of the writing,
the result of that decades-long apprenticeship. John Betjeman snootily
wrote: "An imaginative tale spoiled by too much moralising from a
man and woman whom the author cannot make real."[29]

Experienced science fiction critics disapproved of the way Jack had
set up two initial premises – the triffids combined with the general
blindness – instead of just one. H G Wells had a maxim that a fantasy
author should set up only one believable premise and develop realistic
characters and plot on that basis. Further fantastic assumptions would
result in "irresponsible silliness".[30] Jack had broken this 'rule'.

But this literary niggle meant nothing to the public.

Theirs was a society unbalanced by a changing class structure, fearing a reckless militarised science, and hag-ridden by memories of war.
All these found expression in *The Day of the Triffids*. John Beynon had
been a fantasist ahead of his time: John Wyndham had tapped into
the zeitgeist.

Although nominally set a generation in the future, Jack had made
no attempt to create a world filled with jetpacks and protein pills. London and the Sussex Downs were depicted unchanged. The tightrope
walk of the armed political stalemate between the Soviet Union and
the rest of the world was shown at the moment of tipping into disaster. It was nightmare, prophecy and warning. He wrote directly to his
readers, and they responded in thousands.

A Penguin edition followed the Michael Joseph hardback in the UK
in 1954. It sold 100,000 copies in seven years. It was translated into 11

languages. Worldwide, it sold millions.

Broadcasters spotted a winner. It was read on the BBC Home Service in 1953 and adapted as a radio play for the Light Programme four years later. Albert "Cubby" Broccoli purchased the film rights in 1956, though it was several more years before it was filmed.

For the first time, Jack started receiving fan mail. He replied to many letters, sometimes in great detail, signing himself John Wyndham. He had a new letterhead printed, with his own illustration of a triffid in the bottom corner.

Almost 30 years after his first novel was published, he was a success.

JOHN WYNDHAM

22 BEDFORD PLACE
LONDON
W.C.1

22nd Oct 1951.

Dear Mrs. Lowe,

       It was a great pleasure to have your letter. There is immensely more satisfaction (or could I mean flattery?) in knowing that someone has been interested enough in a thing to take it to pieces and look at the works, than to have anyone say blankly and simply that he 'liked' it.

       And, with this kind of thing, I've always found the taking to pieces to be a part of the game:if it comes to pieces too badly, it should prove salutary for the author -- if it doesn't come to pieces at all, he can consider himself a miracle worker, or at least abnormal. (A similar sort of thing happens with a detective story. There are rules to be observed, and if you are detected in too many slips yourself, or in too many coincidences, or don't play fair, you fail, as even Agatha Christie did, to be elected to the Detective Club.

       The other part of the game is rebuttal - where possible. Though I must admit that yours is the most formidable perception that has turned in a report so far. However, I must try to turn a few thrusts, if I can.

       The doctor's suicide. As you say, the blindness might have been temporary, there might have been a cure -- but surely that is also true of the afflictions of many people who do commit suicide: they happen to be the ones who don't wait to see if there is a cure. A few people behaved in that way in September 1939, rather than face it.

       On the suddenness and completeness of the collapse, I'm not altogether sure. The crux there, of course, is the early failure of the telephone system. Had it remained in working order, various authorities would have been able at least to communicate with one another -- though it is difficult to see that they could have done very much -- but, without it, they were all isolated and helpless. (Opinions seem to vary as to how long the automatic telephone

The first page of a four page letter to a fan who had raised a number of plot queries. He justifies the fast-acting triffid poison by comparing it to centipedes and black widow spiders, saying he made the triffids quick killers "to avoid sheerly morbid horrifics". He adds it did occur to him "or rather, Beadley" to go to a hospital and round up expectant mothers: "but the complications of sudden motherhood in lorries and by roadsides were too much for me, and him." He ends by recommending Ray Bradbury's *The Silver Locusts*.

References

1   *Nineteen Eighty-Four* was released on 9 June. On 12 June, Grace wrote in her diary: ". . . it was too hot to lie on the roof for more than an hour. . . I read the first part of *Nineteen Eighty-Four* by George Orwell. This is very brilliant and important. He stresses the falsification of history that is a necessity of the totalitarian state. J is disappointed (or rather his worst fears are confirmed) because I cannot read the later Gestapo torture part. So I was hurt and angry with him. But a nice evening."

Several people have speculated that Orwell and Jack met. In the 1930s, Orwell worked at a bookshop which Jack may have frequented. During the war, Orwell's wife was working as a censor at the Ministry of Information at the same time as Jack was a censor; and Orwell was working for the BBC at the same time as Jack's friend Howell. But Jack was never part of fashionable literary London, and there is no record of either man mentioning meeting the other. Orwell kept detailed diaries from 1938 to 1942 and Jack described his daily life, including meeting several interesting people, in his letters to Grace. If they had met it seems likely one of them would have noted it.

Orwell's short and difficult post-war life has been exhaustively analysed, but without throwing up any links to Jack as far as I am aware. By the time Jack was better known beyond the science fiction fanbase, Orwell was dead.

2   Vivian Beynon Harris, *My Brother John Wyndham 1903-1969*, manuscript for unfinished biography, held in the University of Liverpool archive.

3   Letter to David Ketterer, 27 August 1998, from Hilary Watt. Held in the University of Liverpool Archive.

4   Diary entry, Thursday September 30, 1948. See note 26, Chapter 3.

5   Mike Ashley (2004) *Time Machines: The story of the science fiction pulp magazines from the beginning to 1950,* Liverpool University Press.

6   John Beynon (1949) "Why Blame Wells?" *Fantasy Review*, 2(12) p.14. Available at http://efanzines.com/FR/fr12.htm

7   Letter from Jack to August Derleth, 3 September 1948. Held in the Liverpool archive, Wyndham 11/5. The remark obviously stung, because he referred to it again in the foreword to *The Seeds of Time*, 1959 Penguin edition.

8   Biographical notes probably written for a magazine publisher. Held in the University of Liverpool archive, Wyndham 13/2/4.

9   The Hays Code was the informal name for the American Motion Picture Code, which became more strictly enforced after the mid-1930s. Its censorship stifled the development of cinema.

10   The Comstock Laws were a series of laws introduced in the US that clamped down on 'obscene literature' and birth control.

11   Reminiscences by Sister Bede, held in the Liverpool archive.

12   Vivian Beynon Harris, ibid.

13   An interview by Derek Hart on the *Tonight* programme, BBC, on 6 September 1960. https://www.bbc.co.uk/programmes/p0162m7x

14   Also known as "Spheres of Hell".

15   Later biographers, including Sam Moskowitz in *Seekers of Tomorrow*, have suggested other influences, including H G Wells' "The Country of the Blind" and various pulp fiction short stories of the 1930s about sentient plants.

16   Letter to Grace, 17 June 1940. Written after a holiday at Fairlight, a seaside town on the South Coast.

17   Letter to Grace, 5 June 1945, held in the University of Liverpool archive.

18   Diary entry, 1 November 1949.

19   Diary entry, 29 August 1949.

20   Q&A interview with Sam Moskowitz, ibid, see note to Chapter 1.

21   It was published by the Liverpool University Press in 2009 and in 2010 by Penguin. It received mixed reviews. It's possible that the unpublished manuscript was an inspiration for *Boys From Brazil*. Ira Levin was friends with Jack's agent Fred Pohl. Fred had offered to try and rework the story in exchange for a joint byline, and may have showed it to Levin. Jack and Levin are also known to have talked and possibly written to each other. The year Jack died, Levin included his name and the Penn Club phone number – Museum 2151 – in his science fiction novel *This Perfect Day*. "Wyndham MU7 2151" is hidden on the back of an old map – a secret joke and tribute to the author who preceded him.

22   Walter H. Gillings, 1969, "The Writer People Believed In", *Cosmos*, No. 2, p. 10.

23   Letter to Frederick Pohl, 25 March 1950. Held in the Liverpool archive.

24   Letter to Frederick Pohl, 3 April 1950. Held in the Liverpool archive. His decision to switch to John Wyndham meant he used it for a short story "The Eternal Eve", which appeared just before *The Day of the Triffids* in *Amazing Stories* in September 1950.

25   Frederick Pohl was then married to science fiction writer and editor Judith Merril. She published two books in 1950, a novel *Shadow on the Hearth*, and an anthology of short stories, *Shot in the Dark,* by authors including her husband, Robert Heinlein and Isaac Asimov.

26   Robert Lusty, 1975, *Bound to be Read*. London, Jonathan Cape, p. 140-141.

27   For an excellent and detailed comparison of the different versions, see Neil Pollard's essay "Early Triffids", available at http://triffidalley. com/ta_research/early_triffids.pdf

28   The serial version, with its original illustrations, can be read on the *Collier's* archive site, beginning with the 6 January 1951 issue at https:// www.unz.com/print/Colliers-1951jan06-00009/

29   Quoted by Walter Gillings in "Modern Masters of Science Fiction, John Wyndham", *Science Fiction Monthly* 1(9) p.8, 1974.

30   Wells' explanation of his 'law' appears in his introduction to *The Scientific Romances of H.G. Wells,* 1933.

10

New Worlds

The 1950s brought a surge of energy to Jack. Still living and working in the spartan surroundings of room number 45, he embarked on a decade-long run of novels and anthologies that would redefine science fiction as a mainstream genre. His writing wasn't his only success: all his enterprises were finally making good.

One of the difficulties of the 1940s for Jack and other writers was the failure of the British science fiction magazine market. Paradoxically, the lack of that outlet had pushed Jack further from spaceships and laser guns and towards the more realistic 'logical fantasies' that had brought him rewards. Nonetheless, he and the old pre-war crowd of writers, editors and fans still wanted to make a success of the British sci-fi scene. Many of its members had been conscripted during the war, but had now returned to London.

Two new British magazines had opened in a burst of post-war enthusiasm. *New Worlds* was edited by Ted Carnell and *Fantasy* by Walter Gillings. *Fantasy* was promptly killed off by paper shortages and *New Worlds* by financial difficulties by the end of 1947, but the sci-fi enthusiasts weren't willing to give up on a high quality British publication.

The original Science Fiction Association haunt in Grays Inn Road was bombed out, so Jack, Arthur C Clarke, William F Temple and other writers and fans had started to meet again at the White Horse pub, near Fleet Street. The landlord was Lew Mordecai, and being a great reader himself, he welcomed his new clientele. On Thursday nights they converted the centre table into a magazine exchange and took over the place.

The two unlucky editors, Gillings and Carnell, decided to combine forces to keep at least one quality magazine alive. Nova Publications was formed in a huddle over a pub table with six directors in early 1948. The quiet chap in the corner, Jack, was chosen as chairman by general consent.

An appeal to fans and friends to invest resulted in enough working capital to produce two more issues of *New Worlds*. Jack bought 25 shares at £1 each. The directors now put their venture on a more formal footing by moving to the private bar.

The whole board was determined that only the best would appear in their magazine. Jack wanted the hackneyed adverts for muscle building programmes to be ditched. The covers were another source of debate. Bulging brassieres and bug-eyed monsters might pull in sales but the board wanted something less brash and adolescent.

A report in the *Fantasy Review* said:[1]

> In the end, after they had seen what the boys in the front room would have out of three suggestions by artist Dennis, they decided (whatever the landlord thought) to ignore "human interest" entirely and appeal to the customers' intelligence. A picture of a space-ship bearing down on the Moon might not be very original, but at least it still has topical value; and it doesn't pull the sordid trick of wheedling one-and-six-pence out of a moron whose roving eye has caught sight of a buxom damsel in a zipper-suit, but who couldn't care less what alien planet she's bound for.

Carnell became editor and one of the first stories to appear was Jack's "Time to Rest", the meditative story of Bert sailing the Martian canals which Margaret Christie had damned as dull. This sale had been enough to keep Jack plugging on through 1949.

Printing problems continued and money was tight. Only five editions appeared sporadically in the first two years, but by 1951, just as *The Day of the Triffids* was published, it settled down to a regular quarterly schedule. Its success would allow Gillings to publish an occasional companion magazine, *Science-Fantasy*, which would also feature Jack's stories.

New Worlds would become one of the most influential science fiction magazines. By 1954 it was a monthly. During the 1950s, it would feature Arthur C Clarke, J G Ballard, Michael Moorcock, Brian Aldiss,

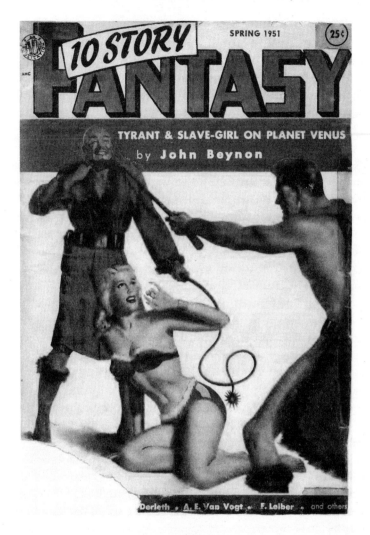

The last appearance of the John Beynon byline, just as *The Day of the Triffids* was published. *10 Story Fantasy* was a short lived publication, despite the lurid covers. This one bears no relation to the story, which is actually a sequel to "Time to Rest", and features no women, bikini-clad or otherwise.

Sam Youd (who wrote under several names including John Christopher) and John Burke (who also wrote under many male and female names).

Later on, it would become a magazine of the avant-garde under the inspired editorship of Michael Moorcock. He would publish some of Terry Pratchett's earliest short stories, along with work by Thomas M Disch which had been refused by more traditional American publishers.

But that was still to come. In the 1950s, the Nova Publications team was simply glad to have a high quality British publication, and their home was the White Horse. The pub was a magnet for scientists, sci-fi fans, writers and editors; in the words of one regular, it was "our home-from-home, our drawing room, our market, parliament and battleground" [2]. In 1953 they moved with the landlord, Lew Mordecai, to the Globe Inn, a few minutes' walk away. This informal club was immortalised by Arthur C Clarke in *Tales from the White Hart*, featuring Jack and his other friends.

In the science fiction crowd, Jack had found another bubble where he could be comfortable. He was known for his modesty and his generosity to younger authors. One American, Everett Franklin Bleiler, met him at the pub through Ted Carnell a year after *The Day of the Triffids* had come out. E F Bleiler, then aged 31, was on a trip to London from Leiden, in the Netherlands, where he was a Fulbright scholar. E F Bleiler would go on to be a prominent editor with Dover Publications and Scribner's.

Jack was then in his late 40s, but Bleiler remembered him as looking older, with thin-rimmed glasses which he took off periodically, while blinking his eyes rapidly. He had a habit of hitching his shirt sleeves up into the sleeves of an elderly plaid jacket: "He created the impression of a highly intelligent, cultured, tolerant, genial but rather shy man."

Jack was interested to meet him because he had been having trouble with Dutch piracy of *The Day of the Triffids*, and asked Bleiler to buy a copy for him if he saw one. Returning to the Netherlands, Bleiler came across one and handed it over next time he was in London, politely refusing payment. In return, Jack invited him to a lavish lunch at the Russell Hotel, close to the Penn Club. Bleiler remembered:[3]

We made our way through a remarkable arrangement of pillars, pilasters, mirrors, marble, crystal, and carved mahogany to the dining room, where there was a full hors d'oeuvres table. Harris ate lightly, but smoked heavily. I am ashamed to say that I gorged myself.

They discussed politics: Jack praised socialised medicine (the NHS was then four years old) and admired Aneurin Bevan, the Labour MP who had championed it. Of course, they talked science fiction, Jack taking the view that American sci-fi was generally better, but that British authors such as Huxley, Orwell and Graves hit higher peaks. He marvelled at American fans' ability to spout titles, authors and dates, seeing sci-fi as something that could be studied like other branches of literature.

Bleiler then made a gaffe that haunted him for a long time:

I lamented the fact that too many writers did not have a feeling for form, and as an example cited a story (author and title of which escaped me) that I had read a year or two earlier when I was working on one of the *Best Science Fiction* volumes. I pontificated away, telling Harris how the author could have done this and that instead of these and those, but had really botched things up.

Harris listened courteously and agreed in a soft way saying that the story demonstrated "bad craftsmanship." I noted a certain diffidence in his manner, but we went on to something else. When I got back to Leiden, memories suddenly clicked. It had been a story of Harris' that I had been knocking! I would guess that it was "Technical Slip," but I am not sure.

Bleiler didn't meet him again, although they exchanged a couple of notes. He remembered:

Harris was a very good talker, witty, perceptive, and genial, with a hearty laugh of the haw-haw sort. He had the gift of seeming to take seriously the perhaps somewhat asinine comments of a much younger person...

Though Jack was now a well-liked member of the sci-fi circle, he still maintained a slight distance. Grace was never a part of this convivial drinking club. They had been together almost 20 years, but still only a very select number of people, such as Viv and Biff, knew about their relationship. At the Penn Club, she was known as Jack's "great friend" – even there not everyone knew they were a couple.

With the sci-fi crowd, he was reticent about his private life. Most of them simply assumed he didn't have one. They were never invited to his room, though Bill Temple once dropped in on him at the Penn Club on a miserable February evening when the pub was empty. At the time, he had known Jack for more than 20 years. He wrote in his diary: "Settled in his room for over 1½ hours, jawing & drinking his brandy & looking at his books. One bed sitter, with a small desk at the window, angle lamp, 2 armchairs, bed against the wall, lav 2 floors down & miles away. So this is his life. I enjoyed the jaw – but I don't know if John did. But he was friendly."[4]

Many years after Jack died, he wrote: "We used to part late at night – often midnight – he to his lonely womb, where everything was taken care of for him, at the Penn Club – me to my suburban home and family. Even then the contrast struck me. He had so few possessions."[5]

The science fiction crowd liked and admired him – after all, he was easy to like – but they didn't really know him, whether they realised it or not. They were permitted to know him only in part. Jack had placed them in a sealed compartment, just as he had sealed off Grace.

This didn't mean they meant nothing to him. Jack may have kept the White Horse crowd at a distance, but they were still a great source of support. Their respect and recognition gave him a confidence and creative freedom that he had never had before. Their conversation was a lighthearted sharing of ideas that benefitted them all.

His writing at this time is notable for its enormous variety of styles and subjects. His enjoyment in playing with the short story form is clear.

Jack's strong heroines are very much to the fore. "The Eternal Eve" (*Amazing Stories*, 1950) opens with one of the last women left alive shooting her would-be rapist. "Survival" (*No Place Like Earth*, 1952, a collection edited by John Carnell) is the gruesome tale of a pregnant girl on a stranded spaceship, determined to outlive the men. "Dumb Martian" (*Galaxy*, 1952) relates the cold-blooded revenge of a beaten wife (see Chapter Twelve for more about this groundbreaking story).

Then there are the comedies. The enterprising future tour operator "Pawley's Peepholes" (*Science-Fantasy*, 1951), projects his clients back in time to laugh at the quaint ways and ridiculous fashions of the 20th century, to the dismay of the locals.

In "Chinese Puzzle" (*Fantasy*, 1953), an Imperial dragon hatches from a souvenir egg sent by a soldier to his Welsh valley home, causing consternation to the local Communists. As the leader of the trade union asks:[6] "What is it that the free people of China will be saying of Llynllawn when they hear of this, I am asking? What is it Mao Tse Tung, glorious leader of the heroic Chinese people in their magnificent fight for peace, will be thinking of South Wales and this imperialist dragon?" The Welsh accent came from his BBC friend Howell Davies, but the politics came from the Penn Club's own "excessively fatheaded Communists".

He wrote hard sci-fi: "And the Walls Came Tumbling Down" (*Startling Stories*, 1951) imagines silicon-based aliens landing in a desert and happily gorging before being destroyed by soundwaves. "Pillar to Post" (*Galaxy*, 1951) is a time-travel fantasy to the distant future of humanity where life is virtually infinite, but births are rare. He still enjoyed writing horror such as "Close Behind Him" (*Fantastic*, January 1953).

Some are simply uncategorisable. What to make of the physicist hero of "Confidence Trick" (*Fantastic*, July/August 1953) who is killed in an Underground crash, then laughs hell out of existence and returns to life to shake the foundations of the Bank of England?

He also published the first of a series of time-travel romances. He had experimented with the idea in the 1930s with "The Man From Beyond". In this unpublished story, the hero returned in time to put right a mistake, by marrying the woman he had loved and lost. It failed to sell, but under the Wyndham name, his whimsical stories were snapped up.

The utterly charming and self-centred heroine of "Chronoclasm", Octavia, has no hesitation in ordering the future of mankind to her personal satisfaction (*Star Science Fiction Stories*, 1953, edited by Fred Pohl). Having stolen a time machine in order to marry her great-great-great uncle, she then sees to it that he will make them both rich:[7]

"All you have to do is get some advanced radio and electronics books, and I'll show you what to invent."

"You'll? Oh, I see. But do you think that would be quite ethical?" I asked doubtfully.

"I don't see why not. After all the things have got to be invented by somebody, or I couldn't have learnt about them at school, could I?"

"Chronoclasm" is pure fun, the flirtiest froth. Octavia is the fantasy of every shy young man: the girl who simply shows up and announces that she is there to fall in love with him, no tricky courtship needed. The resonances of the time-travel/alternate reality romance would deepen as the author got older, through "Opposite Numbers" to "Random Quest" and "A Stitch in Time".

"Random Quest" (in the collection *Consider Her Ways and Others*, 1956) has been filmed three times, twice for television and once for cinema. The hero, thrown into an alternate reality by a laboratory accident, falls in love, but is pulled back to our plane. Back home, he is ruthlessly intent on finding his bride in this reality. It's a satisfying love story with an ending that is happy for everyone, not just the reunited couple.

His next collection, *The Seeds of Time*, 1961, played with more of these paradoxes. It was named for Banquo's challenge to the witches (Macbeth, Act 1, Scene 3): "If you can look into the seeds of time, And say which grain will grow and which will not, Speak then to me, who neither beg nor fear Your favours nor your hate."

One of these stories, "A Stitch in Time" has never been filmed but pondered more interesting anomalies, questioning whether life itself is random or patterned. A scientist guarantees his own existence when he accidentally pulls his mother's young suitor forward through time. But it is the scientist's mother who really understands the implications, whilst knowing nothing of the theory of multi-dimensions.

As she sits in old age, dreaming in the sunshine, she reflects:[8] "How foolish they all were nowadays – trying to tidy everything up, make life secure, while behind, back in everyone's past, stretched the chance-studded line of women who had said 'yes' or 'no', as the fancy took them . . ."

References

1   *Fantasy Review* 3(13), p.4. Unusually, there is no byline. Available at https://efanzines.com/FR/fr13.htm

2   Phil Harbottle (2010), "Fandom and the Post War Boom", *Relapse* 17, p.8. Available at http://efanzines.com/Prolapse/Relapse17.pdf

3   E F Bleiler (1984) "Luncheon with Wyndham", *Extrapolation* 12(4) p.314-317. It is viewable at https://archive.org/stream/Extrapolation_v25n04_1984-Winter/Extrapolation_v25n04_1984-Winter_djvu.txt

4   Joe Patrizio (2010) "Extracts from Bill Temple's Diaries 1955-66", *Relapse* 18, p.20. Available at https://efanzines.com/Prolapse/Relapse18.pdf

5   William Temple's letter to Spanish researcher Angel-Luis Pujante, 22 March 1971, held in the University of Liverpool archive. Bill Temple makes a couple of mistakes in this letter, including referring to Jack as a 100% true blue Tory. Presumably he was misled by Jack's public school background, but it highlights the distance Jack kept between himself and the sci-fi crowd.

6   *Jizzle*, Dennis Dobson, 1954 first edition, p.71.

7   Penguin, 1972 edition, p.25.

8   Penguin, 1976 edition, p.118.

11

Aliens Among Us

Thanks to his unchanged habits – still living in the Penn Club and drinking at the same pubs – Jack was financially secure, but he wasn't quite as wealthy as this surge of publications suggests. He had difficulties accessing money earned abroad due to post-war currency restrictions. Fred Pohl also failed to pass on some of his US revenue – he still owed Jack thousands of dollars ten years after he was no longer his agent.

Fred was a groundbreaking science fiction writer, but an erratic businessman. He had only become an agent to support his friend, and, after his death, his friend's widow. He also had a tumultuous personal life. Soon after the sale of *The Day of the Triffids*, his third wife, writer and editor Judith Merril, divorced him. He was granted joint custody of their one-year-old daughter, but Judith left the state. Fred chased after them. In his letters to Jack, he described how her new boyfriend threatened him with a gun and they ended up grappling on the floor. The following court cases cost him many thousands of dollars, and for a while his assets were frozen.[1]

He had too many financial problems to pay Jack, who allowed the matter to slide. Although some of Fred's other clients deserted him, Jack stuck with him. He refused to respond to offers from other agents. Fred remarried within a year and soon had a son, but the child lived only a few days.

Through these difficulties, Jack continued to send long, affectionate letters, though sometimes he had to wait many weeks for an answer. Fred's belief in Jack's abilities and his success in placing his work was important to Jack as he struggled in February 1953 with the next full length novel:[2]

I did hope to have the full length thing finished well before this, but it drags on, and I don't dare to put it aside. And, boy, does it drag on. My impression of it now is that it has no plot, no story, no suspense, no action, hangs over me like a bloody doom, and reads like a geography book. But I still go on staring grimly at the paper, trying to have done with it. A fortnight, maybe three weeks more, I think. Then type it. After that, with a woof of relief I'll try to do some stories.

Three weeks later he wrote:

Hope also to be sending new book this week THE KRAK-EN AWAKES. Am filled with deep dismay about the whole thing. It practically falls over backwards in the attempt not to be too S.F. for general public, ditto to be unpulpish. About the only thing in its favour is that there does seem to be some interest in the sea lately. Yours as ever, John.[3]

Fred received it warmly: "I like it, John; I like it very well. I do have some reservations, but it's a lovely literate piece, not at all too light-weight to my taste, and I think it's going to make a good book". Most importantly, he sold it promptly to Ballantine Books.

The story concerns a mysterious arrival of fireballs which fall into the deepest parts of the ocean. The icecaps start to melt, and sea levels rise. The aliens who came in the fireballs are never seen and it is not clear what their purpose is. The editor Stanley Kauffman wanted him to describe these mysterious creatures of the deeps and give them a clear motive. Despite repeated urgings, Jack found the confidence to resist:

Now, as I see it, in the usual interplanetary invasion, the invaders are anthropomorphic. Their weapons are superior, and they may be harder to kill, and so on, but their motives, intentions, habits of thought, ways of achieving their ends, the nature of them, are all quite comprehensible, so everybody can meet them on familiar ground, know what's what, how to attack, how to defend, etc, because the invaders are, in fact, the same old human animal with the same old motives just dressed up a bit.

Now the idea here was to get a menace that was alien . . .

So the invaders (if they are invaders) don't follow the conventional pattern expected of interplanetary wars . . . so much so that nobody is even quite certain whether there is an interplanetary war going on, or not. So far from fighting them in the regular way, people can't even reach the things to find out what they really are, let alone get into touch with them to find out hows and whys. They are up against something which is neither approachable nor fully comprehensible, and it has them stumped . . .

This purports to be a story of a mystery rather than that of an interplanetary war, of a menace that went on being successful largely because no one could get a clear idea of its objectives, or what it was up to, or anything much except that it was definitely inimical.[4]

This novel cemented the reputation of John Wyndham and led to more media interest. Jack had avoided personal publicity during the launch of *The Day of the Triffids*. The scars of the humiliating publicity after his parents' separation may have been behind this. He was also aware that his personal life wouldn't bear scrutiny. He couldn't honestly answer even routine questions about his relationships, which led to speculation about thwarted love affairs.

One interviewer asked why he had never married. This was a common euphemism for: "Are you gay?" He replied: "I met the right person twice, but on each occasion, she met a righter person." Given the content of his hundreds of love letters and poems to Grace, this was obviously an evasion, but an unavoidable one given that she would lose her job and reputation if he told the truth.[5]

He was so averse to the limelight that he became known as "the invisible man of science fiction". Fred insisted he at least provide a picture in preparation for the next launch. Jack replied: [6]

Even more than having my hair cut, I hate having my photograph taken. I've been dodging it for years – the photograph, not the haircut. Luckily, I found a self-taken 14 year-old one for use here. However, I've seen this looming, so I'll try to force myself into a Photomaton or something and select the least impossible. Don't you personally think that exhibition of the author's mug is a publicity aberration? I'm sure that it deters more than it invites – the only two exceptions that come to mind being Rupert Brooke and G.B.S [George Bernard Shaw]. However, since we live in a world of advertisers' aberrations, I will conform.

This self-taken picture of a 35-year-old Jack, one eyebrow quizzically raised, would be used on the back of a million Penguins, the defining image of John Wyndham.

Fred wound up his agency shortly after publication of *The Kraken Wakes* to concentrate on his own writing. He went on to have two more children and write many more books. He and Jack remained friends, with Fred making periodic attempts to pay off his debt. He finally managed to in 1966.[7]

Jack's next creative leap came in the mirror-image novels of *The Chrysalids* (1955) and *The Midwich Cuckoos* (1957). They are a pair of morality plays, taking the same situation and replaying it from alternate perspectives. In each case, a group of children with psychic abilities are a threat to mankind. The writing is so subtle, and the plotting so engrossing, that the reader hardly notices as they are manipulated into rooting for the most successful murderers.

They both deal with the themes which had obsessed Jack for years: evolution, and the hive mind, the evolutionary advantage of insects' ability to think and act as a group. They return to the character he had experimented with before: the 'stranger child', the alien, misfit outsider with whom Jack clearly identified.[8]

The first of Wyndham's uncanny children appeared in an unpublished short story from 1931, featuring a little girl, Priscilla, who insists she can see a fairy, Tissifny[9]. Her mother identifies it as the Greek fury Tisiphone, while her father is angry that his wife has been stuffing the child's head with nonsense. He is determined to put a stop to it, but Tisiphone/Priscilla has a terrible revenge, setting a snare on the stairs which sends the father falling to his death.

It's an idea which prefigures by decades Ray Bradbury's haunting short story "The Veldt", in which the children also punish their parents for trying to drag them away from their fantasy world.

The children of *The Chrysalids* are also alienated from their families. They are evolved psychics, a group of genetic mutations scattered amongst a farming community in a Canada of the distant future. It is one of the first post-nuclear dystopias, set many generations after a nuclear war that is barely remembered as 'Tribulation'. Disastrous genetic changes brought about by man was another of Jack's obsessions, but he was very conscious of what his readers would accept.

In his only television interview, he explained the limits that fantasy writers must not transgress if their work was to be accepted:[10]

> What one starts with is the theme and then one works it out to the logical conclusion as far as possible. There is an upward and a lower limit.
>
> The upper limit of sheer invention is really what is acceptable in the circumstances to the public you are hoping to please and whose attention you are hoping to keep. Someone once said that the heart of fantasy is the willing suspension of disbelief. You must not go beyond a certain barrier, if you can find it, in which that willing suspension is shattered. For instance, your English reader does not care for the idea of spaceships, I don't know why. Your American reader loves spaceships.
>
> In the downward limit some of the logical outcomes are not acceptable. In *The Chrysalids* you have a world that has been devastated by atomic bombs and there are a lot of mutations resulting. Now most mutations would naturally be pretty unpleasant but one doesn't want to follow that along, it would swamp the whole story. So one minimises, one leaves out the most unpleasant ones or even tasteless ones. There was in the original a man whose hat was knocked off and he was seen to have a third eye in the top of his head. There's no reason why he shouldn't have a third eye but it just has an unpleasant taste. On the whole the story seemed pleasanter without it.

The details of *The Chrysalids* may be within the limits of what the reading public will accept, but the theme itself is devastating. The population has taken refuge in a fundamentalist Christianity which insists only perfect humans are in the image of God. Narrator David Strorm and his little group of "think-togethers" half-know they do not conform to this image. As they grow they come to understand the penalty of not belonging. "Watch Thou For The Mutant!" proclaims the wooden panel on the back wall of the farmhouse kitchen where David grows up.

He slowly understands more about the dangerous world he inhabits, only half-hidden behind the security of his father's prosperous farm. To be different is to be destroyed. Mutant animals are destroyed with knife and fire. Neither is there mercy for children who are not in the image of God. First, the girls (but not the boys) are sterilised. As in changeling myths, they must not be directly killed, but they can be mutilated or exposed to die. In a nod to the Nazis, the "Purity of the Race" must come before all loyalties, whether friends or family.

David and his friends manage to escape notice for years, but at the cost of constant fear of exposure. It's a vigilance clearly drawn from his own experience of being a well-camouflaged outsider in boarding schools and institutions:[11]

> I don't suppose that there was a single one of us who had not at some time made a slip or two and brought upon himself, or herself, an odd, suspicious look. A few of these looks had been warnings enough to each; it was such looks, not comprehended, but clear enough as signs of disapproval just below the verge of suspicion, that had kept us out of trouble. But now . . . the feeling of a threat was strengthened.

They cannot protect themselves, nor even their youngest member, Petra. They can expect no mercy from their righteous, orthodox families. The only way to survive is by leaving them.

The oppressive religious setting, the brutal punishment of transgressing women and the consequences of environmental damage prefigure Margaret Atwood's *The Handmaid's Tale*. Jack, and his narrator David, see how religion is used to control women:[12]

> A series of memories cut off what my eyes were seeing – my Aunt Harriet's face in the water, her hair gently waving in the current; poor Anne, a limp figure hanging from a beam; Sally, wringing her hands in anguish for Katherine, and in terror for herself; Sophie, degraded to a savage, sliding in the dust, with an arrow in her neck . . . Any of those might have been a picture of Petra's future . . .

Throughout the book, all sympathy lies with the persecuted minority. The sense of them as an oppressed, but rising generation is so strong that rockers Jefferson Airplane used quotes from the book as lyrics: ""In loyalty to their kind / they cannot tolerate our minds. / In loyalty to our kind / we cannot tolerate their obstruction"".

But these lines, from the end of the book, show how the oppressed can themselves become the oppressors. As the book progresses, David and his little band shift their views, bringing the reader with them.

From considering themselves only different, they begin to see themselves as superior. Their parents are no longer to be feared, but to be written off as an evolutionary dead end. Early on, David is unwilling to kill a young neighbour to protect his mutant friend. By the final pages, he is prepared to fight his own father; then he witnesses and accepts the wholesale slaughter of his relatives and countrymen as inevitable.

Critic Rowland Wymer has described this as Wyndham's foretelling of the movement through the 60s and 70s by which "oppressed groups move from a rhetoric of equal rights grounded in a notion of common humanity towards a more militant language of inherent different and superiority – from civil rights to Black Power, from liberal feminism to radical lesbian separatism".

By the end, there is the hint of something even darker. Petra, the youngest, is an archetype of the innocent young girl who must be saved. David's rescue of Petra echoes Bill's rescue of Susan in *The Day of the Triffids*.

Yet Petra is no helpless victim. She is stronger than the rest. She can project thoughts so powerfully as to hurt others. She can hear not just the thoughts others send her, but the thoughts in the hidden recesses of their minds. Have the other psychics helped David save a child, or have they taken control of a weapon? The future lies with Petra. What kind of future will it be?[13]

The ending of *The Chrysalids* outwardly celebrates the realisation of David's dream, and the ascendance of a new kind, but it is ambivalent. It points towards the alternate view, by the dominant, older species, to be found in *The Midwich Cuckoos*.

It was written two years later, just as the press was wringing their hands over the new teenage gangs of teddy boys and the appalling influence of rock'n'roll.[14] Historian Dominic Sandbrook has pointed out that this generation was also physically different; taller, heavier and maturing earlier than before. This may be why *The Midwich Cuckoos'* fast-growing, violent aliens resonated with the readers as they did.[15] Again, John Wyndham was in tune with the zeitgeist.

Like Arthur C Clarke in *Childhood's End*, Wyndham was one of the earliest science fiction authors to see children as the true aliens amongst us. It's a theme that was developed by many others in the 1960s as the new generation veered further and further from the pre-war norms.

The aftermath of the war is present in the book from the start. The narrator and his friend in military intelligence are former soldiers. Like Jack and many of his readers, they have taken active part in the fight against fascism. They have travelled through the aftermath of genocide: "the beaches, the Ardennes, the Reichswald, and the Rhine": Jack's war experiences. They may have seen the concentration camps – they certainly know of them, as Jack was told of them in Germany by a friend who had been to one. Now they have triumphed, they can relax and swap reminiscences in the peace of an English country pub.

It's here, in sleepy Midwich, that the alien threat has arrived. Overnight, the whole village falls into an unbreakable trance, during which the women are impregnated by aliens. The children are born apparently normal but with strange, golden eyes. They develop rapidly, swiftly overtaking their teachers. When threatened, they can use their psychic powers to force their assailants to fight each other, or even kill themselves. In *The Chrysalids*, we were on the side of the minority. Now, the minority is the invading enemy.

Critic Adam Roberts has described how through the narrator – a war hero – Wyndham manipulates the reader into the position of a concentration camp guard.[16] The kindly philosopher Zellaby sums it up: "It is our duty to our race and our culture to liquidate the Children." Armed with a jar of sweets and a case of high explosives, he kills them all.

The stranger children operate on the readers' sensibilities on many levels. One of Jack's great strengths was to place huge catastrophes in a local setting. The Children are specific to a place and time: the aftermath of the war when the Nazis' elimination of whole cultures was fresh in the mind. They are also part of Jack's longstanding belief about how evolution will ultimately leave us all behind, no matter how we fight, even against our own children. But these stranger children are also part of a far older tradition: the changeling.

Changelings were children of fairies or elves left in place of a stolen human child, to be brought up by the unwitting human parents. They physically look like human children, but biologically they are not. Like the Midwich children, they are often intellectually far in advance of their age and even their 'parents', hungry for knowledge and impatient with the routines of childhood. They can be tricked into revealing their true nature by being presented with something astonishing in order to excite their intelligence[17] – exactly as Zellaby reveals the children's psychic powers by presenting them with a Chinese puzzle box.

Karen Renner[18] describes changelings in her work on evil children in popular imagination. Changelings have never been children and never will be. More importantly, they lack the key qualities of a child: innocence and vulnerability. As she says:

> Changelings are disturbing because they directly confront our assumptions about children as merely that – assumptions. Often, changelings hide behind the stereotypes we have of children and control us from this command position. More disturbing, perhaps, is the changeling who no longer feels the need to pretend and reveals that the relationship between adult and child is actually an elaborate dance, which the child has been leading all along . . .
>
> Any child who defaces the image of The Child by refusing to abide by its commandments is too threatening and must be exiled from the realm of childhood . . . And because changelings really are monsters, we have a far easier time justifying our bloody retaliation against them.

This fits with the arc of *The Midwich Cuckoos* narrative, in which the children set the parameters for their relationships with the adults, working every situation to their own advantage. They then reveal their real selves, speaking as a single composite entity, with far greater understanding of the world and their place in it than the adults. And so they invite their terrible fate at the hands of their 'first teacher', Zellaby.

As dehumanised changelings, stranger children throughout Wyndham's fiction can be brutally punished, because they are not 'real' children. But because they are not 'real' children, they can also turn on their parents without remorse.[19]

The Midwich Cuckoos may have carried another barbed message. The alien embryos were implanted in the unconscious host mothers, in several cases, in virgins. They are a negative portrayal of the mystery of the virgin birth. These superior beings aim to destroy humankind rather than lift it up to immortality. This may have come from anger at what was, for Jack, a disturbing event.

In 1948, Biff Barker's wife Eileen had converted to Catholicism. Her daughter Tess later wrote how grieved and upset Jack was when he was told at Easter. For Jack, the organised church had long been the enemy: a brake on mankind's progress and a wellspring of superstition and prejudice with particularly damaging consequences for women. Tess wrote:[20]

> There was earnest argument and persuasions on both sides, and then painful exchange of letters. Since these did not deflect my mother, Jack took the rigid-disapproval stance; and declared that he so disapproved that he could no longer maintain the same friendly relationship with the family.
>
> My father was deeply distressed – as we all were. Jack stayed with the Sykes up at the Red House for the week of the Old Bedalian Meeting that summer. We missed him acutely. He did not come down to Row Cottage. I think my father walked up to visit him at the Sykes.

This hurtful separation continued for several months. For the Barker family, Christmas without Jack was an unhappy, awkward occasion. In the evening, Biff and Jean went to the pub, while Tess followed her mother to church.

Finally, Biff told Eileen that he could not broker a peace between them; it was up to her to make amends. She wrote to him and Jack responded. The breach was repaired, but worse was to come. Tess, the younger daughter, also became a Catholic. In 1956, aged only 23, she became a cloistered nun in a strictly enclosed order. To Jack, it was as if she had committed suicide.

He was both furious and terribly upset. Grace's diaries record conversations about Eileen's "wickedness" which had invited this catastrophe. Jack developed a series of unshakeable colds and eye infections that lasted several months.[21]

The two girls, Jean and Tess, were named as the beneficiaries in his will after the deaths of Grace and Viv. Tess's decision would mean that the Roman Catholic Church would ultimately inherit half his literary estate. He altered his will to skip the generation and leave his estate to the grandchildren. Jean had already married and would go on to have three children.

It may have been Tess's decision to become a nun that provoked Jack to create his mockery of the virgin birth with its ruthless offspring a year later.

The book was an instant hit. It went into reprints within weeks. It was filmed as *Village of the Damned*, one of MGM's most successful horrors and still a cult classic.[22]

MGM was in a bad way when they bought the rights to *The Midwich Cuckoos*. They lost money with a string of poor films in the fifties, with the notable exception of *Forbidden Planet*. This success prompted them to buy more science fiction scripts but they made a serious error with Sam Youd's *Death of Grass* (also known as *No Blade of Grass*). They made a hasty decision believing Columbia was also interested and paid $80,000. It was only later they realised the book was unusable because of the strictures of the Motion Picture Code – in one scene, a mother and daughter are gang-raped as starvation causes societal breakdown.

When a carbon copy of the unpublished manuscript of *The Midwich Cuckoos* found its way to MGM's reading department, they quickly offered £3,000. Jack accepted, thinking it unfilmable due to the multiple clones. The project then languished for two years whilst scripts were written and discarded. Major changes were to reduce the number of 'cuckoos' from 61 to 12, to combine some of the adult characters and to shorten the timespan so the 'cuckoos' were still physically pre-adolescent when they embark on their murderous spree. They were also

Italian poster (top) and Belgian poster (bottom) for *Village of the Damned*. The English strapline was "Beware the stare that will paralyse the will of the world".

given the ability to read human minds as well as each other's. Fearing that Americans wouldn't understand the reference to cuckoos, the title was changed to *Village of the Damned*.

Jack had no part in these changes. He was busy publishing the book version and negotiating with several companies about the *Triffids* film. The first Jack knew about it going ahead was when an article in *The Times* reported villagers' complaints about filming disrupting their lives.

MGM's problematic finances meant it was a low-budget production. About a quarter of the budget went to Jack's old schoolfriend George Sanders in the lead as Zellaby – he received £20,500. Money was so tight that the children were told to dye their hair as it was cheaper than wigs. This left two dark-haired children with orange hair and frantic mothers. The firm relented and fitted them all with the platinum wigs that would be such a feature of the film.

Special effects were kept to a minimum. Overlays were used in post-production to create glowing eyes when the children used their psychic powers on their victims, but this was judged so terrifying that it was removed for the British version. Only the Americans saw the full horror.

The changes were driven by a lack of funds, but in fact the simplicity of the production suited the subject. It underlined the ordinariness of the village and villagers, making the unearthly children yet more eerie. It's exactly this contrast that makes the book so chilling.

Jack was delighted with the result. He sent a letter of congratulation to the lead boy Martin Stephens, aged 11, with a signed copy of the book. Lead girl June Cowell, also 11, received a locket with her face engraved inside with golden eyes.

Jack wrote to Martin: "I did not really believe the story would film – until I saw it. So it was a complete surprise to find how cleverly they had managed it. And a very great part of the pleasantness of that surprise was your work. I do congratulate you, and I do thank you."

MGM went to town with the marketing and the film was a worldwide hit. But whilst the audience treated the children as monsters, Jack himself didn't consider them evil.

In his sole television interview just after the film opened in 1960[23], he repeatedly contradicted the interviewer Derek Hart: "I wouldn't say they are all evil. You know *The Midwich Cuckoos* children look very evil in the film but they aren't so evil in the original story."

To him, the Midwich Cuckoos, like the Chrysalid telepaths and the monsters of the deeps, were just another species in the bloody struggle for survival. They might be the enemy, but he still had sympathy with them.

The film of *The Day of the Triffids*, released three years later, has worn less well. The state of the art special effects have dated badly, as has the dramatic music. It was envisaged as a thriller, but the action sequences seem slow and repetitive to modern eyes, while the script is very light. The pathos of the moment when a teenage girl offers herself to Bill Masen in exchange for help is bowdlerised. But the cast, led by Howard Keel, are solid. The societal breakdown still gives a shiver, especially when a group of blind girls are forced to dance by drunks, before they are all overpowered by triffids.

The plot was changed significantly. The triffids now come to earth with the same meteors that cause blindness: thus, all the political resonance is lost. In the book, the action unfolds over years but as with *Village of the Damned*, the film speeds it up for dramatic effect (a later *Triffids*-inspired film in 2002, *28 Days Later*, also accelerated the plot).

Bill Masen becomes an American navy officer, while the marine biologist who will discover the secrets of the triffids is trapped on a lighthouse with his wife. Bill rescues little Susan and speeds across the channel into France and Spain, rather than into the English countryside. Josella disappears entirely. Bill's love interest is the far more properly behaved Miss Durrant, now a French chateau owner who has taken her villagers into her protection.

The triffids turn out to dissolve in seawater, and mankind is saved. Heaven only knows what Jack made of the final sequence, in which Bill Masen, Susan and Miss Durrant join a procession into church to give thanks for their deliverance.

The making was difficult for director Steve Sekely, a Hungarian who had fled fascism for the USA. Production was cut short in order to have more time and money for special effects. He had to leave part of the production in the charge of a colleague handling a 'second

unit', a separate crew shooting some sequences without the main cast.

Jack was politely enthusiastic about the film in his letter to Sekely but he did query the addition of the lighthouse scenes. Sekely replied:[24]

> To answer your very appropriate question - why it was necessary to 'write in the lighthouse sequences' – I will try to tell it to you (but very confidentially). Our ambitious friend wanted to direct, or at least solely supervise a 'second unit' – a sequence which showed that the Triffids – as the Pied Piper did with the rats at Hamelin – are marched into the sea.
>
> When we saw what he did – in my absence – we realised that it was so terrible that it had to be almost entirely eliminated from the picture. The 'next best' solution was the lighthouse sequence because a repeat of the whole second unit was forbidding in price and in consumed time.
>
> Needless to say, that in some of the highbrow critics in the US I am blamed for the 'inconsistencies' of the screenplay – and also for some technical faults. But, 'that's life' as a director. Anyhow, it seems we have a success on hand, which won't hurt any of us.

Sekely was happy with the reviews, and Jack told his agent Laurence Pollinger that, though it was not what it might have been, it was a lot better than he had feared: "Technically it is often very clever indeed".[25] But some of Jack's hardcore fans were horrified. One wrote to him: "the title was all that remained of the book . . . this is a formal protest that I wish to register against the film."[26]

Jack enjoyed getting letters from fans, and often answered them, sometimes at great length. He was delighted to hear from a Californian couple who had decided to name their daughter Ferrelyn after a *Midwich Cuckoos* character. He would sometimes send books to fans who couldn't get a particular collection in Britain, and was happy to answer long letters about why his characters had made their decisions.

Amongst his contemporaries, Jack had become an elder statesman of the science fiction world, though he remained shy amongst all but his closest friends. One young publisher's assistant, Ron Hall, remembered the first time he met him in the Globe Inn, in the late 1950s. The gang had decamped from the White Horse when the landlord moved.[27]

At the bar three blokes were standing, drinking bottled beer. I ordered a mild and bitter and stood near them with my back to the bar, surveying the somewhat hectic goings on. After a while one of the chaps spoke to me, asking if I were new to the Globe. I explained my situation and that I had been feverishly reading science fiction in order to do reasonably well at picking out new authors. He introduced himself and the others, but, as usual with me I didn't really catch the names.

We talked about what I had been reading. I said that I had been particularly impressed by a writer called John Wyndham. There was a stiffening of attitudes and some strange smiles. The elder of the three seemed to somehow shrink away. I said "Good heavens, you're not John Wyndham?" He nodded. "I thought I caught your name was Bates, or something." "He writes under a penname," said Sam Youd, "he's so ashamed of the stuff he turns out." And so started a life-time friendship with John Burke, Sam Youd (John Christopher) and John Beynon Harris.

I started to meet John H. once a week or so in the afternoon at an Italian restaurant-cum-cafe. He was an intensely shy, I might almost say timid, man, but gradually we became more relaxed and had some wonderful chats.

Jack had found a role as an avuncular figure, well-liked and respected. When the first World Science Fiction Convention to be held in Europe came to London in 1957, Jack was elected president of the committee.

It was a memorable occasion, spanning six days and including a formal luncheon for the presentation of the Hugo Awards. Jack presented Ted Carnell with an award when *New Worlds* won best British professional magazine.[28]

In the evening, Ted gravely announced that the convention gavel had been stolen. This was the cue for a fake gun battle by crime fighters "The Goon Defective Agency". The night went on with a fancy dress ball: aliens and astronauts danced to a jazz band. Jazz musicians are used to being the most off-rail people at any party, but one leaned over and said in tones of wonder "Hey dad, these people are just like us!"

The next day, Cheltenham fans held a ceremony of the Order of St Fantony. Dressed in medieval robes, they initiated fans with glasses of pure Polish spirit under threat of an executioner's axe.

The convention finished with a private event organised by the SF Luncheon Club, which then consisted of John Wyndham, Frank Cooper, Ken Chapman and Les Flood. This was the occasion of the presentation of the final International Fantasy Award to J R R Tolkein. He had just completed *The Lord of the Rings* trilogy. He was rather bemused by the inappropriate prize: a spaceship on a plinth incorporating a cigarette lighter.

There are several galleries of pictures online, but it's notable how little the president of the affair features. Jack is there handing out prizes at the luncheon, and introducing the guest of honour, John W Campbell, but he seems to be missing from the fun. He is not amongst the dancers at the ball, or sitting with the drinkers and merrymakers. He doesn't feature in anecdotes or memories.

He is briefly evident when required to take part in proceedings, then melts away, not even into the background, but into invisibility.

Nor is Grace present. It was by no means an all-male affair: many women attended as fans or guests of fans. The American editor John W Campbell brought his wife Peggy, Sam Moskowitz brought his wife Dr Christine Haydock, but Jack did not bring Grace.

Jack was not easy with his new fame. He still wanted to live a private life. He resisted overtures by biographers, and publishers had to persuade him into interviews at the launch of every book.

And the more John Wyndham became a name and a public property, the more his latest identity became a straitjacket. Publishers didn't just want another story, they wanted a "John Wyndham" novel.

After finishing *The Midwich Cuckoos* in 1957, the year of the Convention, Jack wanted to return to hard science fiction – space rockets and off-world colonies. Russian sputniks had been launched, space travel was becoming closer and closer to a reality. Perhaps his success had helped him return to some of the optimism of his youth. His new stories were of a galactic dynasty, the Troons, spreading out across space over centuries, all inspired in their travels by Rupert Brooke's poem "The Jolly Company".[29]

The stars, a jolly company,
   I envied, straying late and lonely;
And cried upon their revelry:
   "O white companionship! You only
In love, in faith unbroken dwell,
Friends radiant and inseparable!"

Light-heart and glad they seemed to me
   And merry comrades (even so
God out of Heaven may laugh to see
   The happy crowds; and never know
That in his lone obscure distress
Each walketh in a wilderness).

But I, remembering, pitied well
   And loved them, who, with lonely light,
In empty infinite spaces dwell,
   Disconsolate. For, all the night,
I heard the thin gnat-voices cry,
Star to faint star, across the sky.

Written in 1908, Jack probably encountered it at school. After Brooke's death in 1915, his poems were widely read. It must have haunted him as a reflection of himself: looking up at the stars, imagining them as company, whilst spending his own life alone in a crowd. After a decade writing of earthbound disasters, Jack could still hear the thin gnat voices of the stars.

Ted Carnell published the Troon series in *New Worlds* in 1958. Unlike the stories of far-flung galaxies and distant futures that generally filled science fiction magazines, Jack's first instalment imagined the building of the first space station only 35 years ahead. In a guest editorial, he wrote:

> My own preference has been, and remains, for what I call the 'threshold-of-possibility' story. Many of the higher flights of fancy are fine, but still I find the most satisfactory to read . . .

are the kind which the reader finishes, saying to himself: 'Well, there's no reason why it shouldn't happen like that one day.'"[30]

But book publishers were reluctant to disappoint readers looking forward to an earthbound 'logical fantasy', Wyndham's trademark 'what if?' style of chaos and dystopia. The *New Worlds* readers might like to read about space exploration, but the book publishers didn't want to damage the valuable Wyndham brand. The result was one of the weirdest joint authorships in publishing history.

The Outward Urge, the Troon family collection, was published by Michael Joseph in 1959 under two names: John Wyndham and Jack's latest re-invention of himself, 'Lucas Parkes'. Once again, Jack was hiding behind a new alter ego. His compartmentalising had reached the point where it was necessary for his various selves to start formally collaborating with each other.

References

1   Letter from Fred Pohl to John Harris, 4 December 1953. All letters quoted in this section are in the University of Liverpool archive, Wyndham 11/5/5.

2   Letter to Fred Pohl, 22 January 1953.

3   Letter to Fred Pohl, 9 March 1953.

4   Letter to Stanley Kauffman of Ballantine Books, 21 May 1953.

5   John Barrows (1961) "Living Writers: John Wyndham," *John O'London's*, 2 March.

6   Letter to Fred Pohl, 6 December 1952.

7   Letter from Ted Carnell to Jack, 20 January 1966. Ted took over the organising of Fred's payments.

8   David Ketterer (2000) "A Part of the Family", *Learning from Other Worlds*, ed Patrick Parrinder, Liverpool University Press.

9   This unfinished manuscript is in the Liverpool archive. Ketterer, David (2000) "John Wyndham and 'the searing anguishes of childhood': From Fairy Story to Chocky", *Extrapolation* 41(2), p.87-103

10   *Tonight* programme, ibid, see note to Part 3, Chapter 1.

11   *The Chrysalids*, 1961 edition, p.32.

12   Ibid, p.197.

13   Rowland Wymer (1992) "How Safe is John Wyndham? A closer look at his work with Particular Reference to The Chrysalids", *Foundation*, Summer 1992, p.25.

14   Several writers have made this connection including Rowland, above; Colin Greenland (1983) *The Entropy Exhibition*, Routledge; David Pringle (1985) *Science Fiction: The Hundred Best Novels*, Xanadu.

15   Dominic Sandbrook (2015) *The Great British Dream Factory: The Strange History of Our National Imagination*, Allen Lane.

16   Adam Roberts (2006) *The History of Science Fiction*, Palgrave Macmillan, p.310-312.

17   Marte H. Hult (2003) "From the Supernatural to the Human Other: The Marginalized Storytellers of

Norske huldreeventyr og folkesagn", *Framing a National Narrative: The Legend Collections of Peter Christen Asbjornsen*, Wayne State University Press, p.119-140.

18   Karen Renner (2016) *Evil Children in the Popular Imagination*, Springer, p.153-159.

19   This was too bleak for some. When Thai author Kukrit Pramoj re-wrote the story as "Blackbirds at Bangpleng", later a blockbuster film, the alien children learn to cry and say "mother" and "father". This triumph for Buddhist values spelled the failure of their own mission.

20   Reminiscences of Sister Bede, now in the Liverpool archive, Wyndham 14/24.

21   Ketterer (2000) ibid.

22   Anthony McKay (2019) "Beware the Stare!" *Little Shoppe of Horrors*, no 42, p.16-74. This is the fullest account of the making of the film, including the quote from Jack's letter to Martin.

23   *Today* programme, ibid.

24   Letter from Steve Sekely, May 6, 1963.

25   Letter to Laurence Pollinger, 6 May 1963.

26   Letter from Michael Muller, 12 May 1963.

27   *Relapse*, Spring 2010, issue 17. Available at efanzines.com/Prolapse/Relapse17.pdf

28   A full account by fan historian Rob Hansen, with picture galleries, is available at http://www.fiawol.org.uk/FanStuff/THEN%20Archive/1957Worldcon/LonWorld.htm

29   Rupert Brooke, written November 1908, published in *Poems,* 1911.

30   John Wyndham (1958) Profile in *New Worlds*, April, p.2.

12

Wyndham's Women

By the mid-1950s, Jack could afford to relax a little. He was financially secure and his family were less of a drain. He had stopped drawing the allowance from his mother's remaining fortune on the sale of *The Day of the Triffids* in 1950.

His mother had died aged 84 in 1953 in Matlock. Grace's brief diary entry suggests this came as something of a relief: "Thoughtful letter from J about his mother's long and lonely life. A strange exultation death brings."[1]

Gertrude's remaining fortune could support Viv, whose short-lived literary career had stalled. He had written a science fiction novel and Jack did his best to find him a publisher, but without success. Viv and Lila left Derbyshire for Hythe, on the south coast. Mirroring Jack and Grace's relationship, they chose a house split into two flats and lived in one each.

If Jack and Grace had wanted to formalise their relationship, it would now have been very easy to do so. Money was no longer a problem. Nor had their relationship staled: he still wrote her Valentine and birthday poems embellished with lace and hearts. On one occasion they were apart on her birthday and he forgot to mention it in his letter to her. He wrote four pages to apologise:[2]

Darling,

Shaky sanity grows daily more infirm.

Q. Why did I sit down to write to my Sweetle the moment I got back?

A. Because it was important it should arrive on Tuesday.

Q. Why was it so important?

A. Because on that day she closes a sort of gap between us with an annual bound.

Q. Did you, I mean I, tell her that you, meaning I, hoped that this would occur happily many, many times?

A. Well, when I took pen in hand –

Q. Did you – er, I – or not?

A. Well –

Q. Did you not let your own mass of verbiage flourish like a lot of weeds and strangle the very thing you intended to say?

A. I got sort of carried away from the point.

Q. And never got back to it?

A I did say how glad I had been she had come and how I had enjoyed –

Q. That won't do. A birthday is a birthday. And another thing: did you ask her when you were there what she would like for a present?

A. Well, I was on the point of several times, but she's awfully difficult about that, you know. Sort of dodges.

Q. So do you. And after all this I hope she demands a thumping big birthday present as part compensation for neglect. That's fair, don't you think?

A. I don't like 'neglect'. It was more sort of being carried past the station, if you see what I mean.

Q. I don't. Birthdays are sort of black or white. No half measures about them. And I hope you will tell me that you are ashamed of yourself?

A. But the intention was –

Q. Is intention the same as execution?

A. Well, if you put it that way, I suppose –

Q. Then you are ashamed of yourself?

A. Er – yes.

Q. Then will you take your pen and write after me: 'Dear Miss Wilson – '?

A. Shouldn't it be 'Dear Grace' or possibly 'Sweetle'?

Q. Doesn't that depend on the generosity of her nature? It takes great width to be generous on such an occasion, but try if you like.

'Dear Sweetle, I do hope you have had a very happy birthday and will have many happy returns. With love from J.'

And repeat 500 times.

A. I'm not sure that she'd want 500 birthdays.

In the circumstances these particular birthdays are concurrent. Have you done that? NO? Well get on with it.

Dear Sweetle – h'm!

Darling Sweetle,

I did mean to. But now all I can say is I hope you did have a happy birthday, and you will have many, many happy returns. X500.

With all my love, My Sweet, J.

And, p.s. what is that birthday present to be?

Given this obvious affection, why was Miss Wilson not transformed into Mrs Harris?

Jack's views on marriage as an institution had not changed since his horror at Phyllis and Percy's wedding. He thought it, at best, unnecessary and unromantic, as Zellaby made clear on his daughter's engagement in *The Midwich Cuckoos*.[3]

Jack gave an even harsher view of marriage in the short story "Dumb Martian" (*Galaxy*, 1952).[4] It's less than 30 pages long but is one of his strongest narratives: a story of domestic abuse and brutal justice. The parallels between slave and wife are explicit. It's also a satire of the casual racism of the time. Anti-hero Duncan Weaver insists on calling his purchased wife a "dumb Mart", no matter how many

An illustration from "Dumb Martian", by Mac Clellan, in
Galaxy Science Fiction, July 1952

times he is shown proof of her intelligence.

Duncan is a middle-aged boor, mendacious and avaricious. On the cusp of retirement from service in space, he has little to show for his life so far. He accepts a five-year contract on the interplanetary equivalent of a remote one-man filling station to try and build up a nest egg. Warned that the loneliness can drive men crazy, he decides to buy a Martian girl, Lellie, from her unscrupulous parents. He then discovers anti-slavery regulations mean only a wife can come. Grudgingly, he pays for a marriage certificate, all the while totting up the mounting cost of his 'investment'.

For Duncan, the moment of her enslavement is just more proof of her idiocy: "I'd say it's a kind of acid test for dumbness when a girl doesn't know what goes on at her own wedding ceremony."

Her marriage to him does not in any way elevate her to a better status – marriage just legalises her slavery. As Duncan says: "She may be only a dumb Mart, but she's legally my wife: and what I say goes."

Thus Lellie is doubly enslaved, both as a wife and through her membership of the Martian race. She is transferred from daughter to wife without even understanding her own sale.

The story is told entirely from Duncan's point of view, in a style that would be revisited in Alice Sheldon's "Women that Men Don't See" two decades later. We are given few clues to Lellie's inner life. She is naturally expressionless and barely speaks, which irritates Duncan more and more as their confinement progresses. He's also annoyed by her ineptitude in using the cosmetics he has bought her, to make her look like "a real woman". He beats her for failing to live up to his idea of what a wife should be.

Lellie learns to read as the result of a lengthy visit by a scientist, who treats her with respect. At the centre of the story is the first moment Lellie voluntarily speaks: "Lellie lifted her eyes from the book she was reading to ask: 'What does "female emancipation" mean?'"

Now her awareness develops rapidly, and the stage is set for the final act: Lellie's cold-blooded revenge.

To Jack then, marriage was enslavement. But it was not only the ceremony and the legal status that irritated him. He believed the transformation of woman to wife, and in particular to mother, depressed her personality. He did not want to see the woman he loved transformed into a slave.

He expressed this in a poem, "Phyllis Released",[5] a damning view of one woman's "transmutation" from the active woman of wartime, gaily partying with drunken soldiers, but now "dwindled to a wife". The war is painted as her friend "Uncle Mars", but even frowning Hymen can't make her forget the fun she had, though now she must resist it.

> Sweet Phyllis now has lost her Uncle Mars
> To Morpheus, and on that age the bars
> Of Janus gates are shot. From tender bed
> The silver Mercury's forever sped;
> The khaki Corydons are melted in the mist
> And frowning Hymen warns her to resist,
> If not forget, those corybantic halls
> Those bacchic messes, and those messy falls
> When sinatraic voices thick with beer
> Poured scented honey in her thrilling ear,
> Those more (or less) polite tentivities
> On purple passion's pale peripheries.
>
> For Phyllis now those days and dates are gone.
> The washtub's steam bedews the tokalon,
> Uncurls the careful crest for all its clips
> And menaces those rosy finger tips.
> The shopping-bag awaits the busy arm.
> Now every puling cry is an alarm.
> The piddled pram is parked beneath the stair,
> And strings of napkins are her constant care.
>
> No longer set in panoply of strife
> Sweet Phyl's transmuted: dwindled to a wife.

Sweet Phyl wasn't the only one: through the 1950s, women's status was undergoing a reversal. The strong can-do attitude of Rosie the Riveter was no longer in vogue. Corsets were back as part of the New Look to emphasise narrow waists above circle skirts. This was the second time Jack had observed this kind of reactionism – the same thing had happened after the First World War. His irritation with women's failure to engage with the machinery that drove modern life had shown in "Stowaway to Mars" *(Planet Plane).*

It rose again in Coker's lecture in *The Day of the Triffids,* most of which was cut in the American version. Coker fixes a generator, but then castigates a girl who had been sitting in the dark. In a long argument, he points out that women were competent engineers during the war, but had fallen back on "appealing helplessness as a womanly virtue" afterwards.[6]

As the 1950s progressed, Jack became more frustrated with how women failed to shake off their chains, endlessly falling prey to advertising and tradition. In several short stories, he explored worlds in which women broke free.

A decade before the Women's Movement found its voice, Wyndham focussed on the problems of gender by creating the first female utopia. Or is it a dystopia?[7]

"Consider Her Ways" is unusual in Wyndham's fiction in that the narrator is a woman, a recently widowed young doctor, Jane. She has volunteered for trials of a narcotic drug believed by South American tribes to create mystical experiences. Under its influence, she wakes to find herself inhabiting the body of a grossly obese woman, mother of a dozen babies, in a hospital staffed by small but perfectly formed 'servitors' and Amazonian manual workers. There are only a few normally proportioned women, all doctors or academics.

At first, Jane assumes it is a hallucination, but discovers she has been flung forward in time into this all-female world, which was designed by female doctors and scientists after a plague wiped out all the men in Jane's own time. Through intensive research they discovered the means for single-sex reproduction. Remembering how grudgingly they themselves were allowed to study, they do not wish to bring back men and "re-enslave themselves". Instead, they decide to establish a female-only society, modelled on the ant's nest of the title. As the Bible says: "Go to the ant, thou sluggard, consider her ways".

This is much more than just a female world, it is a designed, engineered society, built upon female values with roles assigned at birth to minimise conflict. It is in some ways another example of the strengths of the hive mind that fascinated him, and which surfaces repeatedly in his work from triffids to children.

Jane, along with the typical 1950s reader, is at first horrified by this new world, with its relentless pink placidity and its hints of lesbianism in the sensuous massages delivered by the servitors to the mountainous mothers. Modern readers may wince at the concept of a female world lacking innovation. But this is far from being a straightforward tale of sexist horror.

At the story's heart is a debate between two women, Jane, the representative of the twentieth century, and Laura, a historian of the future who looks on Jane's world with a cold and judgemental eye. Jane has experienced and believes in romantic love. She cannot understand why these women deny themselves partnerships with men. Laura, looking back on a broad sweep of social history, believes Jane is fooling herself.[8]

She delivers a biting description of the women of Jane's time as "ruled by men . . . pets and parasites", exploited by commerce which required them as mass consumers, not producers, and sold a dream of romance. It's an astonishing diatribe, which wouldn't have been out of place decades later on Greenwich Common.

> Women must never for a moment be allowed to forget their sex and compete as equals . . . It would have been unpopular for manufacturers actually to issue an order 'back to the kitchen', but there were other ways. A profession without a difference, called 'housewife', could be invented. The kitchen could be glorified and made more expensive; it could be made to seem desirable, and it could be shown that the way to realize this heart's desire was through marriage. So the presses turned out, by the hundred thousand a week, journals which concentrated the attention of women ceaselessly and relentlessly upon selling themselves to some man in order that they might achieve some small, uneconomic unit of a home upon which money could be spent . . .
>
> The cinema most of all maintained the propaganda, persuading the main and important part of their audience, which was female, that nothing in life was worth achieving but dewy-eyed passivity in the strong arms of Romance.

Jane cannot believe it, claiming it a distorted view, and putting forward her own experience of marriage as evidence:

> How should you understand a love that colours the whole world? How it centres in your heart and reaches out from there to pervade your whole being, how it can affect everything you are, everything you touch, everything you hear . . . It can hurt dreadfully, I know, oh, I know, but it can run like sunlight in your veins . . . oh you don't understand, you don't know . . . you can't . . .

Laura argues love still exists between women, which is stronger and purer when there are no men to introduce jealousy, a feminist viewpoint that would become a rallying cry of the sisterhood in the 1970s: "Do you not begin to understand what it can be like when women are no longer forced to fight one another for the favours of men?"

And she has more to say, about men's violence towards women, the age-long side of suttee, slavery and rape. Jane claims many of these things had disappeared, her world was changing, and that things were getting better.

Then Laura makes the most telling remark of the story: "'Was it?' she said. 'I wonder if the women of Berlin thought so when it fell? Was it, indeed? – Or was it on the edge of a new barbarism?'"

This reference to the mass rapes inflicted on German women by the invading Russian army would have been understood by most of his readers, but it is particularly interesting given Jack's wartime experience. Jack's work as a censor means he would know better than to make a direct reference to atrocities committed by allies, but Laura's remark shows he knew of them.

In the ants' nest of "Consider Her Ways", the debate goes on without resolution. The future historian's judgement is implacable, her answer to all Jane's arguments is that she is too close to her society to see it clearly. But Jane also refuses to cede ground. She has loved and been loved, and she cannot dismiss her own lived experience as a societal construct designed to oppress her. She knows that her marriage did not equate to the historian's view of "being owned by a man".

Some academics have criticised the story for not coming down firmly against Jane's romantic view of 1950s Britain,[9] but this story could be better understood as Jack's continuing attempt to work out his own beliefs as to whether the sexes could live together without the stronger preying on the weaker. He had seen the brutal results of war on civilian women, but he had also had a very happy partnership with Grace that had lasted through decades of both struggle and success, and was still full of love.

This passionate voice comes through when Jane says: "There should be lovers out there under those trees; they should be listening hand in hand to that song while they watch the moon rise."

For Jack, there should be romance, but he also realised the limitations of the life he and Grace had created. Though an equal partnership, they had remained always lovers, and never been transmuted to parents. Children would inevitably have meant Grace leaving her job, Jack becoming the only breadwinner, and the balance of their relationship changing. Though a childfree, communal life at the Penn Club had worked for them, it could not work for humanity as a whole. Reproduction for the vast majority of women in the 1950s inevitably meant them losing their careers, and taking a subservient role washing nappies, "dwindled to a wife" as Jack wrote in his poem.

Childbearing and equality were irreconcilable and so, in "Consider Her Ways", the debate remains unresolved. Is this vision of a female-only world a dystopia or a utopia? Jane and Laura couldn't agree, and Jack seemed undecided too.

But the unfinished themes of "Consider Her Ways" obviously continued to play on his mind, because he made another attempt to solve the puzzle, this time in the full length novel *Trouble with Lichen*, written four years later.

It opens at the end of term party of a modest girls' school, surely modelled on Grace's own, seen through the eyes of a maths teacher. She observes with pleasure her most successful pupil, Diana Brackley, about to leave for Cambridge to study biochemistry. She also observes her beauty and unconventional attitudes to romance. Thus, Jack sets up the central question of the book: how can women combine a successful career with a fulfilling love life?

It's a question that means nothing to Diana herself, floating above the romantic fray on the purer pleasures of the mind. Just like Laura in

"Consider Her Ways", she sees clearly that "being a good housewife" is a con and a drudge, created to turn girls into "advertiser's meat".[10]

But then she falls in love with an unobtainable fellow scientist, Francis Saxover. Previously immune to temptation, now she begins to realise the depth of the problem. As she passes the traditional 'on the shelf' marker of her 25th birthday, her nagging mother wonders when she will produce some grandchildren. Diana understands the central reason for women's failure to take advantage of their hard-won rights – they just don't have enough time. If she had more time, she could have a marriage, children and a career . . .

Meanwhile, Diana and Francis, working in the same lab, have separately stumbled upon a sample of lichen that prolongs life. They both realise its potential for disrupting society. It could destroy the financial basis of pensions; render marriages formed in adolescence into permanent prisons; and create a permanent paradise for the rich while tying the poor to centuries at the factory bench.

Paralysed by indecision and drowning in unhappiness following the death of his wife, Francis chooses to give it to his own children and himself in the guise of an "annual vitamin implant" but does nothing else.

Diana has no such hesitation. Science is her religion and for her, knowledge is the ultimate good. She cannot bury her findings, but she realises she will face chaos if she publishes without a plan. Very possibly the vital species will be destroyed in the gold-rush to secure it. So, with the practicality and energy typical of Wyndham's heroines, she sets off on a trip to Manchuria to establish a reliable supply of the rare lichen, then establishes a beauty parlour catering to the rich and famous. In this way she ensures that when it finally becomes public, she has hundreds of the most influential women in Britain on her side. Diana has no doubt that this new world, after the birth-pangs of homo superior, will be a utopia for women as well as men.

In this way, Jack solves the puzzle of how to liberate women, and this story can have a satisfactorily happy ending.[11]

But even though the problem of how to be both mother and careerist could be solved by science in Jack's imaginary future, there is another issue.

Jack seemed to find it hard to believe that women could ever escape the obliteration of personality brought on by enslavement to a child. As the pregnant Angela Zellaby says in her rant against her husband: "As if one were not a person at all, but just a kind of mechanism, a sort of incubator."

A close reading of "Consider Her Ways" shows the heroine's wandering mind is incorporated into the body of the mother just as she is artificially impregnated – Jane's sharp, educated mind is literally subsumed into Mother Orchis's flesh at the moment of conception.[12]

Mother Orchis and the other gross "mounds of flesh" are some of the least likeable women in all Wyndham's writing: pretty-faced but catty, lazy and luxurious, bored and boring. They expect to be pampered as goddesses while spitefully scoring points off each other. It's an unpleasantly accurate picture of female 'frenemies' that would be recognised in many girls' schools, golf club lounges and private gyms. "Consider Her Ways" was written just after Gertrude's death. Is this Jack's awful judgement on his mother and her hotel acquaintances, living their pointless, leisured lives in a circuit of spa towns?

Many critics from Kingsley Amis onwards have noted that Jack was one of the very few writers to portray strong women. What's less obvious is how rarely they are positive, active mothers.

This placing of motherhood in the background is true in all his stories – perhaps because, having been largely raised by staff and boarding schools, it was even further outside the author's experience than for most men.

Even in "Consider Her Ways", a story based around motherhood, the babies themselves never appear. Jane as 'mother' – like Gertrude – never sees or cares for her children. Her motherhood is of reproduction of babies only, not the creative work of helping a child develop, or even the practical drudgery of care.

In *The Midwich Cuckoos*, all the major female characters escape the alien motherhood – Zellaby's wife Angela because she was already pregnant with his child (like Josella in *The Day of The Triffids*, Angela is barely seen with her son). The narrator's wife Janet escapes because she was away from the village during the Day Out. Zellaby's daughter, Ferrelyn, gives birth to a cuckoo but it dies in an influenza epidemic (this also lets him out of the repugnant situation of having to kill his own 'grandchild' in the final scenes).

The village mothers are bit-players, barely distinguished as individuals. They are compelled to care for their cuckoos but there is no real connection between mother and child.

This is even starker in *The Chrysalids*, where troubled, oppressed mothers are almost divorced from their offspring. The narrator David's remote, cold mother barely features, the caring role being taken by his older sister. Rosalind's mother is also missing except for one mention, when she unexpectedly helps her daughter escape despite guessing at her mutation. Sophie's mother is warmly affectionate, but helpless to save her daughter. But, rare in Wyndham's fiction, there is one heroic, though doomed mother, invisible but audible in a single scene.

Shortly after Petra's birth, David's Aunt Harriet calls, carrying her own newborn. The women congratulate each other while David, bored, eavesdrops in the next room. But Harriet's baby is imperfect. This is no social call, she has really come in a desperate attempt to swap the babies, and so fool the inspector into granting her child a certificate. Though unseen by the narrator, both women seem to snap into focus as Harriet pleads with David's horrified mother Emily.

When David's father appears to genially congratulate his sister-in-law, Emily instinctively conforms to the norm. She betrays her sister, telling her husband of the illegal proposition. With real or simulated shock, he begins on one of his fire and brimstone sermons, telling Harriet that her own hidden impurity has caused her child to be born as a blasphemy and a distortion of the true image, that she is guilty of spreading mutants and abominations, that she should search her heart for her sin and pray for forgiveness. It has no effect on Harriet: [13]

> 'I've done nothing to be ashamed of. I am *not* ashamed – I am only beaten . . .
>
> 'I shall pray,' she said. 'Yes, I shall pray.' She paused, then she went on, her voice steady and harder: 'I shall pray God to send charity into this hideous world, and sympathy for the weak, and love for the unhappy and unfortunate.'

Rowland[14] has pointed out that Harriet's whole speech wouldn't be out of place in Dickens or Forster. It reflects the sermon that provokes it, which is also of a brutal, patriarchal morality of a century earlier. Did Jack still recall listening to his uncle's sermons in those Birmingham chapels?

But as Harriet leaves, the style twists. We return to the subtler characterisations that typify Wyndham. Husband and wife discuss her behaviour. David's father continues his judgemental diatribe, but his mother has already lost her initial anger.

> 'Perhaps, she did not realize what she was saying,' my mother's voice said, uncertainly.
>
> 'Then it is time she did. It is our duty to see that she does.'
>
> My mother started to answer, but her voice cracked. She began to cry: I had never heard her cry before. My father's voice went on explaining about the need for Purity in thought as well as in heart and conduct, and its very particular importance to women. He was still talking when I tiptoed away.

Does Emily, who has herself borne and done penance for two "accursed mutants", regret damning her sister Harriet to another lost child, to being turned out by her husband as an unfit wife? Does she regret not doing more to save her own children? She fades once more into the background, and we never know. Neither does her son. Much later, when Rosalind says her own mother helped her escape, David wonders how many other mothers were concealing children that would officially be judged mutants, and even if his own mother was as righteous and orthodox as she appeared:[15]

> I could not imagine my own mother doing such a thing for Petra's sake. And yet she had cried after my Aunt Harriet had been sent away. And Aunt Harriet had been more than ready to break the Purity Laws. So had Sophie's mother. It made one wonder how many mothers there might be who were turning a blind eye towards matters that did not actually infringe the Definition of the True Image – and perhaps to things that did infringe it, if the inspector could be dodged . . . I wondered, too, whether my mother would, in secret, be glad or sorry that I had taken Petra away . . .

But although mothers figure in all these books, they never dominate the story. They are bit-players, not protagonists. Women are central, children are fascinating, but mothers are neither.

Thus, though we as readers observe motherhood with fascination through the eyes of Zellaby and others, we do not experience it from within. Wyndham appears to understand his own incapacity to describe this through Angela Zellaby, who breaks out during her pregnancy: "It's all very well for a man. He doesn't have to go through this sort of thing, and he knows he never will have to. How *can* he understand? He may *mean* as well as a saint, but he's always on the outside. He can never *know* what it's like, even in a normal way."[16]

It's been suggested that it was Grace who prevented Wyndham having children because of her dedication to her career,[17] but his books suggest he may have been just as reluctant to see the woman he loved transformed to a mother, to see her, as Phyllis of the poem, "dwindled to a wife".

So who are the Wyndham heroines?

They are so similar that they were the genesis of this book. Re-reading his novels many years after I first picked them up, I realised the narrator's other half was the same character over and over. She is so finely drawn, I felt sure she was based on a real person.

His protagonist is energetic, perceptive, determined, and ready to adapt to any disaster. She is taller than average, slim and usually has brown hair. Rosalind in *The Chrysalids*, Phyllis in *The Kraken Wakes*, Diana in *Trouble with Lichen* and Jane in "Consider Her Ways" all follow this pattern. Josella in *The Day of the Triffids* is dark blonde and Octavia, the attractively amoral heroine of "Chronoclasm", is fair with hazel eyes, but they are both tall and slender like the rest: "good looking – not pretty, something better than that".[18] His heroines are usually well-dressed and groomed: even as civilisation ends, Josella moves effortlessly from diamonds and furs to a ski suit, then an elegant dress.

The Wyndham heroine is straightforward, with few traces of feminine wiles and no bitchiness. She may be seen in sharp contrast to this behaviour in other women, as Jane and Diana are. However, she is perfectly capable of managing any man in her life through unarguable good sense.

She is not overtly sexual – never a blonde bombshell type – but neither is she portrayed as virginal or frigid. She is never religious and doesn't have any religion-based sexual morals. She has the same practical attitude to sex as she does to the rest of her life, and is perfectly happy to enjoy and even invite sex. Josella and Octavia are typical of this.

Octavia, visiting from two centuries ahead, is fascinated by the convention of 20th century lovers to marry before sex: "Oh, of course, I remember, there was no probative then – now I mean. You have a sort of rigid, lucky-dip, take-it-or-leave-it system."[19]

Sex with a Wyndham heroine may explicitly occur – in "Chronoclasm" one scene is set in the honeymoon bed – but it is not described. The closest Wyndham comes to describing lovemaking occurs in the "meeting of the souls" between the psychic hero and heroine in *The Chrysalids*. [20]

> Now it was the under-Rosalind calling gently, forlornly, all armour thrown aside, the heart naked.
>
> And again there are no words.
>
> Words exist that can, used by a poet, achieve a dim monochrome of the body's love, but beyond that they fail clumsily.
>
> My love flowed out to her, hers back to me. Mine stroked and soothed. Hers caressed. The distance – and the difference – between us dwindled and vanished. We could meet, mingle and blend. Neither one of us existed any more; for a time there was a single being that was both. There was escape from the solitary cell; a brief symbiosis, sharing all the world...
>
> No one else knew the hidden Rosalind. They did not know at what cost the overt Rosalind had been wrought. None of them knew my dear, tender Rosalind, longing for escape, gentleness, and love; grown afraid now of what she had built for her own protection; yet more afraid still, of facing life without it.
>
> Duration is nothing. Perhaps it was only for an instant we were together again. The importance of a point is in its existence; it has no dimensions.

But despite being neither sexily curvaceous, bitchy or maternal, she *is* entirely feminine. She never has any interest in sport, and is not a head girl type. She is never portrayed as masculine, even when she takes charge of the situation, arms herself and fights or, in *The Kraken Wakes,* takes up bricklaying. She enjoys her clothes and is beautifully groomed in all circumstances. She is intelligent, cool and collected; reserved in public, loving in private.

In other words, his heroine is Grace.

References

1   Diary entry 10 August 1953. The letter itself has not survived. Thanks to Prof Ketterer for finding this reference.

2   Letter to Grace, 27 August 1952, held in Liverpool archive.

3   *The Midwich Cuckoos*, Michael Joseph, 1977 printing, p.19.

4   *Galaxy Science Fiction*, July 1952. Duncan uses American slang, which may be used to point up the similarities with the treatment of black Americans, but it may also be due to the fact that it was published in the American magazine, *Galaxy*. It was made into a television play for the opening episode of the Armchair Theatre series "Out of This World" in 1962.

5   This unpublished poem, in several slightly different versions, is held in the Liverpool archive. The title character was probably based on friends Percy and Phyllis Walsh, who also lived at the Penn Club and married in 1943. Wyndham shared his appalled reaction to their traditional church marriage service in his letters to Grace, see Part 2, Chapter 2.

6   *The Day of the Triffids*, 1981 edition, p.177.

7   Thomas Clareson and Alice Clareson, 1990, "The Neglected Fiction of John Wyndham", *Science Fiction Roots and Branches*, Lumiere Cooperative Press, p.88-100.

8   Quotes come from *Consider Her Ways*, Michael Joseph, 1979 printing, p.70-74.

9   Clareson and Clareson, ibid.

10   *Trouble with Lichen*, Penguin, 1980 edition, p.44.

11   The story has one other quirk, unlikely to be picked up except by the sharpest of readers – an indirect reference to menstruation on p.75. Francis' son Paul, the unknowing recipient of the drug along with his sister Zephanie, is finally told the reason why he rarely needs to shave or cut his nails. His canny wife Jane realises Zephanie must have suspected something amiss much earlier.

> 'I don't see why she should, any more than I. Less in fact; she doesn't have to shave,' Paul replied.
> 'Darling,' Jane told him, using the word edge uppermost,

'you don't have to pretend to be dim with me.'

'I don't – oh, I see what you mean,' Paul said.

Jane knows that if Zephanie's metabolism has been significantly slowed, she must only be having a period once every three months. Though oblique, it's an unusual inclusion in a mainstream book in 1960, when menstruation was taboo, barely mentioned even in women's magazines. Jack has been described as being shy around women, but this shows a confidence vanishingly rare in male science fiction authors. The only other male author I know of the time who references menstruation is George Orwell in *Nineteen Eighty-Four*. Winston is irritated when his date with Julia is cancelled for "the usual reason – it's started earlier this time".

12   *Consider Her Ways and Others*, Penguin, 1976 edition, p.8. Jane slips into Mother Orchis' body as she comes round from a procedure under anaesthetic at a clinic in the future. The doctor notes her slow reaction: "Better make a note of that on her card. What's the number? Oh, only her fourth time. Yes, certainly make a note." Mother Orchis has previously had three successful pregnancies, each producing four babies, as one of the other Mothers says later (p.26). She has given birth several weeks previously; in the interim she has had time for one of the Mothers' routine holidays. If this procedure is "her fourth time", it must be the fourth insemination or implantation of embryos.

13   *The Chrysalids*, Penguin, 1961 edition, p.73-74.

14   Wymer Rowland (1992) "How Safe is John Wyndham? A closer look at his work with Particular Reference to The Chrysalids", *Foundation*, Summer 1992, p.25.

15   *The Chrysalids,* Penguin, 1961 edition, p.126.

16   *The Midwich Cuckoos,* Michael Joseph, 1977 edition, p.91.

17   See Sister Bede's comments in the BBC documentary *The Invisible Man of Science Fiction*. Sister Bede was the daughter of Wyndham's close friend Biff Barker.

18   "Chronoclasm" in *Seeds of Time*, Penguin, p.11.

19   Ibid, p.21.

20   *The Chrysalids*, Penguin, 1961 edition, p.150.

13

Return to Utopia

On 26 July 1963, Jack and Grace walked out of the Penn Club. Accompanied by Grace's cousin Basil Burton and the club warden Ena Thyne, they crossed to the Russell Square Registrar's office. There, almost 30 years after they had fallen in love, they were married.

Grace wrote in her diary: "Very pleasant dignified gentleman did the job professionally well. We in trance, but managed walk to Antoine's top room – melon lobster champagne."[1]

All that remained was to announce the news to the smiling congratulations of the rest of the club and the open-mouthed astonishment of Jack's drinking friends.

Sam Youd said: "He totally shook us when he came in and told us he was getting married. We didn't know Grace existed. We certainly didn't know they'd both been living at the Penn for quite a long time. It was a total shock to us."[2]

Arthur C Clarke wrote: "Incredibly, after years of friendship, I knew very little of John – I had no idea he had a girl friend!"[3]

The wedding had been a long time coming, but was no sudden decision. A year earlier, aged almost 59 and looking ahead to her retirement, Grace had written in her diary "AN IDEA". It was typical of her that although this was momentous enough to use capitals (an unheard-of emphasis in her writing), she did not confide even in her own diary what her idea was. Over the next few days she nursed her idea, finally sharing it with Jack a week later:

> Idea received with comments but not adversely . . . now I feel
> a bit flat and a bit anxious but better than any alternatives.
> Antoine's top room [a favourite restaurant] – additional idea
> received avidly and without reservations. Can hardly believe
> many details easily settled.

Within days "the idea has become a plan" and Jack made several visits to Steep on the lookout for a house that would suit them.

London no longer held the same attractions for Jack. The Blooms-bury neighbourliness had faded as more of his friends retired. The regular sci-fi Thursday night at the White Horse had moved with the landlord to the Globe Inn, in Hatton Garden. A new crowd had arrived and the old friends gradually fell away.

For Grace, her approaching 60th birthday was a major milestone, it meant the end of her career. A new life outside London would allow her full rein for her passion for gardening, so far confined to a patch in the club's back garden.

Their planned marriage was partly a necessity: they couldn't live together unmarried in a country village in the same way as they had in the anonymity of London. Jack was a modest man. His principles were a private matter. He may have ignored society's strictures for 30 years, but he had no desire to publicly flaunt his disregard.

In Steep, Jack fell into conversation in a pub with a local who said the house he had built for his parents didn't suit them. Oakridge was a substantial brick cottage with a large garden backing onto fields, only a few yards from the Bedales school gate. Grace wrote: "J to Petersfield to see Jean and children and perhaps do business – never have I known him so singleminded – only of course wary of chicken counting . . . Reg's house does seem so very desirable considering the alternatives – or want of. J very keen."

Jack took Grace to see it on a summer Saturday in 1962, only six weeks after that first, tentative conversation. Grace wrote:

> Hardly know how to describe these momentous hours set-tling all the rest of my life – but how blessedly . . . everywhere especially the trees looked heavenly. We had been along Mill Lane and I thought [the cottage] pleasantly comical from the outside. Some natter with Reg and wife in the bar and they certainly did not seem to have a refusal in store . . .
>
> Sunday morning Reg came to the cottage. I was charmed with everything about the house – nothing infuriating when the fireplace is changed and a few things done. It might have been tailored for me because it belongs to the meadows . . . Reg began to natter for a bank letter at once, but J fixed three

o'clock and we walked down to the waterfall because he wanted to be sure I really liked it.

I can hardly believe it all for thankfulness.

A week later Jack was back in London and they both threw themselves into the fun of planning the house exactly as they wanted, money no object: "Head full of colours. Persian I think . . . Heal's, now
honeysuckle not Persian. J did kitchens in Harrods! Time goes quickly
because I dream away happily."

By Christmas the house was taking shape. Although they were to
be married, they still planned separate rooms as they had in the Penn
Club:

> Almost too happy to write . . . many things better than we
> expected. I found so much quite heavenly. I will have little
> South room and J middle bedroom. Kitchen fitments will do
> as I wanted. Tried colours and think I am fixed. I have been
> thinking of nothing else during and since, so many things will
> be so simple and nice. J glad that I am so pleased.

By the following summer, the house was almost complete. She received an honoured farewell from Roan School for Girls where she
had been a fixture since 1930. A valediction in the school magazine
said:

> It is difficult to realise that at the end of the Summer term, we
> have to say goodbye to Miss Wilson, and a sorrowful thought
> that the cool and kindly elegance of her presence will no lon-
> ger be with us. Always, through all vagaries of weather and
> whatever the caprices of the Southern Railway may be, one
> can be happily assured of finding Miss Wilson early in the
> staff-room, calm, unruffled, imperturbably good-humoured.

On her last Friday, she was presented with a coffee set by the school
and a set of wine glasses from her own form and was happy to be
away by lunchtime.

The next day, Jack went out in the morning to buy yellow roses for
their buttonholes and they crossed the square to be married. After
lunch at Antoine's restaurant, Grace went to Steep while Jack stayed a
few days to complete formalities in London. Grace wrote:

J said new ceremony – bridegroom seeing off bride! He is so much more pleased and so much more conventional than I would have expected. Flowers from Eileen and Biff and Jean. To Oakridge – entranced – Lillywhites and Vincent have done a wonderful job. Taking down wall means one steps into sunlight any time. Bedroom delicious. Thousands of things to do but all will be heavenly. Rang J and natter natter. Back to supper to Row Cottage. So very tired I could hardly stand. Lovely night with little moon.

One of Jack's jobs in London was to provide greater financial security for Grace. Immediately after the wedding, Jack signed over the deeds of Oakridge to her.[4] He sent a bottle and a signed copy of one of his books as a thank you to the registrar.

He also bought a car. Viv remembered: "He immediately drove in a highly insecure manner to see me. I always remember waving to him in the main road behind our house and he turned to wave back driving along on the wrong side of the road. But he mastered the car as he mastered everything that performed logically and the next time he came with his wife, Grace, he drove all the way from Steep with ease and enjoyment."[5]

Oakridge was the first home of his own Jack had known since he was a child. Grace remained undomestic but for Jack every chore had a charm. Even remembering to put the bins out was a matter of pride: Grace's contribution was to remember to put up a sign in the kitchen that said "DUSTBINS" on the day before.[6]

Now he had plenty of room for new kit, he had a field day with his old love of gadgetry. He bought a new camera, projector and television. He also bought a reel-to-reel tape recorder and microphone, and he and Viv began exchanging weekly tapes in lieu of letters. A few of these remain in the Liverpool archive: two old chums comfortably swapping gossip and recommendations for medicines, signing off "Cheerho, old boy, cheerho". Jack describes his adjustments to the tape recorder, his disembowelling of his new television set and more eccentric projects.

I made a new and improved bird warmer and kept the birds' water liquid even though it was 24 degrees [-4C]. When I pulled back the curtains this morning I scared a bird that was drinking there so I'm regarded as a public benefactor, or a bird benefactor anyway.

We have 12 blue tits in constant association. I bored a hole in a coconut in the hope that they would get inside and eat it out and then use it for a nest. I bought bird seed that said 'attracts all birds' and by God it did. We had starlings and flocks of sparrows . . . Grace puts out a few currants every lunchtime for the blackbirds . . . The robin has grown very tame now. He comes and agitates for crumbs at the end of a meal. Mrs Robin is not being driven off so much now. At least I think it's Mrs Robin. It's very hard to say what's what in robin land.

They discussed cooking and exchanged recipes. Jack had never had his own kitchen before and loved to experiment. The village shop and butcher delivered twice a week, but nonetheless, every Saturday he drove Biff or Eileen, or both, to the market day in Petersfield. He would frequently forget at least one thing and go back the same day. He reported to Viv in great detail on the fluctuating fortunes of the various 'self-service' shops, and their threat from the new Fine Fare. He inspected the stock of every shop to find the most outré ingredients Petersfield had to offer:

I went into one supermarket and they had a tin of something that turned out to be baby clams. I got some turbot and made a sauce with baby clams and it turned out rather well. It's quite a good dish. There's one thing about Grace, she may be a bit timid on the road and in cars but she's very brave in facing my dishes and on the whole they agree with her. When she has an upset it usually turns out not to be my dishes.

Viv responded with a recipe for tripe cooked with onions and milk made of Marvel powder, using a pressure cooker. Grace's reaction to this was not recorded. The new equipment meant Viv could also record *The Archers* for Jack, so he need never miss an episode even when on holiday. Jack had been addicted to it for years.

Despite his marriage, Jack's life remained firmly compartmentalised. No-one in Steep, with the exception of his closest friends, connected him with the world famous writer. Even the local vicar didn't know who he was. Jack and Grace were once embarrassed when the Petersfield literary club chose John Wyndham as the subject for their next meeting, with no idea that he was sitting amongst them.

In Steep, he was happy to be just another retired old Bedalian, drinking at the Cricketers or the Harrow Inn, and attending occasional concerts at the church or school. He sometimes took the train up to London, only an hour away, but he rarely stayed long. Grace barely visited at all.

In the midst of this rural idyll, he produced less work although he was able to sell anything he wrote. Perhaps now the financial pressure had disappeared, he no longer felt the need to push himself: *The Day of the Triffids* alone was still selling by tens of thousands every year. His income from royalties was more than £8,000 a year, the equivalent of about £160,000 today.[7] Perhaps he had less energy: the 40-a-day habit was taking its toll. Perhaps he had said almost everything he wanted to say.

He was working on his final and most autobiographical published novel, *Chocky*. He had written it as a novelette for *Amazing Stories* in the US and *Good Housekeeping* in the UK just before his marriage, but it took him another four years to develop it into a book.

Like *The Chrysalids*, it is a story of a misfit, always on guard against a slip of the tongue, a feeling drawn from Wyndham's own experiences in schools, the censor's office and later the army.

Chocky centres around the Gore family, who were based on Wyndham's close friends in Steep, the Sykes family who lived in the beautiful Red House. Bill and Leslie Sykes, believing themselves unable to have children, adopted a boy, David. Six years later, Leslie gave birth to a daughter and the two children were brought up together.[8] Jack may have been conscious of the need to separate the Sykeses from the fictional Gores: this is the only book to include a disclaimer that the people in the book "are entirely mythical".

In *Chocky*, the son is Matthew Gore, an apparently normal 12-year-old who has acquired the habit of talking to himself. The story is told by his father, David Gore, a typically kind and intelligent Wyndham narrator who encourages Matthew to talk without judging him, and tries hard to understand his sudden changes in behaviour.

Like the Midwich and Chrysalid children, Matthew is a cuckoo in the nest. He is the only adopted child, and so the only stranger in the family. He is also the only one who can hear Chocky, an alien who psychically visits him, almost at times possessing him.

But unlike the Midwich and Chrysalid children, Matthew is truly alone. There is no similar group of young people around him, sharing the same alienating experience of difference from their parents. So he does not wholly welcome Chocky – he also longs to be a normal part of his family.

Who is Chocky? Though neither male nor female, Matthew and his father decide to call her 'she', as she has something of the manner of a bossy, know-it-all older sister. Like many of Wyndham's female protagonists, she is more active than Matthew, decisively saving him and his sister when they nearly drown. She is in some ways an unromantic version of many of Wyndham's heroines, a counterpart to the hesitant, thoughtful narrator.

But she is also something more: an inner part of Matthew, encouraging him, even forcing him to change and learn. Chocky is a representation of an artist's muse; a part she literally plays when teaching Matthew how to paint, and more importantly, how to look at the things he is painting. Chocky and her gifts are a mixed blessing. Though she gives him insight and skills, she also gives him a perspective no-one else can share, rendering him awkward and lonely. Even when she is not present, he is fundamentally changed by knowing her in ways that render him permanently an outsider.

It's not hard to see the young Jack Harris in Matthew Gore, blessed and cursed with an insight and imagination that open up new worlds but separate him from the people he lives amongst.

There is even a sideswipe at the healthy living routine of Bedales when Matthew's mother consults an old-fashioned doctor to try and find a 'cure'. He tells her: "All Matthew needs is plenty of exercise, a cold bath in the morning, plenty of good plain unseasoned food, lots of salads and the window open at night . . . Growing is often more exacting than we realize, but a healthy life, and Nature, the great healer, will soon correct any temporary imbalances."[9]

But all the open windows in the world won't change the fact that Matthew no longer sees things in the same way as everyone else. When Chocky is gone, there is no one else to share this. Talking to his father, he says:[10]

> 'She sort of made me notice things more.'
>
> 'Can't you go on noticing things? The world's quite an interesting place. There's lots to notice.'
>
> 'Oh, I do. More than I did, I mean. Only it's kind of lonely, just noticing by yourself . . .'
>
> 'If you could get what you see down on paper you'd be able to share your noticing with other people,' I suggested.
>
> 'Yes,' Matthew admitted. 'It wouldn't be the same – but it'd be something . . .'

The story almost reads as if John Wyndham, through David Gore, is addressing his childhood self. He is reaching back to him to try and help him from his current state as an adult, to help him with the lessons that he has painfully learned along the way, to reassure him that he can make contact with the rest of the world through getting it "down on paper".

But where David wants to help, his wife Mary, another obtuse Wyndham mother, wants only to deny or even obliterate any strangeness in Matthew. She is a kind and intelligent woman, but is influenced by her awful cabal of sisters, who treat motherhood as a competitive sport in which children are exhibited as prize specimens. Mary has already had the unhappy experience of being judged a 'non-starter' for failing to produce a child within a year of marriage. Now she wants to prove that her adopted son is just as normal as her sisters' children.

David argues that Matthew "isn't *ab*normal: he's perfectly normal, but plus something – which is quite different". Mary is having none of it: "All I want is for him to be normally normal, not plus or minus anything. I just want him to be happy." David wants to tell her that Matthew isn't unhappy being different, only because of the problems the difference causes, but feels he can't argue further when she is so clearly upset. Mary seems unable to imagine someone being happy while not resoundingly normal. [11]

This refusal to see a child as an individual, but only as an offspring which must be physically cared for without requiring mental connection, drifts almost into cruelty. When Matthew loses Chocky, his friend, mentor and literal saviour, Mary insists on making him sandwiches.

As David Gore says of his wife: "I have been astonished before, and doubtless shall be again, how the kindliest and most sympathetic of women can pettify and downgrade the searing anguishes of childhood."[12]

The Gore family may be as imperfect and mismatched as most families, but *Chocky* is a hopeful book. The Gores' misunderstandings don't stop them loving each other. Matthew's long term happiness seems assured despite the loss of his muse. Through her, he has accessed his own talents and forged a closer relationship with his father.

Jack had transformed the pain of his early life into one of the most loved of his books. He himself was unsure about it, saying "Nothing happens". But it struck a chord with everyone who had felt themselves an outsider in their own family. Although written for adults, it became a favourite with younger readers who recognised themselves in the misunderstood Matthew.

The only other book Jack wrote at this time was much darker. *Web* was not published during his lifetime, but it suggests the idyllic retirement Jack described to Vivian did not entirely reflect his inner life.

Its narrator is an older man, grieving for a lost wife and daughter and blindly seeking for a new purpose. Together with a varied group of pioneers, he sets off to build a utopia on a Pacific island. These visionaries seek to create a society similar to Arthur C Clarke's New Athens in *Childhood's End*. From the very start, we know their plans will fail. But the ending goes far beyond this.

The island has been shadily acquired from its native owners through colonial double-dealing during a nuclear testing programme in the Pacific. The white men's tricksy robbery of the island paradise is a darkness at the heart of the project which none of the pioneers acknowledge. They are happy to set up their utopia without inquiring too closely what it is built upon. But that historic injustice has set in motion a terrifying change. The betrayed owners have placed the island under a 'tabu'. Their curse will spread across the world.

The book suffers from some clichés – though well researched, it is clear that the author has never visited such an island. It also revisits some of the set pieces from *The Day of the Triffids:* the malevolent spiders mass silently beyond the pioneers' camp much as the triffids did. The potential dominance of a species that works together was an idea Jack had been playing with for decades.

He was unsure of the book, struggled with it for years and refused to submit it to his publishers. Scott Meredith, his New York agent, and Peter Hebdon at Michael Joseph publishers, both had to beg him to let them see it. Scott Meredith wrote: "I really feel that you ought to at least send it along to us, John, so that we can look it over; it may not be as bad as you think it is. In any case, we might be able to give you some suggestions to fix it up. It is possible, as you say, that it's best buried, but we can't really tell that until we've seen it." [13]

But when he sent it, neither could be enthusiastic. Peter Hebdon wrote: [14]

> I am returning to you the typescript of WEB with a heavy heart and sad misgivings. You know how much I looked forward to reading it. I started happily, enjoying the quality of the writing enormously, but eventually began to wonder when the story proper was going to start . . .
>
> I find this very difficult to write . . . I think this book is way below your best. If you want it published then of course we will publish for you and, I hope, publish it well. In that case you will make money and we shall make money because it will subscribe very well on the strength of your reputation. But it seems to me that the reputation is worth more than the pounds, shillings and pence, and I hope that you may agree to store this typescript, at least for the time being.
>
> I am guilty because I have chivvied you about this book for so long. I feel a cad.

Scott Meredith was more positive: "I think you sold yourself short on this book, John; while it has some flaws, it's not as bad as you seem to think . . . [it is] more a socio-political-historical essay disguised as an adventure novel, again disguised as science fiction." [15]

But even he was not willing to publish it under the John Wyndham

name. In fact, *Web* is just as well written and plotted as his other novels, but its view of colonial guilt, irresponsible use of nuclear weapons
and the price to be paid for this was ahead of its time.

It is also essentially downbeat. *The Day of the Triffids, The Kraken
Wakes* and even *The Chrysalids* foretold an eventual rebuilding of a
better world, after man's hubris had worked its way out in destruction.
Web sees only the coming destruction, with no future beyond it.

Where did this despondency come from?

For an older man, and an accomplished writer, the 1960s were difficult years. The failure of the public prosecution of *Lady Chatterley's
Lover* in 1959 resulted in the lifting of restrictions on sex and violence
in print. The campaigners believed they were fighting for freedom,
a boundless new world in which anything could be possible. In fact,
their victory led to a wave of books, plays and films revelling in gore
and smut with little redeeming literary, artistic or moral value.

The great tradition of storytelling seemed to have lost its way.
Christopher Booker explained:[16]

> The highest terms of praise for a new novel, play or film were
> that it was 'exciting', 'shocking', 'daring', 'disturbing' or 'sick-
> ening' . . . But each time the 'frontiers' were pushed back, it
> would be necessary next time to heighten the dose, to sustain
> the sense of novelty on which the spiral depended . . .
>
> Within just a few years the sentimental, romantic Holly-
> wood movies and respectable 'well-crafted' plays of the post-
> war era were made to seem unimaginably innocent and old
> fashioned, as the cinema and the theatre were taken over by a
> 'new wave' of stories altogether harder, more overtly sensa-
> tional and more surreal in tone.

Though Jack had criticised some of the ridiculous excesses of the
Hays Code, he was innately modest. He had kept his books sufficiently
free of sex to allow them to be recommended for younger readers. He
was protective of this audience.

When selling *Chocky*, he was anxious to include a clause in the contract to prevent it being republished as a paperback without his over-
sight: "A boisterous nude or two on the cover of any of my exceeding-
ly pure books would immediately get it into disfavour with nearly all

schoolmasters and schoolmistresses. They would be unable to recommend it to their pupils, if only for fear of upsetting the parents. And that would upset me."[17]

Such an attitude now was made to seem ridiculous. This was a blow for a writer such as Jack. His style was polished, his storytelling crafted by a decades-long apprenticeship. But such honed skill now looked hopelessly dated. It may be this that depressed him.

The darkness of "the spider book", as Jack always called it, may also have come from ill-health. He still smoked constantly. On one visit to a grand lady in the area, Grace noted in astonishment: "J did not smoke for over an hour!"

In 1965, he had a minor heart attack. Grace wrote: "Great trouble because J had a bad pain in the night. Thought it might be indigestion because of orange peel in orange cream last night; but now he thinks it is more like rheumatism as he has it in left arm as well. Does not want to eat – I never remember his not wanting to shave. Dozing now 5.30. A little Scrabble game."

The next day the doctor came and ordered bed rest for three weeks and a cardiogram. Jack downplayed this, refusing to wallow in self-pity and claiming it was not more than a fainting fit. A few months later, he wrote to his old friend and solicitor Brian Bowcock. He apologised for not having replied to Brian's letter earlier:[18]

> I have been doing a story, and I find a tendency to put everything else aside at such times until I have got rid of the thing, and as it then inevitably seems to be even worse than the last a day or two of self-disgust sets in. However, that's all over now, and I am free again.
>
> It was extremely kind of you to show concern for my indisposition – I call it that because it must have been one of the mildest thromboses (is that the plural?) that ever happened. In fact, I would believe it was all a mistake but that they trotted along one of these cardiograph things, and arguing with machines gets one nowhere. I feel (and felt, except just at the outset) perfectly normal, which makes it difficult to remember to go slow, at times. It seems that they will try me on the machine in March, and then tell me whether I have to go on going slow, or whether I can forget all about it.

I'm glad to hear that you are more or less reconciled to the provincial life, now. I, too, am becoming so. Occasionally I do hanker for London, but when I get there I find that it is not the London that is, that I was hankering for, but the London of 20 or 30 years ago, so then I give up hankering and am glad to be out of the present London which seems to grow more inconvenient with every visit.

Jack wasn't the only one to feel this way. Arthur C Clarke had emigrated to Sri Lanka where he was a keen scuba diver. Sam Youd was also largely living abroad from the late 1950s with his wife Joyce Fairbairn and their growing family, in an attempt to save money.

Although still greatly respected and admired as the old guard, the Thursday meetings at the Globe Inn were not what they had been.

Arthur C Clarke wrote about the new crowd: "Now I don't know one in ten of them, and find their arguments about William Burroughs and the New Wave quite incomprehensible. And it is sometimes necessary to remind them that I was not *personally* acquainted with Jules Verne – or even, alas, H G Wells."[19]

Jack recovered enough to visit old friends in Birmingham in March 1966. These were George and Mollie Barrow – she who had famously knocked out a policeman during the war. George was now Lord Mayor of Birmingham. He asked his old friend to speak at a Literary Luncheon for the first National Library Week. Jack, Grace, George, Mollie and their old friend Bob Lusty (now Sir Robert) sat down with 200 others at the new Pavilion Suite of the Warwickshire County Cricket Club, Edgbaston, just a stroll away from Jack's childhood home.

He and Grace also resumed their annual holidays abroad, flying to Montreux and Geneva. But in 1967, whilst still completing *Chocky*, he had another coronary while mowing the lawn. He again had to spend a period in bed. Viv urged him to be careful, but he told Grace he didn't want to be old and that half a life was no good to him.[20]

He recovered sufficiently for them to be able to fly to the Scottish Isles the following year despite Viv's qualms, telling him stoutly: "Good as new." In Oban he suddenly decided they should hire a car which he attempted to drive with his customary enthusiasm and panache, though he struggled with the gears.

Grace wrote: "Hot and worrying in car, esp. as we crossed wild moor, I thought J would have a heart attack at the least . . . J said later I had been very restrained on the drive – it was my idea of being help-ful, otherwise I could have had hysterics."

Chocky finally appeared in late 1968 and was immediately broadcast as a play on Radio 2 and Radio 4 in November. It was his last pub-lished work.

From his starry-eyed pre-war fantasies, he had matured to write himself and his hopes on to the page in his breakout novel *The Day of the Triffids*. Through his cycle of bestsellers, he had defined the beliefs and fears of his generation. With *Chocky*, he had worked out his own genesis as a writer. It has been described as an "estranged autobi-ography"[21], distorted from reality, unacknowledged but reflecting an inner truth. With its publication, Jack's career as an author, which had defined his life and self, was complete. Ill health was claiming him. It was almost time to go.

Publicly, he was still in demand. He spoke to a few journalists on request in the last year of his life but steered clear of biographers. When he was asked to contribute an interview for a major work on world authors, he politely replied: "My life has been practically devoid of interest to anyone but myself – though I have quite enjoyed it, of course, in those moments when I did not seem to have been sent to occupy a largely lunatic world." [22]

A *Times* journalist, visiting him down in Steep, commented on his ingenious bird feeding devices and the prospect from his garden across the Downs:[23]

> Wyndham is an accommodating and amused man. But he is shy of giving talks and interviews, and has barred the use of his photograph on book jackets. His quizzical expression, accentuated by the sharpish incline of his thick whitening hair back from his forehead, suggests a permanent willingness to appreciate a good try.

Editors still requested stories and comment articles, and his work was being regularly adapted. In February 1969, Jack was very pleased to be able to watch a television adaptation of "Random Quest", an alternate reality love story he had written in 1961, published in the UK as part of the collection *Consider Her Ways,* and in the US in *The Infinite Moment.* It was broadcast as part of the *Out of the Unknown* series. Jack was starting to feel unwell again, but wrote to the producer Owen Holder to congratulate him.

He seemed conscious of his own frailty, telling Viv in his final tapes that he could not accept some invitations such as to attend a film festival in Brazil. With Grace though, he was still outwardly planning for the future, checking hotels in Sark for their next summer holiday.

Grace was not entirely convinced. On 2 March 1969, she tersely recorded: "wretchedly cold and I am very very anxious." The doctor visited and checked his blood pressure. Over the next few days, she recorded every pain: "J by no means in the clear . . . J better but pain after lifting wood, which I must insist on doing . . . J no heart pain today thank god".

Within days, Jack was again up and about, discussing buying a neighbouring property in order to extend: "J has had the idea of offering John D a loan to pay off his mortgage with possible option of buying the house. I have always liked the idea of combining properties . . . J went to see John D about his plan – much enthusiasm – then to a solicitor who thought it feasible."

He was strong enough on 10 March to go to the pub and see his friends as usual, while Grace went to a choral concert at the local church. The next morning, he was making breakfast and called to Grace to get his emergency pills. They didn't do any good. Grace rang the doctor who came quickly and gave him an injection. This didn't work either. The doctor rushed back to his surgery to get something else.

Meantime, Jack lay on the kitchen floor. He wasn't frightened, or in pain, just puzzled. He told Grace: "Those eggs must be boiling dry by now."

Then: "I don't seem able to get enough oxygen."

He died still holding her hand.

Epilogue

In accordance with his wishes, Grace arranged a completely private cremation at Guildford. There was no physical memorial or public service. His ashes were scattered in a field near their home.

Grace lived on alone in Oakridge. She wrote nothing for three months, but then took up her diary again. Her entries in the following months are painful to read. She constantly reminds herself that he would have preferred the death he had than to go through a lengthy illness, but it makes little difference. For the first time she writes more of her emotions: "I dreamed that we were kissing but that I could not go on very well because of a lump in my mouth which came from my throat."

Sometimes she refers to Jack with the name he gave her, Sweetle. Though they had often spent periods apart, her life had been punctuated by the joy of him coming back. Her diaries had always mentioned her preparations: hair washes and trips to the station to meet him. Now he was gone and there would be no reunion. Saturdays, when he used to go to Petersfield shopping, were especially hard: "I miss J terribly on Saturdays. He 'came back' twice. Now a green woodpecker on the lawn and no sweetle to call."

She refused to speak to would-be biographers, though she did give occasional interviews to journalists and academics. In accordance with his wishes, much of his correspondence and his appointment diaries were destroyed, though Grace kept his wartime letters and poems. She died after a long decline on 2 June 1991, 22 years after Jack.

Biff Barker died in 1979. His pension died with him and Eileen found she had very little money. She had to move from Steep to a flat in a communal block. Later, when she was hard pressed for a contribution to repairs to the roof, she turned in desperation to Viv and asked for a loan. Viv insisted on giving her the money as a present from Jack. Despite their differences, Jack had left instructions with him to always help Eileen if she needed anything.[24]

Biff and Eileen's grandchildren, who were living in Australia, were very surprised to find themselves the recipients of the Wyndham estate on Grace's death. Though Grace had told their mother Jean that they would inherit, they had long since assumed it was a family legend. Jean has since died but her sister Tess still lives as a cloistered nun at the Abbey of St Cecilia under the name Sister Bede.

Bill and Leslie Sykes lived on in their beloved Red House. They both died their in their beds, Bill at 74 and Leslie at 93. Both their children still live in the village.

Viv and Lila never married but remained together in their neighbouring flats facing the sea in Hythe. Lila became a pillar of the local branch of the British Red Cross. Viv enjoyed teasing the neighbours who were curious about the exact nature of their relationship. Once, when Lila had done a lot of washing, Viv washed one of his shirts and pegged it out next to Lila's nightdress, safety-pinning the arm of his shirt around the nightdress's waist.[25]

Lila died in 1976. Viv's life had an unexpected new chapter. Aged 70, he fell passionately in love – "spontaneous, simultaneous combustion" – with his district nurse. Friends were doubtful, especially as Corrine was considerably younger and still living with her husband. But Viv, irrepressible to the last, was impervious to criticism. On changing his will, he wrote to his lawyer:[26]

> Even if I hadn't come to love her so deeply, I would still make the same provision for her in my will because of her support and constant pushing of me to do all the things I hadn't been able to do for years. She is a quite scatty, impulsive, kind, devoted, lovely person and I shall never know why she loves me. She must do because she is the only person I know who doesn't say I talk too much.

They were together until Viv's death at the age of 80 in 1987. Viv left money to the National Trust in his will, which resulted in a memorial plaque being erected at Cwrt Farm, North Wales. Viv had specified

North Wales rather than South Wales, because his father's family were from South Wales. George Harris is notable by his absence.

The plaque reads: "The National Trust is grateful for the financial assistance towards the acquisition of Cwrt from . . . a substantial legacy from Vivian Beynon Harris in memory of his brother (who wrote under the name of 'John Wyndham'), Gertrude Harris, Grace Beynon Harris and Lila Mary Grettan."

And so at the last, out of all his many alter egos, it is only John Wyndham who is remembered.

References

1   Grace's diaries are held by David Ketterer, see note 26, Chapter 3

2   Interviewed for "The Invisible Man of Science Fiction", BBC Four, 2005.

3   David Ketterer, 2000, "'A part of the … family [?]': John Wyndham's *The Midwich Cuckoos* as Estranged Autobiography", In *Learning from Other Worlds*, ed Patrick Parrinder. Liverpool University Press.

4   Reminiscences of Sister Bede, now in the Liverpool archive, Wyndham 14/24.

5   Vivian Beynon Harris, ibid.

6   Letter to Viv and Lila, sent by Jack on 26 December 1968, to thank them for their Christmas gift.

7   Accounts prepared for 1968 for tax purposes, held in the Liverpool archive.

8   David Sykes, in a letter to the author.

9   *Chocky*, Puffin 1984 edition, p.68.

10   Ibid, p.153.

11   Ibid, p.69.

12   Ibid, p.118.

13   Letter from Scott Meredith, 5 October. No year given but presumably 1965. Held in the Liverpool Archive.

14   Letter from Peter Hebdon, Michael Joseph publishers, 14 May 1965. Held in the Liverpool Archive.

15   Letter from Scott Meredith, 19 October. No year given but presumably 1965. Held in the Liverpool Archive.

16   Christopher Booker (2004) *The Seven Basic Plots: Why We Tell Stories*, Continuum Books, London, p.471-473.

17   Letter to Jacqueline Korn, 3 June 1967. Liverpool Archive.

18   Letter to Brian Bowcock, 17 Jan 1966. Liverpool Archive.

19   In an introduction to the 1969 edition of the *Tales from the White Hart*. This book of short stories is set in a lightly fictionalised version of their former haunt, The White Horse, and features all the crowd including Jack.

20   This account is taken from Viv's unfinished biography, ibid, and two letters he wrote after Jack's death, all published in *Foundation,* 75, p.18-35.

21   David Ketterer, ibid.

22   Wakeman et al (1975) *World Authors 1950-70*, HW Wilson, p.1574.

23   Pooter (1968) "Talking to John Wyndham", *The Times*, 16 March 1968, p.23.

24   Reminiscences of Sister Bede, ibid.

25   Letter from Dorothy Clegg (friend of Viv and Lila) to Viv's lawyer Brian Bowcock after his death, June 1987.

26   Letter to Brian Bowcock from Viv, 9 September 1976.

List of Works

Novels

The dates and publishers are of first publication. Wyndham stories have been adapted for radio in many countries; for the sake of brevity only British versions are given here.

The Curse of the Burdens, 1927. Published in Aldine's mystery series. The only known copy is in the British Library.

Foul Play Suspected, 1935, George Newnes.

The Secret People, 1935, George Newnes.

Stowaway to Mars, 1936. Serialised in *The Passing Show*, 1936, then published as a book, retitled *Planet Plane*, by George Newnes.

The Day of the Triffids, 1951. Full version published in the UK by Michael Joseph. Edited version published in the US by Doubleday. Abbreviated version with Venusian origin of the triffids published as *Revolt of the Triffids*, a series in *Colliers Weekly*, from January 6 to February 3, 1951. Available at https://www.unz.com/print/Colliers/. Filmed in 1962. Made into a BBC television series in 1981, and again in 2009. Radio adaptations in many countries. Inspiration for 2002 film *28 Days Later*.

The Kraken Wakes, 1953, Michael Joseph. Published in the US as *Out of the Deeps* by Ballantine. BBC Radio adaptations in 1954, 1998 and 2016.

The Chrysalids, 1955, Michael Joseph. Published in the US as *Rebirth* by Ballantine. BBC Radio adaptations in 1982 and 2012. Theatre production in 1999. Jefferson Airplane used the Zealand woman's speech as part of the lyrics in *Crown of Creation*.

The Midwich Cuckoos, 1957, Michael Joseph. Published in the US, 1958, Ballantine. Filmed as *Village of the Damned* in 1960, and again in 1995. Radio adaptations in 1982 and 2003. A further radio adaptation by Graeae, a disabled-led theatre company, was broadcast by the BBC in 2018.

The Outward Urge, 1959. Originally appeared as a series in *New Worlds,* from June to September 1958. A final episode appeared in *New Worlds* in November 1960, written especially for the 100th edition. It was included in subsequent editions of the book.

Trouble with Lichen, 1960, Michael Joseph (UK) and Ballantine (US). BBC radio adaptation in 2011.

Chocky, 1968, Michael Joseph (UK) and Ballantine (US). Previously published as a short story in 1963, see below. Adapted for radio in 1968, 1975 and 1998. Filmed as a children's television series by ITV in 1984.

Web, 1979, Michael Joseph. Completed in 1965. Published posthumously.

Plan for Chaos, 2009, Liverpool University Press. Written c1949. Published posthumously.

Short Fiction

The titles and dates given in brackets are of the first known publication. Many of these stories were published in several magazines and collections, sometimes changing significantly. The same story was often given different titles and published under various pseudonyms. The Internet Speculative Fiction Database lists various versions of most stories.

At time of going to print, stories marked with an asterisk are in magazines which have been scanned and made available through https://archive.org/. Search for them by entering magazine title in quote marks and date in the search bar. Don't bother with the date filter, as this may be missing or incorrect. For example, to find "Worlds to Barter", search: "Wonder Stories" 1931 05. Many titles are also available as pdf downloads on www.luminist.org/archives/SF. Where the first publication magazine is not available online, another title may be given which is available online.

Worlds to Barter (*Wonder Stories*, May 1931).*

The Lost Machine (*Amazing Stories*, April 1932).*

The Venus Adventure (*Wonder Stories,* May 1932).*

The Stare (*The Daily Express*, 15 November 1932).

Wanderers of Time (*Wonder Stories,* March 1933). Available at http://www.luminist.org/archives/SF/WS.htm

The Third Vibrator (*Wonder Stories*, May 1933).*

Spheres of Hell (*Wonder Stories*, October 1933).* Marked as 1933 03 on archive.org, later republished as "The Puff-Ball Menace".

Invisible Monster (*Wonder Stories*, December 1933).*

Exiles on Asperus (*Wonder Stories Quarterly*, Winter 1933).*

The Moon Devils (*Wonder Stories*, April 1934),* also known as "The Last Lunarians".

The Man From Beyond (*Wonder Stories*, September 1934).* Republished as "The Man From Earth". He also used this title for another unpublished time travel story.

The Cathedral Crypt (*Marvel Tales of Science and Fantasy*, March-April 1935)

The Perfect Creature/Una 1937 (Tales of Wonder, first issue, 1937).* This was significantly rewritten and improved when included in the later collection *Jizzle*.

Sleepers of Mars (*Tales of Wonder*, second issue, March 1938).*

Judson's Annihilator (*Fantasy,* 1st issue, 1938). Later published in *Amazing Stories*, October 1939.*

Trojan Beam (*Fantasy,* 2nd issue, March 1939).

The Child of Power (*Fantasy*, 3rd issue, 1939).

Derelict of Space (*Fantasy*, 3rd issue, 1939).

Vengeance by Proxy (*Strange Stories*, February 1940).

Phoney Meteor (*Amazing Stories*, March 1941),* also published as "Meteor".

The Living Lies (*New Worlds*, October 1946).*

Technical Slip (*The Arkham Sampler,* Spring 1949).

Time to Rest (*The Arkham Sampler*, Winter 1949). Also appeared in *New Worlds*, August 1949.* Filmed for the BBC series, *Out of the Unknown,* 1965.

Jizzle (*Colliers Weekly,* January 1949) filmed by Alfred Hitchcock Presents, retitled *Maria*, season 7, episode 3.

Adaptation (*Astounding Science Fiction*, July 1949). Available at http://www.luminist.org/archives/SF/AST.htm

The Eternal Eve (*Amazing Stories,* September 1950 in the US; November 1950 in the UK).*

Pawley's Peepholes (*Science-Fantasy*, Winter 1951).* The magazine version contains a lot of American slang which has been changed for inclusion in the collection *Seeds of Time*.

No Place Like Earth (*New Worlds*, Spring 1951).*

The Red Stuff (*Marvel,* February 1951 in the US; May 1951 in the UK).*

And the Walls Came Tumbling Down (*Startling Stories,* May 1951).*

A Present from Brunswick (*The Magazine of Fantasy and Science Fiction*, June 1951). Available at http://www.luminist.org/archives/SF/FSF.htm

Pillar to Post (*Galaxy Science Fiction,* December 1951).*

The Wheel (*Startling Stories,* January 1952).*

Survival (*Thrilling Wonder Stories,* February 1952).*

Dumb Martian (*Galaxy Science Fiction*, July 1952).* Filmed for the TV Series *Armchair Theatre*, 1962.

Time Out, in the collection *The Infinite Moment*.

Close Behind Him (*Fantastic*, January-February 1953).*

Time Stops Today (*Future Science Fiction*, January 1953). Available at http://www.luminist.org/archives/SF/FUT.htm

Chinese Puzzle, as A Stray From Cathay (*Fantasy Fiction*, August 1953).*

Chronoclasm (*Star Science Fiction*, February 1953). Later published in *Science Fantasy*, September 1954.*

Reservation Deferred (*Fantastic*, May June 1953).*

More Spinned Against (*Fantasy Fiction*, June 1953).*

Confidence Trick (*Fantastic*, July-August 1953).*

How Do I Do? (*Beyond Fantasy Fiction*, September 1953). Available at http://www.luminist.org/archives/SF/#FUK

Esmerelda, in the collection *Jizzle*.

Heaven Scent, in the collection *Jizzle* and *Tales of Gooseflesh and Laughter*.

Look Natural Please! in the collection *Jizzle*.

Never on Mars (*Fantastic Universe*, January 1954).*

Perforce to Dream (*Beyond Fantasy Fiction*, January 1954).*

Opposite Numbers (*New Worlds*, April 1954).*

Compassion Circuit (*Fantastic Universe*, December 1954).*

Wild Flower (*Fantastic Universe*, November 1955).*

Consider Her Ways, first in multi-authored collection *Sometime, Never*; then in Wyndham collection *Consider Her Ways and Others*. Filmed for the *Alfred Hitchcock Hour* in December 1964.

But a Kind of Ghost (*Tales of the Frightened*, Spring 1957).

The Troons series (*New Worlds,* from June to September 1958. A final episode appeared in *New Worlds* in November 1960, written especially for the 100th edition). The series, without the final episode, was published as *The Outward Urge* in 1959. The final episode was included in subsequent editions.

The Killer on the Hill (*Argosy*, October 1958). Later published as The Meddler.

A Long Spoon, in the collection *Consider Her Ways and Others*. Filmed for the *Storyboard* series, 1961.

Odd, in the collection *Consider Her Ways and Others*.

Oh, Where, Now, is Peggy MacRafferty? in the collection *Consider Her Ways and Others*.

Random Quest, in the collection *Consider Her Ways and Others*. Filmed three times: in 1969 for the TV series *Out of the Unknown*; in 1971 as *Quest for Love*; and in 2006 by BBC Four.

Stitch in Time, in the collection *Consider Her Ways and Others*. (*Magazine of Fantasy and Science Fiction*, July 1961).*

It's a Wise Child (*Argosy*, November 1962).

Chocky (*Amazing Stories*, March 1963).* Appeared in Good Housekeeping in the same year. Later revised and extended to a full-length novel.

In Outer Space There Shone a Star (*TV Times Xmas Extra*, December 1965).

A Life Postponed (*Galaxy*, December 1968).*

Blackmoil, commissioned by Esquire magazine and submitted in April 1967 but unpublished. First appeared in a posthumous collection, *No Place Like Earth*, Darkside Press.

Collections

During his lifetime, five collections of Wyndham short stories were published, with slightly different content in the US and the UK. Other collections including his earlier stories were published after his death.

Jizzle, 1954, Dennis Dobson, London. Contains: "Jizzle", "Technical Slip", "A Present from Brunswick", "Chinese Puzzle", "Esmeralda", "How Do I Do?", "Una", "Affair of the Heart", "Confidence Trick", "The Wheel", "Look Natural, Please!", "Perforce to Dream", "Reservation Deferred", "Heaven Scent" and "More Spinned Against".

The Seeds of Time, 1956, Michael Joseph, London. Contains: "Chronoclasm", "Time to Rest", "Meteor", "Survival", "Pawley's Peepholes", "Opposite Number", "Pillar to Post", "Dumb Martian", "Compassion Circuit" and "Wild Flower".

Tales of Gooseflesh and Laughter, 1956, Ballantine Books, New York. Contains a selection from *Jizzle* and *The Seeds of Time*, including: "Chinese Puzzle", "Una", "The Wheel", "Jizzle", "Heaven Scent", "Compassion Circuit", "More Spinned Against", "A Present from Brunswick", "Confidence Trick", "Opposite Numbers" and "Wild Flower".

Consider Her Ways and Others, 1961, Michael Joseph, London. Contains: "Consider Her Ways", "Odd", "Stitch in Time", "Oh, Where, Now, is Peggy MacRafferty?", "Random Quest" and "A Long Spoon".

The Infinite Moment, 1961, Ballantine Books, New York. This was the American version of *Consider Her Ways and Others*. Contains: "Consider Her Ways", "Odd", "How Do I Do", "Stitch in Time", "Random Quest" and "Time Out".

Acknowledgements

Many people have assisted in the production of this book, by giving time, expertise, or sharing memories or materials. I would like to thank the following:

Mike Ashley, author and science fiction historian, who fact checked several chapters; **Nick Blincoe**, author and editor, who read early drafts and provided encouragement; **Gary Buckland**, for the beautiful cover concept; **Bill Burns**, fan historian, who sent copies of his archived pictures; **Jonathan, Kate and Virginia Case**, Biff Barker's grandchildren, who kindly gave permission to use material; **Fergal Crossan**, manager of the Penn Club, who gave me access to the club archives; **David Ketterer,** author, who has done a great deal of excellent research on Wyndham, and who kindly let me read some of Grace Wilson's diaries; **Jane Kirby**, archivist of Bedales School, who sent me school pictures and fact checked the Utopia chapter; **Nicholas Levin**, son of Ira Levin, who found Wyndham's phone number in his late father's address book; **Wayne Noble**, for gifting me the title; **Neil Pollard**, author, who analysed the various versions of the *Triffids* and sent scans of several Wyndham photographs; **Ken Smith**, author, who shared his unpublished work and kindly allowed me to scan Wyndham's family photograph album; **David Sykes,** son of Bill and Leslie, who identified many people in the pictures and shared his memories; the **University of Liverpool librarians Caitlin Fleming** and **Robyn Orr**, who were unfailingly helpful; **Ann Wilson**, widow of Grace's nephew, and **Hilary Wilson**, Grace's niece, who shared their photographs, letters and memories, and gave permission to use material; **Morgan Wallace** and **Philip Harbottle**, collectors, who tracked down material about the versions of *Planet Plane*; the many **anonymous contributors** to the Internet Speculative Fiction Database and other online resources mentioned in the text.

I would also like to thank **my family, friends and colleagues at the University of Central Lancashire**, who have borne with me droning on about John Wyndham for two years.

Illustrations

Main Body:

Scans of Jack's letters in Chapters 5, 7 and 9 were kindly provided by the University of Liverpool Special Collections Archive.

Postcard of Bedales in Chapter 2 was kindly provided by Bedales School.

Illustrations from most magazines in Chapter 3 were taken from downloads from archive.org. Copyrights originally belonged to Gernsback Publications but were not renewed and are now in the public domain. The scans of Modern Wonder (Chapter 3) and Galaxy (Chapter 12) were taken from personal copies.

Illustration section:

Pictures on pages 1, 3, 6-9, 11, bottom of p12, and 16 are courtesy of Dr Ken Smith, who owns John Wyndham's family album and other pictures.

P2, pictures courtesy of Bedales School.

P4 and 5, top of p12 and top of p13, pictures courtesy of Anne and Hilary Wilson, Grace's relatives.

P10, picture courtesy of The Penn Club.

P13, bottom, photograph of Senate House, credit Wellcome Collection, CC BY, available at https://wellcomecollection.org/works/q3z4dc2r

P14, pictures taken by Peter West, and kindly provided by fan historian Bill Burns.

P15, pictures courtesy of Neil Pollard, who owns some of John Wyndham's own photographs.

About the Author

Dr Amy Binns teaches journalism at the University of Central Lancashire, Preston. She has a wide range of research interests, including difficult behaviour on social media, interwar feminism and local reporting. She is the author of one previous book, *Valley of a Hundred Chapels: the Lives and Legacies of the Nonconformists*. She lives with her husband and children in West Yorkshire. She said:

> I don't recall when I first read a John Wyndham book. I must have found the battered paperbacks on one of many rainy days sitting on the landing before my parents' bookcases. His strong, witty heroines did not strike me as unusual then. I attended a Northern girls' grammar where self-doubt was not part of the curriculum. Josella, Rosalind and Diana could have been any of my bloody-minded friends.
>
> It was many years later that I realised these women, sparkling from the pages in book after book, had to be based on a real person. Online biographies only said Wyndham had married late in life. I felt sure this could not be the whole story, and decided to investigate.
>
> But even as a child, I recall the sense that these were truly adult books. They had perception, intelligence and the driest of humour. They recognised the oddities of the most everyday experiences, and presented the extraordinary without melodrama.
>
> This was the same voice I found in hundreds of letters in the University of Liverpool archive. In writing this book, it has been an honour to make the acquaintance of Jack and Grace.

Index

Index